What Can I Do Now?

Science

Books in the
What Can I Do Now? Series

Animal Careers
Animation
Art
Business and Finance
Computers
Education
Engineering, Second Edition
Environment, Second Edition
Fashion
Film
Health Care
Journalism, Second Edition
Law
Music
Nursing, Second Edition
Radio and Television, Second Edition
Safety and Security, Second Edition
Science
Sports, Second Edition
Travel and Tourism, Second Edition

What Can I Do Now?

Science

Ferguson Publishing
An imprint of Infobase Publishing

What Can I Do Now? Science

Ferguson
An imprint of Infobase Publishing
132 West 31st Street
New York NY 10001

Library of Congress Cataloging-in-Publication Data

What can I do now? Science.
    p. cm. — (What can I do now?)
  Includes bibliographical references and index.
  ISBN-13: 978-0-8160-8082-3 (hardcover : alk. paper)
  ISBN-10: 0-8160-8082-8 (hardcover : alk. paper) 1. Science—Vocational guidance—Juvenile
literature. I. Title: Science.
  Q147.W425 2010
  502.3—dc22

                        2009046478

3 1218 00442 3571

Ferguson books are available at special discounts when purchased in bulk quantities for businesses, associations, institutions, or sales promotions. Please call our Special Sales Department in New York at (212) 967-8800 or (800) 322-8755.

You can find Ferguson on the World Wide Web at http://www.fergpubco.com

Text design by Kerry Casey
Composition by Mary Susan Ryan-Flynn
Cover printed by Sheridan Books, Ann Arbor, Mich.
Book printed and bound by Sheridan Books, Ann Arbor, Mich.
Date printed: April 2010
Printed in the United States of America

10 9 8 7 6 5 4 3 2 1

This book is printed on acid-free paper.

All links and Web addresses were checked and verified to be correct at the time of publication. Because of the dynamic nature of the Web, some addresses and links may have changed since publication and may no longer be valid.

Contents

Introduction

There are many people just like you who want to pursue a career in science, whether in a lab, in the field, in a classroom, or in another setting. You may see a science-related career in your future and wonder how you can start exploring right away, while still in high school. There are countless areas of science in which you can work. All you need to begin is a general interest in a science-related field. Although most science careers require a combination of formal training and experience, there is absolutely no reason to wait until you get out of high school to get serious about a career. That doesn't mean you have to make a firm, undying commitment right now. Indeed, one of the biggest fears most people face at some point (sometimes more than once) is choosing the right career. Frankly, many people don't choose at all. They take a job because they need one, and all of a sudden 10 years have gone by and they wonder why they're stuck doing something they hate, like being an accountant rather than being a physicist. Don't be one of those people! You have the opportunity right now, while you're still in high school and still relatively unencumbered with major adult responsibilities, to explore, to experience, to try out a work path. Wouldn't you really rather

find out sooner than later that you're not cut out to be an ecologist after all and that you'd actually prefer to be a geologist, or a meteorologist?

There are many ways to explore science careers. What we've tried to do in this book is give you an idea of some of your options. Section 1, What Do I Need to Know about Science?, will give you an overview of the field—a little history, where it is at today, and promises of the future; as well as a breakdown of its structure (how it is organized) and a glimpse of some of its many career options.

The Careers section includes 10 chapters, each describing in detail one or more career options: astronomers, biologists, chemists, ecologists, forensic scientists, genetic scientists, geologists, meteorologists, physicists, and science technicians. These chapters rely heavily on firsthand accounts from real people on the job. They'll tell you what skills you need, what personal qualities you need to have, and what the ups and downs of the jobs are. You'll also find out about educational requirements—including specific high school and college classes—advancement possibilities, related jobs, salary ranges, and the employment outlook.

In keeping with the secondary theme of this book (the primary theme, for those of you who still don't get it, is "You can do something now"), Section 3, Do It Yourself, urges you to take charge and learn about science-related careers on your own and start your own programs and activities where none exist—school, community, or the nation. Why not?

The real meat of the book is in Section 4, What Can I Do Right Now? This is where you get busy and *do something*. The chapter "Get Involved" will clue you in on the obvious volunteer and intern positions, the not-so-obvious summer camps and summer college study, and other opportunities.

"Read a Book" is an annotated bibliography of books (some new, some old) and periodicals. If you're even considering a career in science, reading a few books and checking out a few magazines or professional journals is the easiest thing you can do. Don't stop with our list. Ask your librarian to point you to more materials. Keep reading!

While we think the best way to investigate science-related careers is to jump right in and start exploring, there are plenty of other ways to get into the science mind-set. "Surf the Web" offers a short annotated list of Web sites where you can explore everything from job listings (start getting an idea of what employers are looking for now), to educational requirements, to on-the-job accounts, to blogs and podcasts from science professionals.

"Ask for Money" is a sampling of scholarships for people who are interested in pursuing science careers. You need to be familiar with these because you're going to need money for school. You have to actively pursue scholarships; no one is going to come up to you one day and present you with a check because you're such a wonderful student. Applying for scholarships is work, and it takes effort. And it must be done right and often as much as a year in advance of when you need the money.

"Look to the Pros" is the final chapter. It lists professional organizations you can turn to for more information about accredited schools, education requirements, career descriptions, salary information, union membership, job listings, scholarships, and more. Once you become a college student in a science-related field, you'll be able to join many of these organizations. Time after time, professionals say that membership and active participation in a professional organization is one of the best ways to network (make valuable contacts) and gain recognition in your field.

High school can be a lot of fun. There are dances and football games; maybe you're in band or play a sport. Great! Maybe you hate school and are just biding your time until you graduate. Whoever you are, take a minute and try to imagine your life five years from now. Ten years from now. Where will you be? What will you be doing? Whether you realize it or not, how you choose to spend your time now—studying, playing, watching TV, working at a fast food restaurant, hanging out, whatever—will have an impact on your future. Take a look at how you're spending your time now and ask yourself, "Where is this getting me?" If you can't come up with an answer, it's probably "nowhere." The choice is yours. No one is going to take you by the hand and lead you in the right direction. It's up to you. It's your life. You can do something about it right now!

SECTION 1

What Do I Need to Know About Science?

Our world would be a very different place without scientists. Without scientists, our air and water would be more polluted. More plants and animals would be endangered—many more would be extinct. Fewer crimes would be solved. We would have less warning that killer heat waves, cold snaps, and tornados and hurricanes were about to strike our cities and towns. Outbreaks of infectious diseases would quickly become epidemics. Miracle drugs and cures would just be a dream. Space exploration and the discoveries made by space scientists we now take for granted would just be science fiction. And that's just the tip of the iceberg (which we wouldn't even know is melting—as a result of global warming—without the work of scientists). Without scientists, there would be no Internet, no increasing life spans, no new products and discoveries, no renewable energy...you get the idea.

Science involves constant research and investigation, and if you have an inquisitive personality and like to solve problems, there are a wide variety of career options available in countless fields. There are jobs for people with every educational background—from medical degrees (pathologists), to master's and bachelor's degrees (scientists), to those with some college training or just a high school diploma (science technicians and laboratory testing personnel). Science professionals work in a variety of settings, including laboratories, offices, factories, classrooms, home-based settings, and many other locations. They also work outdoors conducting research and other tasks. In short, the field of science offers opportunities for people with every interest, skill, and educational background. Now it's up to you to decide which career path is right for you. The following sections provide more information about scientific subspecialties, typical career paths and employers, and the employment outlook for the field.

GENERAL INFORMATION

According to the American Association of Physics Teachers, science is "the systematic enterprise of gathering knowledge about the universe and organizing and condensing that knowledge into testable laws and theories." More practically, we use science to help solve problems, develop products and processes, understand the earth and the universe, and make the world a healthier and safer place. The following paragraphs detail some of the most popular areas of scientific study that are covered in this book.

Astronomy. The term *astronomy* is derived from two Greek words: *astron,* meaning star, and *nemein,* meaning to arrange or distribute. Astronomy, one of the oldest sciences, is the study of the universe and its celestial bodies such as planets, moons, suns, galaxies, black holes, and other phenomena.

Biology/life sciences. Life has many different levels of organization, from the atom to complex organisms to whole populations. The biological sciences look at life on one or more of these levels—at anything that is or has been alive. The field of biology also looks at the effects of the environment and humanity on living things. Because living things vary greatly in how they live and where they came from, the field of biology is divided into many different specialty areas. Biology subfields are many and varied and include microbiology, anatomy, morphology, plant and animal physiology, pathology, cell biology, molecular biology, marine biology, and genetics, just to name a few. There are also fields of specialization for different classifications of living things: herpetology (reptiles and amphibians), entomology (insects), and ornithology (birds), for example.

Chemistry. The science of chemistry is concerned with the composition, changes, reactions, and transformations of matter. Major specialties in chemistry include analytical, biological, inorganic, organic, and physical chemistry.

Earth sciences/geosciences. People have always been curious about the physical world around them, and this curiosity inspired the development of the earth sciences, sometimes called geosciences. The earth sciences include the atmospheric sciences, ecology, environmental science, geography, geology, geophysics, hydrology, meteorology, oceanography, paleontology, petrology, seismology, and soil science, among other specialties.

Forensic sciences. The American Academy of Forensic Sciences defines forensic science as any science that is "used in public, in a court, or in the justice system." The academy has the following discipline sections: Criminalistics, Digital and Multimedia Sciences, Engineering Sciences, General, Jurisprudence, Odontology, Pathology/Biology, Physical Anthropology, Psychiatry and Behavioral Science, Questioned Documents, and Toxicology.

Mathematics and physics. Mathematics and physics are closely related natural sciences. Mathematics is the science and study of numbers and how they relate with each other. Physics is the study of the basic elements and laws of the universe. Physicists study the structure of matter, energy in all forms, and the relationship between matter and energy. Physics sub-specialties—many of which are linked with other scientific disciplines—include biophysics, geophysics, optics, quantum physics, and thermodynamics.

STRUCTURE OF THE INDUSTRY

As mentioned earlier in this article, there is no single umbrella industry that employs science professionals. In fact, scientists and science technicians work in multiple industries such as biology, biotechnology, aeronautics and aviation, pharmaceuticals, genetics, earth sciences, chemicals, space exploration, medical research, criminal justice, and a variety of other industries. In these industries, there are companies of all sizes that conduct research, solve problems, and make groundbreaking discoveries that change the way we live, as well as small breakthroughs that make our lives easier and lead the way for even bigger discoveries down the line. A large amount of research is also conducted by government agencies.

Lingo to Learn

agronomy The science of soil management and the production of field crops.

anatomy The study of living structures, chiefly internal.

animal husbandry The study of the care and breeding of farm animals.

barometer An instrument that measures atmospheric pressure.

bioremediation Use of living organisms to clean up oil spills or remove other pollutants from soil, water, wastewater; use of organisms such as nonharmful insects to remove agricultural pests or counteract diseases of trees, plants, and garden soil.

biotechnology The use of live organisms (plant and animal cells) to manufacture new products.

catalysis Speeding up a chemical reaction by addition of a substance that does not undergo a permanent chemical change.

chromosomes Threadlike structures of nucleic acids and protein that carry genes.

DNA profiling Using biological residue from the scene of a crime to make genetic comparisons in identifying suspects.

Doppler radar An electronic instrument that measures atmospheric motion of objects such as precipitation.

ecology The study of living things in relation to each other and in relation to their surroundings.

ecosystem A community of various species that interact with one another and with the chemical and physical factors making up the nonliving environment.

endangered species A species having so few individual survivors that it may become extinct over all or most of its natural range.

Generally, those working in scientific fields do one of four types of work: basic research, applied research, testing, or support. Basic research seeks knowledge for its own sake, uncovering fundamental truths and transforming the unknown into the known. Often done at universities, basic research includes all areas of science. Applied research deals with translating basic knowledge into practical, useful products and processes for use in areas such as medicine, agriculture, the chemical pharmaceutical industries, and other specialized fields. Most scientific research uses a team approach. Team members review previous research and experiments, then set a goal for their project. They may form a hypothesis (an educated guess) to prove or disprove a current theory or set an open-ended objective, such as finding out what happens over time to people who smoke or drink. An experiment may prove something or not. After experimentation, the scientist analyzes the results, often publishing his or her findings in a scientific journal article. Publishing results is a key part of doing research, for only by sharing data and evaluations can the scientific community make the most of research. Scientists working under contracts with research companies do not own their discoveries; their research becomes the prop-

genes The units of heredity that are transmitted from parents to offspring and control or determine a single characteristic in the offspring.

genetics The study of inheritance, or how living things resemble or differ from their ancestors.

genetic manipulation Changing the hereditary characteristics of a plant or animal, as in seedless grapes. Also known as genetic engineering.

gravity Natural force that pulls objects on or near earth toward earth.

groundwater The supply of fresh water found beneath the earth's surface, usually in aquifers, that supplies wells and springs.

hazardous waste Any discarded substance, usually chemical, that can cause harm to humans.

horticulture The study of all ornamental or food plants except field crops.

pathology The study of diseases. It is both a biological and a medical subject.

physiology The study of the functions of living cells, tissues, organs, and systems.

pollution The presence of a substance in the environment that because of its chemical composition or quantity prevents the functioning of natural processes and produces undesirable environmental and health effects.

space Begins where earth's atmosphere is too thin to affect objects moving through it, about 100 miles above earth.

synthetic Produced by chemical reaction rather than being of natural origin.

taxonomy The classification of organisms into orderly groups according to their physical structure and other traits.

erty of the employer. Scientists working independently can keep their discoveries as their own and have the right to patent and charge others for using their research.

Another important specialty area in science is testing. Although scientists may perform tests to determine if their hypotheses are correct, they are often assisted by laboratory testing technicians or field technicians who conduct tests on many substances and products.

Finally, scientists and science technicians would never be able to conduct research or solve problems without the assistance of support personnel such as secretaries, receptionists, laboratory managers, clerks, computer support specialists, and a variety of other specialized workers. These professionals keep labs running and make sure that grants are applied for, ensure that computers and other technology are working correctly, and handle any other task that allows scientists and technicians to focus on scientific investigation.

CAREERS

There are many different career opportunities in science-related industries, from becoming a biologist or chemist to working as an astronomer, meteorologist, or science technician. A short sampling of

Quotes

"Science is a wonderful thing if one does not have to earn one's living at it."

—Albert Einstein, Nobel Prize-winning physicist

"Science is simply common sense at its best—that is, rigidly accurate in observation, and merciless to fallacy in logic."

—Thomas Henry Huxley, English biologist

"Equipped with his five senses, man explores the universe around him and calls the adventure 'Science.'"

—Edwin Powell Hubble, American astronomer

"Those who dwell, as scientists or laymen, among the beauties and mysteries of the earth are never alone or weary of life."

—Rachel Carson, American marine biologist and environmentalist

the many career options in science follows in the paragraphs below.

Agricultural scientists study all aspects of living organisms and the relationships of plants and animals to their environment. They apply the results to such tasks as increasing crop yields and improving the environment. Some agricultural scientists plan and administer programs for testing foods, drugs, and other products. Others direct activities at public exhib-

its at such places as zoos and botanical gardens.

Agronomists are agricultural scientists who investigate large-scale food-crop problems, conduct experiments, and develop new methods of growing crops to ensure more efficient production, higher yields, and improved quality. They use genetic engineering to develop crops that are resistant to pests, drought, and plant diseases.

Animal scientists are agricultural scientists who conduct research and develop improved methods for housing, breeding, feeding, and controlling diseases of domestic farm animals. They inspect and grade livestock food products, purchase livestock, or work in sales and marketing of livestock products. They often consult agricultural businesses on such areas as upgrading animal housing, lowering mortality rates, or increasing production of animal products such as milk and eggs.

Astrobiologists, also known as *exobiologists*, *life scientists*, and *space scientists*, study the origin of all life forms—from a simple one-celled organism, to plants, to human beings. They study and research the evolution, distribution, and future of these life forms, on earth as well as on other planets in our solar system and beyond.

Astronomers study the universe and its celestial bodies by collecting and analyzing data obtained through observation and through information obtained by means of spacecraft, telescopes, and earth satellites.

Astrophysicists use the principles of physics to study the solar system, stars, galaxies, and the universe.

Biochemists explore the tiny world of the cell, study how illnesses develop, and search for ways to improve life on earth.

Through studying the chemical makeup of living organisms, biochemists strive to understand the dynamics of life, from the secrets of cell-to-cell communication to the chemical changes in our brains that give us memories.

Biological technicians, assist biologists, often working on teams in laboratory experiments. They may work with lab animals, record data, and use lab equipment such as microscopes and centrifuges.

Biologists study all types of living organisms—including humans, micro-organisms, plants, and animals—and the relationship of each organism to its environment. They focus on the origin, development, anatomy, function, distribution, and other basic principles of living organisms.

Botanists study all different aspects of plant life, from cell structure to reproduction, to how plants are distributed, to how rainfall or other conditions affect them, and more.

Chemical engineers take chemistry out of the laboratory and into the real world. They are involved in evaluating methods and equipment for the mass production of chemicals and other materials requiring chemical processing. They also develop products from these materials, such as plastics, metals, gasoline, detergents, pharmaceuticals, and foodstuffs. They develop or improve safe, environmentally sound processes, determine the least costly production method, and formulate the material for easy use and safe, economic transportation.

Chemical technicians assist chemists and chemical engineers in the research, development, testing, and manufacturing of chemicals and chemical-based products.

Chemists study the composition, changes, reactions, and transformations of matter. They may specialize in analytical, biological, inorganic, organic, or physical chemistry.

Ecologists examine the complex relationships between living organisms and the physical environment. They combine biology, which includes the study of both plants and animals, with physical sciences, such as geology and geography.

Engineers use scientific knowledge and tools to design products, structures, and machines. Most engineers specialize in a particular area but have a base of knowledge and training that can be applied in many fields.

Environmental technicians, also known as *pollution control technicians,* conduct tests and field investigations to obtain soil samples and other data. Their research is used by engineers, scientists, and others who help clean up, monitor, control, or prevent pollution. An environmental technician usually specializes in air, water, or soil pollution.

Forensic science technicians help forensic scientists analyze, identify, and classify physical evidence relating to criminal cases. They may work in laboratories or they may travel to crime scenes to collect evidence.

Forensic scientists apply scientific principles and methods to the analysis, identification, and classification of physical evidence relating to criminal (or suspected criminal) cases. They do much of their work in laboratories, where they subject evidence to tests and then record the results. They may travel to crime scenes to collect evidence and record the physical facts of the site. Forensic scientists may also be called upon to testify as expert witnesses and to present scientific findings in court.

Foresters protect and manage forest resources through various biological techniques. Using their specialized knowledge of tree biology and ecology, wood science, and manufacturing processes, they manage forests for timber production, protect them from fire and pest damage, harvest mature forests, and re-establish new forests after harvesting.

Forestry technicians work as members of a forest management team under the direction of a professional forester. They collect data and information needed to make decisions about resources and resource depletion. They also help plan, supervise, and conduct the operations necessary to maintain and protect forest growth, including harvesting, replanting, and marketing of forest products.

Genetic counselors are genetic scientists who work with individuals who may be at risk for a variety of inherited conditions or who have family members with birth defects or genetic disorders.

Genetic scientists, also known as *geneticists,* study heredity. They study plants as well as animals, including humans. Geneticists conduct research on how characteristics are passed from one generation to the next through the genes present in each cell of an organism. This research often involves manipulating or altering particular genetic characteristics to better understand how genetic systems work.

Geological technicians assist geologists in their studies of the earth's physical makeup and history. This includes the exploration of a wide variety of phenomena, such as mountain uplifting, rock formations, min-

eral deposition, earthquakes, and volcanic eruptions. Modern geology is particularly concerned with the exploration for mineral and petroleum deposits in the earth and with minimizing the effects of human-made structures on the environment.

Geologists study the origin, history, composition, and structure of the earth. They may also help locate oil, groundwater, minerals, and other natural resources and play an increasingly important role in studying, preserving, and cleaning up the environment.

Geophysicists are concerned with matter and energy and how they interact. They study the physical properties and structure of the earth, from its interior to its upper atmosphere, including land surfaces, subsurfaces, and bodies of water.

Groundwater professionals are different types of scientists and engineers concerned with water supplies beneath the earth's surface. For example, they search for new water sources and ensure safe water supplies. *Hydrogeologists* study the science of groundwater supplies. *Hydrologists* study underground and surface water and its properties, including how water is distributed and how it moves through land.

Horticulturists are agricultural scientists who study fruit and nut orchards as well as garden plants such as vegetables and flowers. They conduct experiments to develop new and improved varieties and to increase crop quality and yields. They also work to improve plant culture methods for the landscaping and beautification of communities, parks, and homes.

Laboratory testing technicians conduct tests on countless substances and products. Their laboratory duties include measuring and evaluating materials and running quality control tests. They work in a variety of unrelated fields, such as medicine, metallurgy, manufacturing, geology, and meteorology.

Marine biologists study species of plants and animals living in saltwater, their interactions with one another, and how they influence and are influenced by environmental factors.

Mathematicians solve or direct the solution of problems in higher mathematics, including algebra, geometry, number theory, logic, and topology. *Theoretical mathematicians* work with the relationships among mathematical forms and the underlying principles that can be applied to problems, including electronic data processing and military planning. *Applied mathematicians* develop the techniques and approaches to problem solving in the physical, biological, and social sciences.

Meteorologists study the physical and chemical characteristics of the atmosphere. They also study the way in which the atmosphere affects the rest of the natural environment. Many meteorologists forecast the weather. Meteorologists are also known as *atmospheric scientists.*

Microbiologists are scientists who study living things that cannot be seen with the naked eye, such as bacteria, fungi, protozoans, and viruses, as well as human and animal cells. They examine the effects these microorganisms and infectious agents have on people, animals, plants, and the environment. They are interested in learning about microorganisms that cause diseases, how microorganisms can be used to treat and prevent diseases, and ways microorganisms can be used in developing products.

Naturalists educate the public about the environment and maintain the natural environment on land specifically dedicated to wilderness populations. Their primary responsibilities are preserving, restoring, maintaining, and protecting a natural habitat. Among the related responsibilities in these jobs are teaching, public speaking, writing, giving scientific and ecological demonstrations, and handling public relations and administrative tasks.

Oceanographers obtain information about the ocean through observations, surveys, and experiments. They study the biological, physical, and chemical composition of the ocean and the geological structure of the seabed. They also analyze phenomena involving the water itself, the atmosphere above it, the land beneath it, and the coastal borders. They study acoustical properties of water so that a comprehensive and unified picture of the ocean's behavior may be developed. A *limnologist* is a specialist who studies freshwater life.

Paleontologists study the fossils of ancient life-forms, including human life, found in sedimentary rocks on or within the earth's crust. Paleontological analyses range from the description of large, easily visible features to biochemical analysis of incompletely fossilized tissue. The observations are used to infer relationships between past and present groups of organisms (taxonomy), to investigate the origins of life, and to investigate the ecology of the past (paleoecology) from which implications for the sustainability of life under present ecological conditions can be drawn.

Pathologists are physicians who analyze tissue specimens to identify abnormalities and diagnose diseases.

Petroleum technicians measure and record the conditions of oil and gas wells. They use instruments lowered into the wells, and evaluate mud from the wells. They examine data to determine petroleum and mineral content.

Petrologists are specialized geologists who focus specifically upon the analysis of the composition, structure, and history of rocks and rock formations. Petrologists are also interested in the formation of particular types of rocks that contain economically important materials such as gold, copper, and uranium. They also study the formation and composition of metals, precious stones, minerals, and meteorites, and they analyze a wide variety of substances, ranging from diamonds and gold to petroleum deposits that may be locked in rock formations beneath the earth's surface.   ✳

Pharmacologists play an important role in medicine and in science by studying the effects of drugs, chemicals, and other substances on humans, animals, and plants. These highly educated scientists conduct research on living tissues and organs to determine how drugs and other chemicals act at the cellular level. Their results help to discover how drugs and other chemicals should be most effectively used.

Physicists are concerned with the study of energy in all its forms, the structure of matter, and the relationship between energy and matter. They investigate and attempt to understand the fundamental laws of nature and how these laws may be formulated and put to use.

Physiologists are biologists who specialize in studying all the life stages of plants or animals. Some specialize in a particular body system or a particular function, such as respiration.

Range managers work to maintain and improve grazing lands on public and private property. They research, develop, and carry out methods to improve and increase the production of forage plants, livestock, and wildlife without damaging the environment; develop and carry out plans for water facilities, erosion control, and soil treatments; restore rangelands that have been damaged by fire, pests, and undesirable plants; and manage the upkeep of range improvements, such as fences, corrals, and reservoirs.

Science teachers instruct students in specific subjects—such as biology, chemistry, earth science, forensic science, physics, or astronomy. They lecture classes, lead small seminar groups, and create and grade examinations. They also may conduct research, write for publication, and aid in administration.

Science writers translate technical scientific information so it can be disseminated to the general public and professionals in the field. Science writers research, interpret, write, and edit scientific information. Their work often appears in books, technical studies and reports, magazine and trade journal articles, newspapers, company newsletters, and on Web sites and may be used for radio and television broadcasts.

Soil conservation technicians work directly with land users by putting the ideas and plans of soil conservationists into action. In their work they use basic engineering and surveying tools, instruments, and techniques. They perform engineering surveys and design and implement conservation practices like terraces and grassed waterways. Soil conservation technicians monitor projects during and after construction and periodically revisit the site to evaluate the practices and plans.

Soil conservationists develop conservation plans to help farmers and ranchers, developers, homeowners, and government officials best use their land while adhering to government conservation regulations.

Soil scientists study the physical, chemical, and biological characteristics of soils to determine the most productive and effective planting strategies. Their research aids in producing larger, healthier crops and more environmentally sound farming procedures.

Statisticians use mathematical theories to collect and interpret information. This information is used to help various agencies, industries, and researchers determine the best ways to produce results in their work.

Toxicologists design and conduct studies to determine the potential toxicity of substances to humans, plants, and animals. They provide information on the hazards of these substances to the federal government, private businesses, and the public. Toxicologists may suggest alternatives to using products that contain dangerous amounts of toxins, often by testifying at official hearings.

Zoologists are biologists who study animals. They often select a particular type of animal to study, and they may study an entire animal, one part or aspect of an animal, or a whole animal society. There are many areas of specialization from which a zoologist can choose, such as origins,

Profile: Lucy Braun (1889–1971)

● ● ● ● ● ●

E. Lucy Braun was an American botanist and ecologist. She is famous for studying forests of deciduous trees (trees with leaves that fall off) in the eastern part of the United States. She is also famous for her efforts to conserve land and was a pioneer in the field of ecology.

Braun was born in Cincinnati, Ohio, in 1889. When Braun was a young girl, she was interested in nature and the wildflowers she found growing outside of the city. Braun later studied botany at the University of Cincinnati and received a bachelor's degree in 1910. She continued her studies and received a master's degree in geology and a Ph.D. in botany. In 1917 she founded the Wildflower Preservation Society of North America. Braun taught at the University of Cincinnati for many years but retired in 1948 so she could spend more time doing research. She wrote many books during her lifetime and some of them, like *Deciduous Forests of Eastern North America* (published in 1950), are still used today.

Braun was honored for her contributions to botany and ecology during her life, receiving the Mary Soper Pope Medal in Botany in 1952 and the Certificate of Merit from the Botanical Society of America in 1956. She became the first woman to be named president of the Ohio Academy of Science in 1933 and of the Ecological Society of America in 1950. In 1971 Braun was the first woman to be named to the Ohio Conservation Hall of Fame.

Sources: Western Kentucky University, Ecological Society of America, Botanical Society of America

genetics, characteristics, classifications, behaviors, life processes, and distribution of animals.

EMPLOYMENT OPPORTUNITIES

Science professionals are employed in the private sector by companies of all sizes. They also work for nonprofit research organizations. Many scientists hold faculty positions at colleges and universities and most of these combine their teaching with research.

Scientists are also employed by government agencies at the local, regional, and federal levels. Federal government agencies that employ a large number of scientists include the National Aeronautics and Space Administration, the Centers for Disease Control and Prevention, the U.S. Environmental Protection Agency, the Federal Bureau of Investigation, the National Institute of Standards and Technology, and the U.S. Departments of Agriculture, Commerce, Defense, Energy, Health and Human Services, and Interior. Scientists also work for the U.S. military.

INDUSTRY OUTLOOK

Because science is such a broad category, it is difficult to project future employment growth for the field as a whole. Depending on economic conditions, government funding, and other factors, it is common for one scientific specialization to suffer slow growth or decline while another specialization thrives.

Overall, the U.S. Department of Labor predicts that the following scientific careers will enjoy the strongest growth through 2016: biochemists, biological technicians, biophysicists, environmental science and protection technicians, environmental scientists, forensic science technicians, forensic scientists, and medical scientists (a category that includes pathologists). Average growth is predicted for agricultural and food scientists, atmospheric and space scientists, chemists, geological and petroleum technicians, microbiologists, physicists, wildlife biologists, and zoologists. Slower than average employment growth is predicted for astronomers, chemical technicians, conservation scientists, and foresters.

On the whole, employment in the private sector is expected to be stronger than at government agencies due to cuts in funding for government-sponsored research programs.

As with most industries, science professionals with advanced education and considerable experience will have the best employment prospects.

SECTION 2

Careers

Astronomers

SUMMARY

Definition
Astronomers study the universe and its celestial bodies by collecting and analyzing data. They strive to explain how the universe came to exist, how elements formed, why galaxies look the way they do, and whether there is other life in the universe. They also compute positions of stars and planets and calculate orbits of comets, asteroids, and artificial satellites.

Alternative Job Titles
Astronomical scientists

Salary Range
$45,330 to $101,300 to $156,720+

Educational Requirements
Bachelor's degree; doctoral degree required for top positions

Certification or Licensing
None available

Employment Outlook
About as fast as the average

High School Subjects
Computer science
Mathematics
Physics

Personal Interests
Computers
Science
Travel

Astronomer Tod Lauer says that one of the most rewarding experiences of his career was serving as a member of the Hubble Space Telescope Wide Field and Planetary Camera-1 Team. "The team operated the first camera on board the Hubble," he says. "I wrote the first research paper ever done with the Hubble, and over the years got to see new things in the centers of galaxies that had never been seen before. I also was deeply involved in finding a way to do science with the Hubble right after its launch when we discovered that its optics were flawed. I was able to use my skills to use the Hubble as a sharp tool, even in its compromised condition.

As someone who grew up with the Apollo missions and had a lifetime of watching space missions, it was fantastic not only to be involved in one, but to do work that made a real difference to its success."

WHAT DOES AN ASTRONOMER DO?

Astronomers study the universe and all of its celestial bodies. They collect and analyze information about the moon, planets, sun, and stars, which they use to predict their shapes, sizes, brightness, and motions.

They are interested in the orbits of comets, asteroids, and even artificial satellites. Information on the size and shape, the luminosity and position, the composition, characteristics, and structure as well as temperature, distance, motion, and orbit of all celestial bodies is of great relevance to their work.

Practical application of activity in space is used for a variety of purposes. The launching of space vehicles and satellites has increased the importance of the information astronomers gather. For example, the public couldn't enjoy the benefits of accurate predictions of weather as early if satellites weren't keeping an eye on our atmosphere. Without astronomical data, satellite placement wouldn't be possible. Knowledge of the orbits of planets and their moons, as well as asteroid activity, is also vital to astronauts exploring space.

Astronomers are usually expected to specialize in some particular branch of astronomy. The *astrophysicist* is concerned with applying the concepts of physics to planets, stellar atmospheres and interiors, galaxies, the universe as a whole, and the formation and evolution of these systems. *Radio astronomers* study the source and nature of celestial radio waves with extremely sensitive radio telescopes. The majority of astronomers either teach or do research or a combination of both. Astronomers in many universities are expected to teach such subjects as physics and mathematics in addition to astronomy. Other astronomers are engaged in such activities as the development of astronomical instruments, administration, technical writing, and consulting.

Astronomers who make observations may spend long periods of time in observatories. Astronomers who teach or work in laboratories may work eight-hour days. However, those who make observations, especially during celestial events or other peak viewing times, may spend long evening hours in observatories. Paperwork is a necessary part of the job. For teachers, it can include lesson planning and paper grading. Astronomers conducting research independently or for a university can expect to spend a considerable amount of time writing grant proposals to secure funding for their work. For any scientist, sharing the knowledge acquired is a vital part of the work. Astronomers are expected to painstakingly document their observations and eventually combine them into a coherent report, often for peer review or publication.

Although the telescope is the major instrument used in observation, many other devices are also used by astronomers in carrying out these studies, including spectrometers for the measurement of wavelengths of radiant energy, photometers for the measurement of light intensity, balloons, rockets and airplanes for carrying various measuring devices, and computers for processing and analyzing all the information gathered.

Astronomers use ground-based telescopes for night observation of the skies at optical and infrared wavelengths. Most ground-based telescopes are located high on a hill or mountain and normally in a fairly remote area, where the air is clean and the view is not affected by lights from unrelated sources. There are

To Be a Successful Astronomer, You Should...

- have a good imagination
- have an analytical personality
- be an excellent researcher
- have strong communication skills
- enjoy traveling
- have good mathematical skills

Those astronomers in administrative positions, such as director of an observatory or planetarium, will maintain fairly steady office hours but may also work during the evening and night. They usually are more involved in administrative details, however, spending less time in observation and research.

Those employed as teachers will usually have good facilities available to them, and their hours will vary according to class hours assigned. Astronomers who are employed by colleges and universities may often work more than 40 hours per week.

approximately 300 of these observatories in the United States. Telescopes in space have become an important tool for the work of many astronomers. They provide access to wavelengths not accessible from the ground, such as far-infrared, submillimeter, ultraviolet, X ray, and gamma ray, and, as in the case of the Hubble Space Telescope, can provide much sharper vision even at optical wavelengths than land-based capability allows.

Astronomers working in these observatories usually are assigned to observation from three to six nights per month and spend the remainder of their time in an office or laboratory, where they study and analyze their data. They also must prepare reports. They may work with others on one segment of their research or writing and then work entirely alone on the next. Their work is normally carried on in clean, quiet, well-ventilated, and well-lighted facilities.

WHAT IS IT LIKE TO BE AN ASTRONOMER?

Dr. Tod Lauer is an astronomer at the National Optical Astronomy Observatory in Tucson, Arizona. "I grew up with the race to the moon," he recalls, "and space exploration was a strong influence in the popular culture of the time. My first curiosities go back to when we made papier-maché models of the planets in first grade, and an older kid drew out a map of the solar system on the playground. I started reading about astronomy just as I was learning to read, and by the second grade I decided that this was what I wanted to do. I think that there was no real 'why,' I was just swept up into the fantastic universe revealed by astronomy, and always wanted to get more of it. There was a special magic to astronomy and science overall that revealed a bright path that was irresistible. By the time I was a teenager, I was an avid amateur astronomer and hoped to major in it in college. I was an undergrad at Caltech [California Institute of Technology], which hosts one of the top astronomy departments in the world, and was able to get involved in professional research after my freshman year, so if I add it all up, I've been doing research for 33 years.

"It often surprises people," Tod continues, "but doing astronomy superficially looks like any number of professional 'office jobs.' Most of the time you work at a desk in front of a computer. A key part of science in general is how much it centers on communication. Research communicates new and interesting findings about the universe, but in practical details this means writing long and richly detailed papers. The work includes reading and digesting other astronomers' written works. There are proposals to be written, collaborators and colleagues that you work with through email and phone calls, and so on. Much of the daily work involves a lot of paper shuffling! The good part of the day, though, is when you can work with your data and projects. This often involves running complex analysis software on the computer. Some of the day requires making time to think creatively. Other parts of the days are devoted to working within your organization to work to support the research of other astronomers."

Tod says that one of the best parts of his job is the enjoyment of discovering new things. He least likes the steps one must take to get to that point of discovery. "In astronomy, like every other field of science," he explains, "there is the 'doing' and the doing what you have to do to get to the 'doing!' Actually working on new data to find new things is the part that I enjoy most—this is the 'doing' of the science. To get to this point, however, one has to do a tremendous amount of setup work. This includes writing and reviewing research proposals, looking ahead to what new telescopes and instruments will be required in the future, seeing that new capabilities are developed, working hard to get the telescopes and their instruments into shape to support their use, and so on and so on. These are the 'get to the doing things.' Much of this can be fun, but the hardest parts and the least fun parts are probably all the tedium that these things can sometimes involve."

Dr. Heidi Newberg is an astronomer and associate professor in the Department of Physics, Applied Physics, and Astronomy at Rensselaer Polytechnic Institute in Troy, New York. She has worked as an astronomer for 17 years. She says that she became an astronomer through a series of small decisions. "In high school," she explains, "I particularly liked science and math. I entered undergraduate school as an engineering major, since my father recommended that I pursue a major that would result in solid job opportunities. But after my first year I switched my major to physics since I realized I wanted to know 'why' things are the way they are, not 'how' to build things. For example, an engineer will create tables or charts that show how much steel will stretch as a function of the weight applied to it, since that is required to design buildings or bridges.

A physicist will ask what it is about the steel material that causes that behavior. In my senior year of college, I interviewed at a few companies, but after interviewing me they thought I really should go to graduate school—even though I had not yet come to that realization myself. I was excited to be admitted to the University of California—Berkeley physics program, since it was large, varied (good for a student who was not sure what area of physics she wanted to do), and from my perspective it was in an exotic, exciting location. After my first year there, I got a summer job working with the Berkeley Automated Supernova Search, and liked it there, so I ended up doing my Ph.D. research project in astronomy. I'm not sure I ever made a conscious decision to become an astronomer; it is just what happened."

Dr. Newberg has taught astronomy classes for science majors, for non-science majors, and introductory physics courses for engineers. "A typical day for a professor involves constant interruptions," she says. "I constantly keep my tasks prioritized to make sure the most important ones get done. I prepare and deliver lectures, write grant proposals, write science papers, advise students, consult with colleagues, and attend meetings. The best part of my job is when I have a little time to look through the data myself and try to discover new knowledge. I also like working individually with students. I travel quite a bit for conferences and collaborations—on average three days per month. I think people tend to think of scientists as reclusive people who are stuck

in a laboratory. But the most successful ones are excellent communicators. I have worked mainly in large, international collaborations. Right now, I am helping to organize a collaboration between astronomers in the United States and China. If you looked at me during the day, I would either be talking to someone or typing at my computer, which is pretty much the same as most professionals these days."

Dr. Newberg says the least favorite part of her job is the pressure to obtain grant money to support her research and her students. "This is somewhat like working in sales," she explains. "I need to produce written proposals that convince panels that my research is important and likely to succeed and worthy of support." Dr. Newberg cites the opportunity to be creative as the best part of her job. "That is really the most important thing for me," she says. "It is very exciting when I think I am discovering something new. Much of the time, the possible discoveries do not hold up to further testing, but sometimes they do!"

Dr. Michael Hauser has worked in the fields of astronomy and astrophysics since 1970. He is currently the deputy director of the Space Telescope Science Institute (STScI) in Baltimore, Maryland. "The deputy director is the second-ranking management official at the STScI," he explains. "As such, a basic responsibility is to work with the director to assure that STScI meets its responsibilities to NASA and to serve as acting director when the director is not available. I have been deputy director during the terms of three directors, and my specific responsibilities have varied as the desires of the director and the nature of STScI have changed. In all cases I have been closely involved in strategic planning for STScI. Though I have assisted the director in interactions with external groups, such as NASA, the scientific community, advisory groups, and STScI governance groups, most of my responsibility has been inwardly focused. I have at times managed processes associated with the research staff, such as recruitment, evaluation, and promotion. When I was hired, STScI was responsible for one mission, the Hubble Space Telescope (HST). STScI is now a multi-mission organization, with responsibility for HST, the James Webb Space Telescope, and the Kepler mission, among other things. The organization has evolved from a Hubble-centric structure to a matrixed structure, with staff organized into divisions according to discipline, with each division providing its expertise to multiple missions. I am now responsible for overseeing the management of the Instruments Division, Operations and Engineering Division, and the office that carries out our education and public outreach programs. This responsibility includes recruiting, selecting, and evaluating the performance of the senior managers of these organizations, as well as monitoring the accomplishment of their mission goals. At times, I have modified organizational structures or reassigned managers to accomplish better the institute's responsibilities. Though I am allowed time for scientific research, in practice there is very limited time for that.

Good Advice I

Dr. Tod Lauer offers the following advice to young people who want to become astronomers:

First, keep your curiosity. It's the most important tool that you will have, but it's one of the first things that people will try to beat out of you as part of "growing up." It's also good to keep your interests as broad as possible. Astronomy has lots of connections to other fields in science, as well as engineering and computer science. Likewise, it's good to get your hands on technical things. Lots of astronomers got their first exposure to astronomy by playing with telescopes, electronics, computers, and so on. Amateur astronomy is a fun hobby, as is building electronics, getting computers to do real work (as opposed to just surfing the Web), and leads to deeper understanding of the tools you'll use later. In school you'll need to be rock solid in mathematics and physics; but what really surprised me is that you also need to be strong in writing composition, given how much of this you'll do.

"What I like least [about my job]," he continues, "is the gap between what it is now possible to do and what available resources allow us to pursue. While this statement probably could be made in most fields, astronomy is now in a golden age of discovery and understanding enabled by remarkable technologies and computational capability. This gap is both frustrating and conducive to sometimes overly competitive behavior. What

I like best is the participation in a venture that allows us to bring scientific methods to bear on some of the oldest and most profound questions that humans have pondered since the dawn of time, and to actually find answers to some of them."

DO I HAVE WHAT IT TAKES TO BE AN ASTRONOMER?

To be a successful astronomer, you should have a strong, but controlled, imagination. You must be able to see relationships between what may appear to be, on the surface, unrelated facts, and you must be able to form various hypotheses regarding these relationships. You must be able to concentrate over long periods of time. You should also express yourself well in both writing and verbally.

"Perseverance is the most important trait for an astronomer, or any researcher for that matter," says Dr. Newberg. "Good mathematical and analytical skills are important, as are communication skills (both written and verbal). Many astronomers enjoy traveling. Astronomers often travel to beautiful, remote locations where there is little light pollution for better observations of the skies."

HOW DO I BECOME AN ASTRONOMER?
Education

High School

While in high school, prospective astronomers should take mathematics (including analytical geometry and trigonometry),

---

Good Advice II

Dr. Heidi Newberg offers the following advice to young people who want to become astronomers:

I sometimes see young people who want to be astronomers because they have been exposed to a lot of pretty pictures and "gee whiz" facts. Or they like to look at the sky through small telescopes. These are activities that I associate with amateur astronomy. Although many professional astronomers are also avid amateur astronomers, it is more important for a professional astronomer to be interested in math, physics, analytical reasoning, and to have a strong inner drive to learn new information about how our universe works. If you want to be a professional astronomer, you should pursue an undergraduate degree in physics, and get research experience with a professional astronomer as early in your career as possible. Computer skills are becoming more important in professional astronomy, and can make it easier to contribute to research projects early in your career.

---

science courses (including chemistry and physics), English, foreign languages, and courses in the humanities and social sciences. Students should also be well grounded in the use of computers and in computer programming.

"I would advise students interested in careers in astronomy to study as much physics and mathematics as possible," says Dr. Hauser. "Courses in astronomy are, of course, also important, but these require the basics of math and physics. Modern astronomy often involves analysis of large and complex bodies of data, so skill in computing and numerical analysis is also very valuable. Skill in written and oral presentation is also an essential element for a research career. I would advise students to engage in hands-on training as soon as possible, be it in instrument or telescope building, observing, data analysis, modeling, theory, or laboratory measurements to aid in the interpretation of astronomical data. Experience in most or all of these areas will be valuable regardless of the particular astronomical career track one takes. On the basis of my own experiences, I would emphasize that one cannot really predict the wonderful opportunities that will become available if one is broadly prepared at the outset."

Postsecondary Training

All astronomers are required to have postsecondary training, with a doctoral degree being the usual educational requirement because most jobs are in research and development. A master's degree is sufficient for some jobs in applied research and development, and a bachelor's degree is adequate for some nonresearch jobs. Students should select a college program with wide offerings in physics, mathematics, and astronomy and take as many of these courses as possible. Graduate training will normally take about three years beyond the bachelor's degree. Some astronomers participate in postdoctoral fellowships to gain more experience in their specialty. "My first real job after graduate school was as a postdoctoral fellow at Princeton University," says Tod Lauer. "As I was finishing my Ph.D., I did the standard thing of applying to a number of astronomical research departments that were offering fellowships. The position at Princeton was attractive because it was to work with James Gunn, an exceptionally talented astronomer, and involved astronomical image processing, a specialty that was somewhat arcane at the time, but which was central to the research that I had done in graduate school. The job seemed an excellent chance to learn more and was matched to my talents and interests. It was also different from the standard path for a Santa Cruz Ph.D., which generally was to go on to another department strongly focused on observational work. The Princeton department was known for its strengths in theoretical work, and I thought that I would gain the most from this very different emphasis on problems, than what I was used to in graduate school."

Bachelor's degrees in astronomy are offered by about 80 institutions in the United States, and 40 institutions offer master's degrees or doctorates in the field, often combined with physics departments. Some of the astronomy courses typically offered in graduate school are celestial mechanics, galactic structure, radio astronomy, stellar atmospheres and interiors, theoretical astrophysics, and binary and variable stars. Some graduate schools require that an applicant for a doctorate spend several months in residence at an observatory. In most institutions the student's graduate courses will reflect his or her chosen astronomical specialty or particular field of interest.

Certification or Licensing

No certification or licensing is available for this profession.

Internships and Volunteerships

Internships are an excellent way of learning more about a career in astronomy while you are still in school. This experience allows you to gain valuable exposure to the field and practical applications of your studies, as well as providing you with future networking contacts. Internships are usually nonpaying, but do count toward semester credit hours. NASA is just one organization that offers internships for students with some postsecondary training. To find out more about NASA internships and other opportunities, explore its Web site (http://www.nasajobs.nasa.gov).

Volunteering at a planetarium is another good way to learn more about astronomy. Contact your local planetarium or science museum to inquire about available opportunities.

WHO WILL HIRE ME?

Approximately 1,700 astronomers are employed in the United States. About 38 percent of all physicists and astronomers work for scientific research and development companies. Another 21 percent work for the federal government. Astronomers represent only a small portion of these workers. The federal government employs astronomers in agencies such as NASA, the U.S Naval Observatory, the Naval Research Laboratory, and the U.S. Departments of Defense, Health and Human Services, and Energy.

In the private sector, astronomers are hired by consulting firms that supply astronomical talent to the government for specific tasks. In addition, a number of companies in the aerospace industry hire astronomers to work in related areas in order to use their background and talents in instrumentation, remote sensing, spectral observations, and computer applications.

A chief method of entry for astronomers with a doctorate is to register with the college's career services office, which provides contacts with the agencies looking for astronomers. Astronomers can also apply directly to universities, colleges, planetariums, government agencies, aerospace industry manufacturers, and others who hire astronomers. Many positions are advertised in professional and scientific journals devoted to astronomy and astrophysics.

Graduates with bachelor's or master's degrees can normally obtain semiprofessional positions in observatories, planetariums, or some of the larger colleges and universities offering training in astronomy. Their work assignments might be as research assistants, optical workers, observers, or technical assistants. Those employed by colleges or universities might well begin as instructors. Federal government positions in astronomy are usually earned on the basis of competitive examinations. Jobs with some municipal organizations employing astronomers are often based on competitive examinations. The examinations are usually open to those with bachelor's degrees.

WHERE CAN I GO FROM HERE?

Because of the relatively small size of the field, advancement for astronomers may be somewhat limited. A professional position in a large university or governmental agency is often considered the most desirable post available to an astronomer because of the opportunities it offers for additional study and research. Those employed in a college may well advance from instructor to assistant professor to associate professor and then to professor. There is also the possibility of eventually becoming a department head.

Opportunities also exist for advancement in observatories or industries employing people in astronomy. In these situations, as in those in colleges and universities, advancement depends to a great extent on the astronomer's ability, education, and experience. Peer recognition, in particular for discoveries that broaden the understanding of the field, is often a determinant of advancement. Publishing articles in professional journals, such as *Science* and the *Astrophysical Journal,* is a way for astronomers to become known and respected in the field. Advancement isn't usually speedy; an astronomer may spend years devoted to a specific research problem before being able to publish conclusions or discoveries in a scientific journal.

WHAT ARE THE SALARY RANGES?

Astronomers had median annual earnings of $101,300 in 2008, according to the U.S. Department of Labor. Salaries ranged from less than $45,330 to $156,720 or more annually. The average for astronomers employed by the federal government in 2008 was $124,810, according to the U.S. Department of Labor.

A 2007 survey conducted by the National Association of Colleges and Employers focuses on professionals who hold physics doctoral degrees, which covers many astronomers. According to the survey, the average starting salary offered to physics doctoral candidates was $52,469.

In educational institutions, salaries are normally regulated by the salary schedule prevailing in that particular institution. As the astronomer advances to higher-level teaching positions, his or her salary increases significantly.

Opportunities also exist in private industry for well-trained and experienced astronomers, who often find their services in demand as consultants. Fees for this type of work may run as high as $200 per day in some of the more specialized fields of astronomy.

Benefits for astronomers depend on the employer; however, they usually include such items as health insurance, retirement or 401(k) plans, and paid vacation days.

WHAT IS THE JOB OUTLOOK?

Employment for astronomers will grow about as fast as the average for all careers through 2016, according to the U.S. Department of Labor. Astronomy is one of the

Educational Path

Dr. Michael Hauser details the training he undertook to become an astronomer:

My academic training was a bachelor's degree in engineering–physics at Cornell, followed by a Ph.D. in physics at Caltech, with an experimental thesis on pion photoproduction.

It is worth noting that, beginning with the summer after high school graduation, I worked in the Radiation Physics Division at the National Bureau of Standards [now known as the National Institute of Standards and Technology] each summer until I entered graduate school. The first year was an excepted appointment as a student trainee; thereafter I had the title of physicist. That experience was an invaluable part of my training and had a significant influence on my choice of field of graduate study and subsequent early career.

After shifting my attention to astronomy, I did some reading of basic texts in the field, having had no astronomy courses during my college and graduate school years. I also began looking into promising detector technologies for measuring the high-frequency spectrum of the CMB, and undertook studies of the statistics of existing galaxy catalogs in collaboration with Jim Peebles. These activities were effectively the start of my graduate training in astronomy.

I then elected to further that training by returning to Caltech [California Institute of Technology] to work jointly with Gerry Neugebauer's infrared astronomy group and the low-temperature physics group with the aim of pursuing millimeter-wave detector development. After two years, during which I learned a lot about infrared astronomy and developed detectors that were the basis of the design used later on NASA's Cosmic Background Explorer mission, I accepted an offer to start a space infrared astronomy program at NASA's Goddard Space Flight Center. My years at Goddard were the scientifically most productive years of my astronomy career.

smallest science fields. Job openings result from the normal turnover when workers retire or leave the field for other reasons. Competition for these jobs, particularly among new people entering the profession, will continue to be strong. In recent years the number of new openings in this field have not kept pace with the number of astronomers graduating from the universities, and this trend is likely to continue for the near future. Furthermore, there will likely be few new positions made, since funding in this area is hard to come by.

The federal government will continue to provide employment opportunities for astronomers. Defense expenditures are expected to increase over the next decade, and this should provide stronger employment opportunities for astronomers who work on defense-related research projects. However, government agencies, particularly NASA, may find their budgets reduced in the coming years, and the number of new positions created for astronomers will likely drop as well. Few new observatories will be constructed, and those currently in existence are not expected to greatly increase the size of their staffs.

The greatest growth in employment of astronomers is expected to occur in business and industry. Companies in the aerospace field will need more astronomers to do research to help them develop new equipment and technology.

"Astronomy is not the subject that you major in because it is the easiest path to a high-paying job," says Dr. Newberg. "It is hard work to finish graduate school with a Ph.D., and it can be difficult to find a post-doc position afterward—especially if the search is geographically limited, and also difficult to find a research faculty position (most of which do pay very well) after that.

I know many people who did not stay on the research track for quite a variety of reasons. But fear that you will not be able to financially support yourself should not keep you from pursuing an astronomy career. The good news is that the skills you learn in astronomy are applicable many other places, and everyone I know who has decided to leave astronomy has done well in life. Many become programmers or teachers (high school or college), financial analysts, work in education and outreach at a museum or NASA center, or start their own businesses. Most of us have more things we would like to do, and are capable of doing, than we could finish in several lifetimes."

Biologists

SUMMARY

Definition
Biologists study the origin, development, anatomy, function, distribution, and other basic principles of living organisms. They are concerned with the nature of life itself in humans, microorganisms, plants, and animals, and with the relationship of each organism to its environment.

Alternative Job Titles
Biological scientists
Life scientists

Salary Range
$34,953 to $65,080 to $101,130+

Educational Requirements
Bachelor's degree; advanced degree required for top positions

Certification or Licensing
Voluntary (certification)
Required for certain positions (licensing)

Employment Outlook
About as fast as the average

High School Subjects
Biology
Chemistry
Mathematics
Physiology

Personal Interests
The environment
Science

"Every day as a microbiologist is rewarding," says Dr. Gary Toranzos, a professor of microbiology at the University of Puerto Rico. "But writing and publishing scientific journal articles as well as books and seeing the result of your work is probably one of the most rewarding things that can happen to a scientist. Of course, being recognized by your peers is also very rewarding. Awards and other recognitions are also rewarding, but they are simply the cherry on top of the dessert."

WHAT DOES A BIOLOGIST DO?

Biology can be divided into many specialties. *Biologists*, or *life scientists*, may be identified by their specialties. Following is a breakdown of the many kinds of biologists and their specific fields of study.

Anatomists study animal bodies from basic cell structure to complex tissues and organs. They determine the ability of body parts to regenerate and investigate the possibility of transplanting organs and

skin. Their research is applied to human medicine.

Aquatic biologists study animals and plants that live in water and how they are affected by their environmental conditions, such as the salt, acid, and oxygen content of the water and temperature, light, and other factors.

Biochemists study the chemical composition of living organisms. They attempt to understand the complex reactions involved in reproduction, growth, metabolism, and heredity.

Biophysicists apply physical principles to biological problems. They study the mechanics, heat, light, radiation, sound, electricity, and energetics of living cells and organisms and do research in the areas of vision, hearing, brain function, nerve conduction, muscle reflex, and damaged cells and tissues.

Bio-technicians, or *biological technicians,* assist the cornucopia of biological scientists in their endeavors.

Botanists study plant life. Some specialize in plant biochemistry, the structure and function of plant parts, and identification and classification, among other topics.

Cytologists, sometimes called *cell biologists,* examine the cells of plants and animals, including those cells involved in reproduction. They use microscopes and other instruments to observe the growth and division of cells and to study the influences of physical and chemical factors on both normal and malignant cells.

Ecologists examine such factors as pollutants, rainfall, altitude, temperature, and population size in order to study the distribution and abundance of organisms and their relation to their environment.

Entomologists study insects and their relationship to other life forms.

Geneticists study heredity in various forms of life. They are concerned with how biological traits such as color, size, and resistance to disease originate and are transmitted from one generation to another. They also try to develop ways to alter or produce new traits, using chemicals, heat, light, or other means.

Histopathologists investigate diseased tissue in humans and animals.

Immunologists study the manner in which the human body resists disease.

Limnologists study freshwater organisms and their environment.

Marine biologists specialize in the study of marine species and their environment. They gather specimens at different times, taking into account tidal cycles, seasons, and exposure to atmospheric elements, in order to answer questions concerning the overall health of sea organisms and their environment.

Microbiologists study bacteria, viruses, molds, algae, yeasts, and other organisms of microscopic or submicroscopic size. Some microorganisms are useful to humans; they are studied and used in the production of food, such as cheese, bread, and tofu. Other microorganisms have been used to preserve food and tenderize meat. Some microbiologists work with microorganisms that cause disease. They work to diagnose, treat, and prevent disease. Microbiologists have helped prevent typhoid fever, influenza, measles, polio, whooping cough, and smallpox. Today, they work on cures for AIDS, cancer, cystic fibrosis, and Alzheimer's disease, among others.

Molecular biologists apply their research on animal and bacterial systems toward the goal of improving and better understanding human health.

Mycologists study edible, poisonous, and parasitic fungi, such as mushrooms, molds, yeasts, and mildews, to determine which are useful to medicine, agriculture, and industry. Their research has resulted in benefits such as the development of antibiotics, the propagation of mushrooms, and methods of retarding fabric deterioration.

Nematologists study nematodes (roundworms), which are parasitic in animals and plants. Nematodes transmit diseases, attack insects, or attack other nematodes that exist in soil or water. Nematologists investigate and develop methods of controlling these organisms.

Parasitologists study animal parasites and their effects on humans and other animals.

Pharmacologists may be employed as researchers by pharmaceutical companies. They often spend most of their time working in the laboratory, where they study the effects of various drugs and medical compounds on mice or rabbits. Working within controlled environments, pharmacologists precisely note the types, quantities, and timing of medicines administered as a part of their experiments. Periodically, they make blood smears or perform autopsies to study dif-ferent reactions. They usually work with a team of researchers, headed by one with a doctorate and consisting of several biologists with master's and bachelor's degrees and some laboratory technicians.

Physiologists are biologists who specialize in studying all the life stages of plants or animals. Some specialize in a particular body system or a particular function, such as respiration.

Wildlife biologists study the habitats and the conditions necessary for the survival of birds and other wildlife. Their goal is to find ways to ensure the continuation of healthy wildlife populations, while lessening the impact and growth of civilization around them.

Zoologists study all types of animals to learn their origin, interrelationships, classifications, life histories, habits, diseases, relation to the environment, growth, genetics, and distribution. Zoologists are usually identified by the animals they study: *ichthyologists* (fish), *mammalogists* (mammals), *ornithologists* (birds), and *herpetologists* (reptiles and amphibians).

Biologists may also work for government agencies concerned with public health. *Toxicologists*, for example, study the effects of toxic substances on humans, animals, and plants. The data they gather are used in consumer protection and industrial safety programs to reduce the hazards of accidental exposure or ingestion. *Public health microbiologists* conduct experiments on water, foods, and the general environment of a community to detect the presence of harmful bacteria so pollution and contagious diseases can be controlled or eliminated.

The biologist's work environment varies greatly depending upon the position and type of employer. One biologist may work outdoors or travel much of the time. Another wears a white smock and spends years working in a laboratory. Some work with toxic substances and disease cultures; strict safety measures must be observed.

Biologists frequently work under pressure. For example, those employed by pharmaceutical houses work in an atmosphere of keen competition for sales that encourages the development of new drug products, and, as they are identified, the rapid testing and early marketing of these products. The work is very exacting, however, and pharmaceutical biologists must exercise great care to ensure that adequate testing of products has been properly conducted.

Some biologists, including botanists, ecologists, and zoologists, may undertake strenuous, sometimes dangerous, fieldwork in primitive conditions. Marine biologists work in the field, on research ships or in laboratories, in tropical seas and ocean areas with considerably cooler climates. They will be required to perform some strenuous work, such as carrying a net, digging, chipping, or hauling equipment or specimens. Marine biologists who work underwater must be able to avoid hazards, such as razor-sharp coral reefs and other underwater dangers. Wildlife biologists work in all types of weather and in all types of terrain and ecosystems. They may work alone or with a group in inhospitable surroundings in order to gather information.

To Be a Successful Biologist, You Should...

- have a systematic approach to solving problems
- have an inquisitive nature
- have an aptitude for biology, chemistry, and mathematics
- have patience in order to conduct time-consuming research and analysis
- be a good communicator
- have good observational skills

WHAT IS IT LIKE TO BE A BIOLOGIST?

Dr. Gary Toranzos is a professor of microbiology at the University of Puerto Rico. He has been a professor for 22 years. "I started college studies as pre-med, as most students do," he recalls, "because of the lack of information regarding science as a career, and total misinformation that physicians are scientists. In my third year of college, I had a life-changing professor of microbiology; he was nice, understanding, and presented his lectures with true passion, giving the impression that he was actually enjoying his chosen profession. By my fourth year, I started working in a research laboratory, where I had another professor who, by his passion for molecular microbiology, also changed my life, and I have not looked back since.

"I am an environmental microbiologist," Dr. Toranzos continues, "and as such, I do research on microorganisms that can be transmitted by water, food, and air. We are currently doing studies at several beaches looking at the microbiological quality of the waters and trying to develop new indicators of risk to bathers. Having passion for my job, I can hardly wait to get to my laboratory, and the first thing I do is check the results from the experiments done the previous day. Looking at the results, then I get together with my students to discuss these and plan for the next set of experiments. My typical responsibilities include doing the experiments designed to answer specific questions, discussing them with graduate and undergraduate students, and, of course, the other passion of my life: teaching. I regard teaching actually as a 50-50 contract with the students: I will teach 50 percent but I also want them to teach me the equivalent of 50 percent."

Dr. Toranzos says that the worst part of his job is occasionally not having the funds to carry out research. "And the best part of being a microbiologist," he says, "just about everything [else]. They pay me to play, and I get to do this every day of my life! But, actually, what I enjoy the most is going to conferences the world over to intellectually spar with my peers; I come back full of energy and new ideas from every single one of the trips."

Dr. Marshall Sundberg is a botany professor at Emporia State University and the editor of *Plant Science Bulletin.* He has been a teaching botanist for 31 years: seven on the Eau Claire campus of the University of Wisconsin and 12 each at Louisiana State University, Baton Rouge, Louisiana, and Emporia State University, Emporia, Kansas. His research focuses on structure and development of flowering plants. "Even as a high school student," Dr. Sundberg recalls, "I was fascinated with biology and especially the structural beauty and complexity that can be observed through the microscope. However, it wasn't until my sophomore year in college that I became aware of the fantastic diversity of plants. As a biology major at Carleton College I was required to take at least one botany course. It was during my first botany course that Professor Bill Muir introduced me to the touch, smell, taste, and sound of plants. Dr. Muir had been losing his sight for many years (a side-effect of diabetes), but he taught himself to observe with his other senses and passed some of this along to us in the laboratory and on campus field trips—the rustle of quaking aspen leaves, the smell of juniper, the taste of willow twigs. Of course, he would also make us describe the visual appearance of what we observed, always prompting us to observe more carefully and describe more explicitly so that he could be sure of what we were (or were not) seeing. Plants were intriguing and alive—and much less well known than animals. I decided to focus on a botany emphasis and took every course Dr. Muir offered.

"Most of my career has been at regional, comprehensive public universities that offer bachelor's and master's degrees, but not a doctorate," continues Dr. Sundberg. "Faculty at these schools have a heavier teaching responsibility than our colleagues at the major research universities, but we also have expectations for conducting research—especially during the summer. During the academic year I may teach two or three different lecture courses and one or two laboratory sections each semester. The hours are regularly scheduled but account for only 10 to 16 hours per week in class with students. This leaves considerable flexibility for me and my colleagues to arrange our schedules. This flexibility is one of the attractions of an academic career. If my first class is not until 10 A.M., I could come in at 7 in the morning to have a couple of 'quality hours' to myself before class—or I could come in at 9:40 just to get things together before heading to class. I may decide to teach one of my courses at night—or occasionally setup an experiment that runs into the night. During school breaks, including summer, I may schedule fieldwork or laboratory work, or I may decide to take a vacation. As long as I meet my classes and regularly publish my research results, I have a lot of flexibility in setting my schedule."

Dr. Sundberg says that the "most disappointing aspect of being a botanist is that many people do not understand what that means. Most people know that a zoologist is a biologist who studies animals but many fewer people know that botanists are scientists who study plants. In fact, many people do not even realize that plants are living organisms! The best part about being a botanist is that I have the freedom to study and work every day on what I like doing. The best job is one that is fun and doesn't feel like 'work.'"

Dr. Crystal Johnson is a research assistant professor at the Gulf Coast Research Laboratory at the University of Southern Mississippi in Ocean Springs, Mississippi. "I was always a germophobe and yet fascinated by germs," she recalls, "and after I took a microbiology course in college, I decided to study them. So, my fear of germs and obsession to get rid of them led me to study them and learn that they are not all bad and some are even good for you."

Dr. Johnson says that she has few typical days on the job and that her job responsibilities change drastically depending on the day. "I will give two scenarios," she says, "one as a postdoc and one as a research assistant professor, that highlight this variety. As a postdoc, on sampling days, we (a technician or student and I) arrive around 7:30 A.M. to prepare to go out in the field. We load the boat with coolers and pre-labeled collection containers, go to our sampling site, collect water, oysters, and sediment, transport them back on cold packs so that the bacteria do not continue to grow (we want to get a snapshot of the environment at one point in time), and then we process the samples. This involves shucking oysters and placing them in a blender to get a homogenate, and then placing a small amount of this homogenate, or water or sediment, on agar in a Petri dish. The Petri dishes are incubated overnight and the colonies are lifted and then probed for a specific gene that we are targeting. As a research assistant professor, by the time I arrive, the lab is already up and running, and I spend more time writing and reviewing manuscripts, teaching and training students or technicians in the lab, writing grant proposals, writing reports, communicating with collaborators (other scientists doing similar experiments), advising other scientists on projects and providing technical support, optimizing parameters on experiments, and reading scientific articles."

Dr. Johnson says that one thing that has surprised her about becoming a research assistant professor is how the further she advances in her career, the less involved she becomes with lab work. "I have had to learn to let go and allow students and technicians to carry out the experiments that I help establish while my actual lab time has decreased,"

she says. "As I progress over the years, I know that my students and technicians will become my hands. So one thing I like least is having to let go and live vicariously as an outsider to projects that I design. What I like most is the freedom to ask almost any scientific question I want. I love the fact that each question that gets answered raises more interesting questions. I love bouncing ideas off other scientists and discussing the ins and outs of one approach versus another. I love watching students grow and learn and take ownership of a project."

DO I HAVE WHAT IT TAKES TO BE A BIOLOGIST?

To be a successful biologist, you must be systematic in your approach to solving problems. You should also have an inquisitive, probing mind and an aptitude for biology, chemistry, and mathematics. You should also have patience since you will spend much time in observation and analysis. Developing good communication skills will help you gather and exchange data and solve problems that arise in your work.

"The skills required of a botanist are the same as required for any modern biologist," says Dr. Sundberg. "Most important are good critical thinking and observational skills. It is ironic that good observational skills tend to decrease the more time you spend passively watching images and pictures. Artists learn early that to really see something, they must try to sketch it. That's also good advice for budding botanists!"

HOW DO I BECOME A BIOLOGIST?

Education

High School

High school students interested in a career in biology should take English, biology, earth science, physics, chemistry, Latin, geometry, computer science, and algebra.

Postsecondary Training

Prospective biologists should also obtain a broad undergraduate college training. In addition to courses in all phases of biology, useful related courses include organic and inorganic chemistry, physics, and mathematics. Modern languages, English, biometrics (the use of mathematics in biological measurements), and statistics are also useful. Courses in computers will be extremely beneficial. Students should take advantage of courses that require laboratory, field, or collecting work. "In terms of course preparation," says Dr. Sundberg, "you must have a solid foundation in mathematics as well as chemistry and physics. College algebra is the bare minimum for math. Basic statistics is necessary for field studies and research design and calculus is important for studying growth and development. Studies of physiology and development both depend on understanding basic chemistry, through biochemistry, and a year of introductory physics."

Dr. Johnson took a microbiology class as an undergraduate, and when she entered graduate school she took more advanced courses in microbiology, immunology, virology, and immunology, and then additional electives later in graduate school, such as bacterial pathogenesis. "During the first year," she recalls, "I did rotations, where I spent 40 to 60 hours per week working in a lab doing scientific experiments for my own project or assisting with other, older graduate students' projects. After the rotations, I chose a lab that was focused on studying a particular bacterium called *Streptococcus pneumoniae.* The experiments I did over the course of six years to study this organism were later published in scientific journals, and at the end of 6.5 years, I compiled these papers into one dissertation that told a story about antibiotic resistance in this bacterium."

Nearly all colleges and universities offer undergraduate training in one or more of the biological sciences. These vary from

A Rewarding Experience

Dr. Crystal Johnson details one of her most rewarding experiences as a microbiologist:

One of the most rewarding things that happened to me as a microbiologist was the time I was in the mall and I happened to see a student I had taught through the National Science Foundation GK-12 program. She was still excited about the lessons that I had taught and the fact that she had struggled to understand a concept (calculating concentration and volume) for so long until I explained it to her in the GK-12 lab, and it was like a light bulb went off. She was talking about it even with all of her "cool" friends around right there in the mall. That was very satisfying.

liberal arts schools that offer basic majors in botany and zoology to large universities that permit specialization in areas such as entomology, bacteriology, and physiology at the undergraduate level.

The best way to become a biologist is to earn a bachelor's degree in biology or one of its specialized fields, such as anatomy, bacteriology, botany, ecology, or microbiology. For the highest professional status, a doctorate is required. This is particularly true of top research positions and most higher-level college teaching openings. Many colleges and universities offer courses leading to a master's degree and a doctorate.

Candidates for a doctorate specialize in one of the subdivisions of biology. A number of sources of financial assistance are available to finance graduate work. Most major universities have highly developed fellowship (scholarship) or assistantship (part-time teaching or research) programs.

Organizations, such as the U.S. Public Health Service and the National Science Foundation, make awards to support graduate students. In addition, major universities often hold research contracts or have their own projects that provide part-time and summer employment for undergraduate and graduate students.

Dr. Johnson participated in a National Science Foundation (NSF) program called the NSF GK-12 Fellowship (for grades K–12). "I dedicated 10 hours per week teaching junior high school and high school students," she says. "In some semesters, I delivered modules to the schools that included fruit flies, DNA, Petri dishes, pipets, and other items to teach students about microbiology and genetics. In other semesters, the students came to visit the local science museum, and we held daylong labs for the students that introduced them to microbiology, cell biology, and molecular biology, e.g, a sickle cell anemia project and HIV testing. Although a distraction from grad school at first, the NSF GK-12 program changed my life because teaching younger students, some of them not otherwise attentive or engaged, forced me to make them pay attention and explain my research in a way that they understood. This, in turn, led me to write better papers, give better talks, and write better grant proposals, some of which have now been funded. I believe this experience is a big part of what made me into the now-funded scientist that I am today."

Certification or Licensing

Several professional associations, such as the Ecological Society of America and the American Society for Microbiology, offer voluntary professional certification to biologists who specialize in a particular field.

A state license may be required for biologists who are employed as technicians in general service health organizations, such as hospitals or clinics. To qualify for this license, proof of suitable educational background is necessary.

Internships and Volunteerships

You will most likely participate in an internship as part of your college education. Internships allow you to learn more about the field and work closely with professionals. Most internships are unpaid, but many colleges convey course credit for their successful completion.

High school students may have the opportunity to join volunteer service groups at local hospitals or laboratories. Student science training programs (SSTPs) allow qualified high school students to spend a summer doing research under the supervision of a scientist.

"Science, and in my case, microbiology, has been the most fulfilling career I could have ever imagined," says Dr. Toranzos. "The love for science can only be acquired by doing science. Young people should get involved in research at all levels; it is never too early to start. I have had high school students and even junior high students doing summer projects. Many of these are now accomplished professors/scientists or working for industry, but they all got an early start. Do your homework using the Web, look at your local university to see what microbiological research is being done, and volunteer your time to learn. It will be an incredibly fulfilling effort, and one that will pay off in the long run."

WHO WILL HIRE ME?

Approximately 39 percent of all biological scientists work for the government at the federal, state, or local level. The majority of those who do not work for the government are involved in the drug industry, which includes pharmaceutical companies, hospitals, biotechnology companies, and laboratories. The area in which biologists work is influenced by their specialties. Marine biologists, for example, can find employment with the U.S. Department of Interior, the U.S. Fish and Wildlife Service, and the National Oceanic and Atmospheric Administration. They may also find employment in nongovernmental agencies, such as the Scripps Institution of Oceanography in California and the Marine Biological Laboratory in Massachusetts. Microbiologists can find employment with the U.S. Department of Health and Human Services, the Environmental Protection Agency, and the Department of Agriculture, among others. They may also work for pharmaceutical, food, agricultural, geological, environmental, and pollution control companies. Wildlife biologists can find employment in the U.S. Public Health Service, the U.S. Fish and Wildlife Service, and the Forest Service, among many other sources.

Biologists who are interested in becoming teachers should consult their college career services office. Public and private high schools and an increasing number of colleges hire teachers through the colleges at which they studied. Private employment agencies also place a significant number of teachers. Some teaching positions are filled through direct application.

Biologists interested in private industry and nonprofit organizations may also apply directly for employment. Major organizations that employ biologists often interview college seniors on campus. Private and public employment offices frequently have listings from these employers. Experienced biologists often change positions as a result of contacts made at professional seminars and national conventions.

Special application procedures are required for positions with government agencies. Civil service applications for

Did You Know?

The editors of *What Can I Do Now? Science* asked Dr. Crystal Johnson, a microbiologist and research assistant professor at the Gulf Coast Research Laboratory, to detail one thing that young people may not know about the field of microbiology:

One thing many young people don't know is that there are actually many different ways to be a microbiologist, and these depend on a person's interests, the sector they choose, the degree a person gets, and other factors. A person may be a microbiologist with an associate's degree, a bachelor's degree, a Ph.D., an MD, a master's degree, an MPH (master's of public health), or even an MBA. Major sectors include academia (colleges and universities), government (e.g., the Food and Drug Administration, the Centers for Disease Control, the Environmental Protection Agency, state agencies, etc.), and industry (e.g., working for a company like Johnson & Johnson or Bayer). In academia, doctorate-level microbiologists typically do research, teach courses, and train undergraduate and graduate students. Associate's-, bachelor's-, and master's-level microbiologists analyze bacterial samples, diagnose the cause of human or animal disease, perform genetic testing of microbes, determine whether spinach is safe to eat, etc. In government agencies, a microbiologist does research and is typically more involved in regulatory work, such as ensuring that the nation's spinach is safe, figuring out where the 2001 anthrax spores came from, or figuring out what type of flu vaccine needs to be produced from year to year. In industry, a microbiologist typically uses research to discover new antimicrobial compounds, such as the next penicillin. There are also microbiologists who focus on scientific writing, and some go on to become major authors of both fiction and nonfiction.

federal, state, and municipal positions may be obtained by writing to the agency involved and from high school and college guidance and placement bureaus, public employment agencies, and post offices.

WHERE CAN I GO FROM HERE?

In a field as broad as biology, numerous opportunities for advancement exist. In many instances, however, advancement depends on the individual's level of education. A doctorate is generally required for college teaching, independent research, and top-level administrative and management jobs. A master's degree is sufficient for some jobs in applied research, and a bachelor's degree may qualify for some entry-level jobs.

With the right qualifications, the biologist may advance to the position of project chief and direct a team of other biologists. Many use their knowledge and experience as background for administrative and management positions. Often, as they develop professional expertise, biologists move from strictly technical assignments into positions in which they interpret biological knowledge.

The usual path of advancement in biology, as in other sciences, comes from specialization and the development of the status of an expert in a given field. Biologists may work with professionals in other major fields to explore problems that require an interdisciplinary approach, such as biochemistry, biophysics, biostatistics (or biometrics). Biochemistry, for example, uses the methods of chemistry to study the composition of biological materials and the molecular mechanisms of biological processes.

WHAT ARE THE SALARY RANGES?

Earnings for biological scientists vary extensively based on the type and size of their employer, the individual's level of education and experience, and the area of biology in which the scientist specializes. The U.S. Department of Labor (DoL) reports that biologists earned the following mean annual salaries in 2008 by specialty: biochemistry and biophysics, $88,450; microbiology, $70,150; soil and plant science, $64,110; and zoology and wildlife biology, $58,820. The DoL reports that the median salary for biological scientists, not otherwise classified was $65,080 in 2008. Salaries ranged from less than $35,620 to $101,130 or more.

According to the National Association of Colleges and Employers, those with bachelor's degrees in the biological and life sciences had beginning salaries averaging $34,953 in 2007.

Biologists are usually eligible for health and dental insurance, paid vacations and sick days, and retirement plans. Some employers may offer reimbursement for continuing education, seminars, and travel.

WHAT IS THE JOB OUTLOOK?

Employment for biological scientists is expected to grow about as fast as the average for all careers through 2016, according to the U.S. Department of Labor. Despite this prediction, competition will be stiff for some positions. For example, those with Ph.D.'s looking for research positions will find strong competition for a limited number of openings. In addition, certain government jobs as well as government funding for research may also be less plentiful. A recession or shift in political power can cause the loss of funding for grants and the decline of research and development endeavors.

Private industry will need biologists to work in sales, marketing, and research management. Companies developing new drugs, environmentally friendly products, modified crops, and the like will need the expertise of biological scientists. The U.S. Department of Labor also predicts that even companies not solely involved in biotechnology will be increasingly using biotechnology developments and techniques in their businesses. This should create more job opportunities for biological scientists in a variety of industries.

"Employment opportunities for botanists (and biologists in general) are reasonably good even in the current economic conditions," says Dr. Sundberg, "but vary considerably depending on level of education attained. Entry-level jobs exist for those with a bachelor's degree in state and federal agencies for those with taxonomic and ecological training. These days there is strength in areas associated with ecological monitoring (associated with climate change). There are also opportunities in biotechnology, again starting at the introductory level with positions for technicians in industry and agriculture. A botanist with training in molecular biology will also have access to opportunities in biomedical and health-related fields—another boom area even in today's economy. A surprising number of botany undergraduates end up in medical school!"

Dr. Toranzos says that the employment outlook for microbiologists is very good at most levels. "There are university or college positions for those who love to teach, research positions at universities or institutes, or employment with local government or the federal government. There is always the possibility of doing consulting work as well. If we take into consideration the clinical field, the outlook is even better."

Biologists with advanced degrees will be best qualified for the most lucrative and challenging jobs, although this varies by specialty, with genetic, cellular, and biochemical research showing the most promise. Scientists with bachelor's degrees may find openings as science or engineering technicians, health technologists and technicians, and high school biology teachers. Many colleges and universities are cutting back on their faculties, but high schools and two-year colleges may have teaching positions available. Employment in marine biology is predicted to be especially competitive.

Chemists

SUMMARY

Definition
Chemists are scientists who study the composition, changes, reactions, and transformations of matter. They may specialize in analytical, biological, inorganic, organic, or physical chemistry; chemical engineering; or other areas.

Alternative Job Titles
Scientists

Salary Range
$37,840 to $66,230 to $139,440+

Educational Requirements
Bachelor's degree; advanced degree required for top positions

Certification or Licensing
None available

Employment Outlook
About as fast as the average

High School Subjects
Chemistry
Mathematics

Personal Interests
Science

A few years ago, chemical/environmental engineer Dr. Dianne Gates-Anderson worked on a project that studied how surfaces would become contaminated if a "dirty bomb" were to be set off in an urban environment. "For my study," she recalls, "we built a 'mock' dirty bomb with real explosives but fake contaminants. As I was standing inside the bomb chamber working with explosive experts on a live bomb I thought to myself 'wow, who could have ever imagined me doing this.' I really liked the combination of blowing things up but doing it for a good cause that this project provided me."

WHAT DOES A CHEMIST DO?

There are many branches of chemistry, each with a different set of work responsibilities and requirements. The following paragraphs detail some of the major specialties in the field.

The distinction between organic and inorganic chemistry is based on carbon-hydrogen compounds. Ninety-nine percent of all chemicals that occur naturally contain carbon. *Organic chemists* study the chemical compounds that contain carbon and hydrogen, while *inorganic chemists* study all other substances.

Analytical chemists study the composition and nature of rocks, soils, materials that may be used in pharmaceuticals, and other substances and develop procedures for analyzing them. They also identify the presence of pollutants in soil, water, and air.

Physical and theoretical chemists study the physical characteristics of atoms and molecules. A physical chemist working in a nuclear power plant, for example, may study the properties of the radioactive materials involved in the production of electricity derived from nuclear fission reactions. *Macromolecular chemists* study the properties of atoms and molecules.

Another major specialty is biochemistry. *Biological chemists,* also known as *biochemists,* study the composition and actions of complex chemicals in living organisms. They identify and analyze the chemical processes related to biological functions, such as metabolism or reproduction, and they are often involved directly in genetics studies.

Generally, biochemists employed in the United States work in one of three major fields: medicine, nutrition, or agriculture. In medicine, biochemists mass-produce life-saving chemicals usually found only in minuscule amounts in the body. Some of these chemicals have helped diabetics and heart attack victims for years. Biochemists employed in the field of medicine might work to identify chemical changes in organs or cells that signal the development of such diseases as cancer, diabetes, or schizophrenia. Or they may look for chemical explanations for why certain people develop muscular dystrophy or become obese. While studying chemical makeup and changes in these situations, biochemists may work to discover a treatment or a prevention for a disease. For instance, biochemists discovering how certain diseases such as AIDS and cancer escape detection by the immune system are also devising ways to enhance immunity to fight these diseases. Biochemists are also finding out the chemical basis of fertility and how to improve the success of in vitro fertilization to help couples have children or to preserve endangered species.

Biochemists in the pharmaceutical industry design, develop, and evaluate drugs, antibiotics, diagnostic kits, and other medical devices. They may search out ways to produce antibiotics, hormones, enzymes, or other drug components, or they may do quality control on the way in which drugs and dosages are made and determined.

In the field of nutrition, biochemists examine the effects of food on the body. For example, they might study the relationship between diet and diabetes. Biochemists doing this study could look at the nutrition content of certain foods eaten by people with diabetes and study how these foods affect the functioning of the pancreas and other organs. Biochemists in the nutrition field also look at vitamin and mineral deficiencies and how they affect the human body. They examine these deficiencies in relation to body performance, and they may study anything from how the liver is affected by a lack of vitamin B to the effects of poor nutrition on the ability to learn.

Biochemists involved in agriculture undertake studies to discover more efficient methods of crop cultivation, storage, and pest control. For example, they might create genetically engineered crops that are more resistant to frost, drought, spoilage, disease, and pests. They might focus on helping to create fruit trees that produce more fruit by studying the biochemical composition of the plant and determining how to alter or select for this desirable trait. Biochemists may study the chemical composition of insects to determine better and more efficient methods of controlling the pest population and the damage they do to crops. Or they could work on programming bacteria to clean up the environment by "eating" toxic chemicals.

Chemical engineers take chemistry out of the laboratory and into the real world. They are involved in evaluating methods and equipment for the mass production of chemicals and other materials requiring chemical processing. They also develop products from these materials, such as plastics, metals, gasoline, detergents, pharmaceuticals, and foodstuffs. They develop or improve safe, environmentally sound processes, determine the least costly production method, and formulate the material for easy use and safe, economic transportation.

Some chemists pursue careers as educators, writers, or in management at pharmaceutical companies, chemical manufacturing companies, and other businesses.

Because chemistry is such a diverse field, central to every reaction and the transformation of all matter, it is necessary for chemists to specialize in specific areas. Still, each field covers a wide range of work and presents almost limitless possibilities for experimentation and study. Often, chemists will team up with colleagues in other specialties to seek solutions to their common problems.

Most chemists work in clean, well-lighted laboratories that are well organized and neatly kept. They may have their own offices and share laboratory space with

To Be a Successful Chemist, You Should...

- be detail-oriented and precise
- have a good imagination
- be highly organized
- enjoy solving problems
- be able to work alone or in groups
- have good written and oral communication skills
- be willing to continue to learn throughout your career

other chemists. Some chemists work at such locations as oil wells or refineries, where their working conditions may be uncomfortable. Occasionally, chemical reactions or substances being tested may have strong odors. Other chemicals may be extremely dangerous to the touch, and chemists will have to wear protective devices such as goggles, gloves, and protective clothing and work in special, well-ventilated hoods.

WHAT IS IT LIKE TO BE A CHEMIST?

Dr. Judith Klinman is a professor of chemistry at the University of California —Berkeley. "My first love of chemistry was stimulated by a teacher I had in high school," she says. "That was the spark that convinced me to change a planned major in French language and literature to chemistry. I have had no regrets since. I received my Ph.D. in physical organic chemistry at the University of Pennsylvania-Philadelphia, and did not start to do biochemistry until my postdoctoral work with Irwin Rose at Fox Chase Cancer Center in Philadelphia. I immediately realized that the application of chemistry to biological problems was a fantastically interesting field and one I have followed ever since."

Dr. Klinman says that each day as a chemistry professor is different. "When I am teaching, my week is structured by the course that I am teaching (these days either a biochemistry course or a graduate course on enzyme structure and function). I run a research group of about 15 people (about half graduate students and half postdocs) and we meet twice a week as a group for intense discussions about the research literature and our own research. I spend a lot of time analyzing experimental data and designing new research directions and then on writing up the research results for publication. At a major research university like the University of California—Berkeley, faculty also spend time interacting with graduate students in other research groups (especially around the time that these graduate students must pass a Ph.D. qualifying exam and then at annual Ph.D. thesis committee meetings). There is also advising of undergraduate students and training them in the laboratory (so that they can have a research experience as part of their education). As a practicing scientist I find myself 'on the road' a fair amount, in order to attend scientific conferences and to give research seminars at other universities. Bottom line: there is never a dull moment."

Dr. Klinman says that the downsides to a career as a biochemist are "being busier than one can manage in any day and the continuing need to make sure there are sufficient funds to run the research program. On the positive side, I absolutely love the scientific process of discovery."

Dr. Dianne Gates-Anderson is a chemist and chemical engineer who has worked in the field of environmental engineering for 18 years. She is currently employed at the Lawrence Livermore National Laboratory in Livermore, California. (Visit http://www.chemheritage.org/women_chemistry/enviro/anderson.html to learn more about her career.) "I develop processes to treat hazardous and radioactive waste," she explains. "My academic background includes a BS in chemical engineering from Oklahoma State University and a MS and Ph.D. in environmental engineering from the University of California—Berkeley. My typical workday can vary a lot. I divide my time between researching and gathering information, designing studies and equipment, performing studies in a laboratory, and writing up and presenting the results of my work. As my career has advanced I find myself spending more time sharing my knowledge with others as a 'subject matter expert' and less time in the laboratory. I also spend time working with safety professionals to make sure that the work I propose is done safely and writing and presenting research proposals to get funding for my work. My work hours also vary; when I am on-site my typical workday is from 7:00 A.M. until 4:30 P.M.

When I am off-site I can work some very long days."

Dr. Gates-Anderson says that technical writing is the least favorite aspect of her career. "It takes a lot of time to write and publish the results of your work," she explains, "and I would much rather spend my time in the lab than at my desk writing. What I like the most about my career is the flexibility I have had to contribute to the projects that I find interesting and meaningful. I also like the fact that what I do would never be considered routine. I work on really challenging problems and find that very rewarding. I do not like doing the same thing over and over again. I typically work on a project from the bench-scale through pilot-scale."

DO I HAVE WHAT IT TAKES TO BE A CHEMIST?

Chemists must be detail-oriented and precise. They will often work with minute quantities, taking minute measurements. They must record all details and reaction changes that may seem insignificant and unimportant to the untrained observer. Chemists must keep careful records of their work and have the patience to repeat experiments over and over again, perhaps varying the conditions in only a small way each time. "I think the key to success in the field is being thorough and meticulous with the work that you do," says Dr. Gates-Anderson. "The key to being a good chemist or research engineer is not just knowing that you have to split a lot of hairs in order to do quality work. If you try to split every hair you will

be very inefficient; a good chemist knows which hairs to split."

Chemists should be inquisitive and have an interest in what makes things work and how things fit together. Chemists may work alone or in groups. A successful chemist is not only self-motivated but should be a team player and have good written and oral communication skills.

HOW DO I BECOME A CHEMIST?
Education
High School

In high school, you can begin preparing for a chemistry career by taking advanced-level courses in the physical sciences, mathematics, and English. A year each of physics, chemistry, and biology is essential, as are the abilities to

---

Good Advice

Dr. Judith Klinman offers the following advice to young people who want to become biochemists:

Make sure that you find this discipline fascinating and exciting. You will know once you start to study this subject whether you find it exciting and are anxious to learn more. You will need to master the basic sciences to provide the foundation for more cutting edge work. After that, there are many directions to pursue in biochemistry; take a variety of different classes and see if you can find a lab that will allow you the opportunity to do some research.

Mean Annual Earnings for Chemists by Industry, 2008

Federal government: $98,060

Scientific research and
    development services: $79,560

Pharmaceutical and medicine
    manufacturing: $70,570

Basic chemical manufacturing:
    $67,490

Architectural, engineering,
    and related services: $59,010

Source: U.S. Department of Labor

---

read graphs and charts, perform difficult mathematical calculations, and write scientific reports. Computer science courses are also important to take, since much of your documentation and other work will involve using computers.

Postsecondary Training

Chemists need at least a bachelor's degree in chemistry or a science-related field. However, in the upper levels of basic and applied research, and especially in a university setting, most positions are filled by people with doctoral degrees.

More than 640 bachelor's, 310 master's, and 200 doctoral degree programs are accredited by the American Chemical Society (ACS). Many colleges and universities also offer advanced degree programs in chemistry. Upon entering college, students majoring in chemistry must expect to take classes in several branches of the field, such as organic, inorganic, analytical, physical chemistry, and biochemistry. Chemistry majors must advance their skills in mathematics, physics, and biology, and be proficient with computers.

A bachelor's degree in chemical engineering is the minimum educational requirement to become a chemical engineer. For some positions, an MS, an MBA, or a Ph.D. may be required. A Ph.D. may be essential for advancement in research, teaching, and administration.

Certification or Licensing

No certification or licensing is available for this profession.

Internships and Volunteerships

Many schools require that their chemistry students fulfill an internship. Intended to provide students with hands-on work experience, the internship experience also grants students the opportunity to network and gain a deeper insight into careers in the field. If an internship is required, it usually lasts from four to 12 months, or roughly somewhere between one and two semesters. Schools are usually instrumental in locating internships, but placing cold calls or writing query letters to companies you have already carefully researched can also be an effective way of locating a quality internship. The American Chemical Society offers a list of internships at its Web site (http://www.chemistry.org).

Due to the extensive training involved, it is very unlikely that a high school student will be able to get a summer job or internship working in a laboratory.

However, you may want to contact local manufacturers or research institutions to explore the possibility.

WHO WILL HIRE ME?

About 41 percent of the approximately 84,000 chemists employed in the United States work for manufacturing companies. Most of these companies are involved in chemical manufacturing, producing such products as plastics, soaps, paints, drugs, and synthetic materials. Chemists are also needed in industrial manufacturing and pilot plant locations. Examples of large companies that employ many chemists are Dow Chemical, DuPont, Monsanto, and Campbell Soup Company.

Chemists also work for government agencies, such as the Department of Health and Human Services, the Department of Agriculture, the Department of Energy, and the National Institute of Standards and Technology. Chemists may find positions in laboratories at institutions of higher learning that are devoted to research. In addition, some chemists work in full-time teaching positions in high schools and universities.

Once you have a degree in chemistry, job opportunities will begin to open up. Summer jobs may become available after your sophomore or junior year of college. You can attend chemical trade fairs and science and engineering fairs to meet and perhaps interview prospective employers. Professors or faculty advisors may know of job openings, and you can begin breaking into the field by using these connections.

If you are a senior and are interested in pursuing an academic career at a col-

Best Chemistry Graduate Schools, 2007

The following schools are ranked by *US News & World Report* as having the best graduate chemistry programs:

1. California Institute of Technology (http://chemistry.caltech.edu)
1. Massachusetts Institute of Technology (http://web.mit.edu/chemistry/www)
1. Stanford University (http://www.stanford.edu/dept/chemistry/grad)
1. University of California—Berkeley (http://chem.berkeley.edu/grad_info)
2. Harvard University (http://www.chem.harvard.edu)

lege or university, you should apply to graduate schools. You will want to begin focusing even more on the specific type of chemistry you wish to practice and teach (for example, inorganic chemistry or analytical chemistry). Look for universities that have strong programs and eminent professors in your intended field of specialty. By getting involved with the basic research of a specific branch of chemistry while in graduate school, you can become a highly employable expert in your field.

WHERE CAN I GO FROM HERE?

In nonacademic careers, advancement usually takes the form of increased job responsibilities accompanied by salary increases. For example, a chemist may rise from doing basic research in a laboratory to being a group leader, overseeing and directing the work of others. Some chemists eventually leave the laboratory and set up their own consulting businesses, serving the needs of private manufacturing companies or government agencies. Others may accept university faculty positions.

Chemists who work in a university setting follow the advancement procedures for that institution. Typically, a chemist in academia with a doctoral degree will go from instructor to assistant professor to associate professor and finally to full professor. In order to advance through these ranks, faculty members at most colleges and universities are expected to perform original research and publish their papers in scientific journals of chemistry and/or other sciences. As the rank of faculty members increases, so do their duties, salaries, responsibilities, and reputations.

WHAT ARE THE SALARY RANGES?

Salary levels for chemists vary based on education, experience, and the area in which they work. Median annual earnings for all chemists in 2008 were $66,230, according to the U.S. Department of Labor (DoL). The lowest paid 10 percent earned less than $37,840, and the highest paid 10 percent made more than $113,080 annually. Chemists working for the federal government had mean incomes of $98,060 in 2008. Biochemists earned salaries that ranged from less than $44,320 to $139,440 or more.

According to a salary survey conducted by the American Chemical Society in 2008, the median salary of its members with Ph.D.'s was $101,000; those with master's degrees, $82,000; and those with bachelor's degrees, $72,600. Salaries tend to be highest on the East and West Coasts. In addition, those working in industry usually have the highest earnings, while those in academia have the lowest.

The median annual salary for chemical engineers was $84,680 in 2008, according to the DoL. The lowest paid 10 percent earned less than $53,730; the highest paid 10 percent earned more than $130,240 annually.

As highly trained, full-time professionals, most chemists receive health insurance, paid vacations, and sick leave. The specifics of these benefits vary from employer to employer. Chemists who teach at the college or university level usually work on an academic calendar, which means they get extensive breaks from teaching classes during summer and winter recesses.

WHAT IS THE JOB OUTLOOK?

Employment of chemists is expected to grow about as fast as the average for all careers through 2016, according to the U.S. Department of Labor. Opportunities will be best for researchers who are interested in working in pharmaceutical and medicine manufacturing, biotechnology, and in professional, scientific, and technical services firms. Employment in nonpharmaceutical chemical manufacturing industries is expected to decline. Aspiring chemists are strongly encouraged to get doctoral degrees to maximize their opportunities for employment and advancement. The ACS reports that 40.3 percent of 2007 chemistry master's graduates found full-time jobs (as opposed to only 27.3 percent of bachelor's graduates).

Dr. Klinman says that opportunities for biochemists are "absolutely excellent. Biochemistry is the underpinning of modern medicine and human/animal health, and plays an essential role in drug development. Biochemistry is also important for the development of alternate fuels to replace fossil fuels. There are so many fields that require a knowledge of biochemistry, e.g., nutrition/wine making, etc. There is also much opportunity for basic research at the university level."

Those wishing to teach full time at the university or college level should find opportunities but also strong competition. Many of these institutions are choosing to hire people for adjunct faculty positions (part-time positions without benefits) instead of for full-time, tenure-track positions. Nevertheless, a well-trained chemist should have little trouble finding some type of employment.

Ecologists

SUMMARY

Definition
Ecologists examine the complex relationships between living organisms and the physical environment. They combine biology, which includes the study of both plants and animals, with physical sciences, such as geology and geography.

Alternative Job Titles
Environmental scientists

Salary Range
$36,310 to $59,750 to $102,610+

Educational Requirements
Bachelor's degree; master's or Ph.D. recommended

Certification or Licensing
Voluntary

Employment Outlook
About as fast as the average

High School Subjects
Biology
Chemistry
Earth science
Geology
Mathematics

Personal Interests
Botany
The environment
Science
Zoology

In the filtered light of the rainforest, professor Tim Schowalter and Mark, a graduate student, hike along a crudely cut trail. They pause briefly at a predetermined point. Tim fights his way through dense undergrowth to a tree growing several yards from the trail. Using a long, closeable net lined with a plastic bag, he is able to snap an upper branch from the 30-foot tree and quickly uses the drawstring on the net to close the bag to prevent the escape of any organisms and returns to the trail with the sample. Later, Tim and his assistant will examine the sample to identify and record the organisms living or resting on the branch.

"A sample is like a snapshot," Tim explains. "It gives you a good idea of what's living on or associated with the plant."

A professor and head of the Department of Entomology at Louisiana State University, Tim is conducting ecological research in the Luquillo Experimental Forest in Puerto Rico. He is studying the recovery of the tropical forest in the wake of Hurricanes Hugo and Georges. He is also examining the impact of the hurricane on species diversity.

When Tim and Mark return to camp after several hours of collecting samples, they learn that the electricity is not working. "Well," says Tim with a laugh, "it's not the first time I've had to sort samples by the light of a lantern."

WHAT DOES AN ECOLOGIST DO?

Ecologists study the relationships between living organisms and their environment. They try to understand the way changes in the environment affect living organisms. An ecologist might, for example, study the effect of pollutants on the diversity of species within a river. Another ecologist might explore the impact logging practices have on arthropods (an organism with a hard skeleton and a jointed body and limbs) and plant life within a forest.

Because the connections between living organisms and the environment are so diverse and intricate, most ecologists concentrate on studying one ecosystem or many ecosystems that share similar characteristics. An ecosystem is a single community of organisms that interacts with a specific environment. Physical characteristics, such as climate, altitude, and topography, define an ecosystem's environment. Coniferous forests, rain forests, rivers, savannas, and tundras are all different types of ecosystems.

Because the relationships within an ecosystem are extremely complex and delicate, even small environmental changes can upset the delicate balance within the ecosystem. The survival of each species within an ecosystem is dependent, to some degree, on the survival of every other species within that ecosystem. Each organism plays a vital role in the food chain. Green plants "fix" energy through photosynthesis. That is, they capture solar energy in the chemical bonds of

Lingo to Learn
arthropod An animal with an exoskeleton, a segmented body, and jointed appendages.
canopy The upper layer of a forest, created by the foliage and branches of the tallest trees.
coniferous A coniferous forest is composed of trees that bear cones.
ecosystem A community of animals and plants and their interaction with the environment.
effluent Wastewater or sewage that flows into a river, lake, or ocean.
entomology The study of insects.
invertebrate An organism that does not have a backbone.
riparian zone Forest or grass growing on the banks of a stream. The riparian zone can prevent soil erosion.
savanna A flat, grassy plain found in tropical areas.
tundra A cold region where the soil under the surface of the ground is permanently frozen.
watershed The gathering ground of a river system, a ridge that separates two river basins, or an area of land that slopes into a river or lake.

carbohydrates synthesized from water and carbon dioxide. Some insects and animals obtain that energy by eating the plants. Others obtain energy by eating insects or animals that have consumed plants. If one species fails, the organisms that feed on that species may, in turn, become endangered. Living organisms also release chemicals into the atmosphere, water, and soil (depending on where they live) as they fix, consume, or process energy. Each of these chemicals plays an important role in sustaining life within an ecosystem.

Many ecologists devote their careers to studying the forces that can upset ecosystems. They attempt to find ways to prevent disruption from occurring. If ecosystems already have been damaged, ecologists look for ways to help them recover.

In order to understand any ecosystem, ecologists must consider many factors. To understand events within a single river ecosystem, for example, ecologists must study the types of the living organisms within the river and look for evidence of disease or pollutants within the organisms' cells. They must evaluate the quality of the water in the river. They must study the river's banks for traces of soil erosion. They also must consider the slope of the river, the proximity of any heavy

industry or sewage treatment plants, and local farming practices. To understand just one ecosystem, ecologists must combine many different areas of knowledge, including zoology, cellular biology, geography, and geology.

Ecologists gather information in many ways. They usually collect samples from the ecosystem or ecosystems they are studying. Using nets lined with plastic bags, they collect samples of plant life and the invertebrates and other organisms that dwell on or amidst plant life. Small containers are used to gather soil and water samples. In addition to collecting samples, ecologists rely on satellite data about an ecosystem's geography. They compare data collected from one ecosystem to immense databases of information about comparable ecosystems. This comparison enables ecologists to determine whether an ecosystem is deviating from normal standards.

Once an ecologist has gathered significant data about an ecosystem, he or she must interpret the data, which can be a painstaking process. Ecologists draw conclusions about measurable changes within an ecosystem, about their causes, and about their possible long-term consequences. Ecologists also make recommendations for protecting or restoring ecosystems.

WHAT IS IT LIKE TO BE AN ECOLOGIST?

Although ecologists study interactions between organisms and the environment of their ecosystem, most spend the majority of their time indoors, working in laboratories, offices, or classrooms. Tim Schowalter estimates that he spends approximately 90 percent of his time on administrative responsibilities (e.g., financial management; supervision of faculty, staff and students; recruiting new students; curriculum development and course scheduling; conflict resolution; interpreting and applying institutional goals to the department; evaluating personnel; and reporting and promoting departmental accomplishments). His remaining time is devoted to research. In addition to conducting research in the Luquillo Experimental Forest in Puerto Rico, he has visited Taiwan to conduct comparable research on forest recovery from typhoons in its tropical/subtropical forests, and also works closer to home. "I'm working on forest recovery from Hurricanes Katrina (2005) and Gustav (2008) that caused similar levels of forest disturbance in Louisiana to that resulting from Hugo (1989) in Puerto Rico," he explains. "Results from similar forests in different parts of the world will help us to understand what recovery processes are common among these forests and which are unique to particular forest types or regions." Tim is quick to note, however, that he conducts only a fraction of his research in the field. He spends most of his time in his office analyzing data, or in laboratories sorting samples.

Bruce Boler is an ecologist for the National Park Service. He works as a project manager for Everglades National Park's South Florida Natural Resource Center. "The Center is a collection of leading scientists in many fields," Bruce explains, "who work on Everglades restoration through federal and state funding.

As project manager, I love the freedom to plan how I will spend my time each day. I also love working with so many other scientists who are similarly committed to restoration of the Everglades. I also like the fact that decisions I make are making a difference and this is why I wanted to become an ecologist in the first place. My least favorite aspect is having to address political issues that permeate Everglades restoration projects."

As a project manager, Bruce manages a team of scientists who work on individual restoration projects. "The hydrologists and engineers," he explains, "develop, modify, or review models that are used to simulate and predict how changes in flows of water to Everglades National Park (ENP) will affect the park as well as surrounding public and private lands. The ecologists evaluate how changes in the timing, distribution, and volume of flows will affect ecological responses. As the project manager, I am responsible for developing a project management plan that identifies the tasks, responsibilities, resources (scientists), and budget needed to complete each individual project, as directed by Congress. For example, the 2009 Omnibus Appropriations Act directed the National Park Service to evaluate the additional bridging of the Tamiami Trail needed to fully restore flows to ENP and ecologically reconnect ENP to the natural areas north of the trail. Each day I review the progress of my individual team members in the completion of specific tasks and how the completion of specific tasks are contributing to the overall progress of the project. Also, I have contracts with private corporations and the U.S. Army Corps of Engineers to

Important Skills

Tim Schowalter, professor and head of the Department of Entomology at Louisiana State University, believes that the most important personal and professional qualities for ecologists are curiosity, creativity, flexibility, and the ability to get along with people. In the following paragraphs, he details why:

Curiosity is a driver for any scientist. It is what allows scientists to see what others miss and to ask the questions that result in hypothesis testing and, eventually, policy recommendations. Probably the first indicator that this is the right career to pursue is an insatiable curiosity to learn more about all aspects of ecology.

Creativity is necessary to think outside of cultural boxes (to not take what is currently "known" for granted), in order to conceive new hypotheses, and to develop methodology to test those hypotheses.

Flexibility is necessary to permit . . . adjustment to unexpected (often adverse) field conditions and . . . change in perspective when anomalous data require a new interpretation.

The ability to get along with people helps in several ways. First, as the article emphasizes, ecology is necessarily multidisciplinary. The ability to get along with scientists in other disciplines clearly facilitates research. However, the ability to get along with people also can be extremely important when making arrangements for field activities, especially in remote areas with people from different cultures (this, in itself, has been a tremendous stimulus to my work—I'm as curious about cultural characteristics and how people adapt to their environment as about the overall ecology of an area). The ability to get along with people also helps in presenting policy recommendations, often to politicians or groups not eager to hear or apply these recommendations. I emphasize this quality, because I think many (perhaps most) ecologists (including me) are attracted to this field because of the opportunities for work in isolated ecosystems and often undervalue personal interactions. I have had to work to overcome this particular limitation.

complete different tasks. I also frequently meet with different public interest groups to discuss how this project may affect their interests, this includes environmental groups, stakeholders who have specific interest in the project, e.g., airboat operators along the trail, fishermen, Indian tribes, etc." Bruce also spends a portion of each day writing or editing sections of the final report that is due to Congress next year. "This is of critical importance," he says, "because I must clearly convey the importance of this project in language bureaucrats can understand in order to improve its chances of receiving funding during a time when competition for federal dollars is intense. I generally work about 40 hours a week."

DO I HAVE WHAT IT TAKES TO BE AN ECOLOGIST?

Ecologists, like other scientists, must be intelligent and possess intellectual curiosity and must be able to think both analytically and creatively about complex issues. Most importantly, they must be excited about understanding the environment and committed to preserving it.

To the surprise of many would-be ecologists, communication skills are every bit as important as the ability to take accurate measurements and conduct good research. Ecologists must be able to communicate ideas to other scientists, to regulatory agencies, and to the public. They must, therefore, be able to speak and write clearly. According the Princeton Review, most ecologists consider writing skills the second or third most important skill for succeeding in this field.

Most science is collaborative. Ecologists must be able to work closely with others in their field and should enjoy sharing ideas and being challenged by others' questions.

"Professionally," says Bruce Boler, "ecologists need to have a broad understanding of ecological principles, particularly the effects of anthrogenic activities on ecological responses. It is also critical that aspiring ecologists learn to express this understanding in clear and concise written and oral arguments. While the purely academic pursuit of this understanding is still very valuable, it is becoming more important that we train ecologists to work within federal, state, and local governments to better protect and restore our dwindling natural resources. To be effective in these positions, ecologists need to have strong communication skills and be effective working on interdisciplinary teams."

HOW DO I BECOME AN ECOLOGIST?
Education
High School
High school students who are interested in becoming ecologists should concentrate on science and math classes. They should not, however, neglect other disciplines. English, for example, can provide students with useful experience in writing well and easily.

Postsecondary Training
Once in college, students should continue to study science. Ecology courses are important, but students should take biology, chemistry, meteorology, and zoology courses, as well. Geography and geology can be equally helpful in preparing a student for a career as an ecologist. Because ecologists amass and analyze immense amounts of data, students should also take math, computer, and statistics courses.

While people with undergraduate degrees in ecology can find employment as laboratory technicians or field researchers, the vast majority of ecologists have master's or doctoral degrees. "If you want to be in a decision-making position, you pretty much have to have an advanced degree," says Tim Schowalter. "Most ecologists who are conducting their own research have Ph.D. degrees."

Many colleges and universities throughout the United States offer doctoral degrees in ecology or related fields. According to the Ecological Society of America, a great many practicing ecologists received doctoral degrees from the University of California, Berkeley; the

University of Wisconsin, Madison; Cornell University; the University of Washington; and Duke University. In Canada, many ecologists received doctoral degrees from the University of British Columbia, the University of Alberta, and the University of Toronto.

Certification or Licensing

The Ecological Society of America offers professional certification at three levels: associate ecologist, ecologist, and senior ecologist. A candidate's certifica-

tion level will depend on the amount of education and professional experience he or she has. Contact the society for more information.

Internships and Volunteerships

Students also should strive to gain as much practical experience as possible by volunteering for environmental organizations or by helping an ecologist conduct research. Research positions for high school students are not abundant, but some ecologists will hire students to

Rewarding Experiences

Bruce Boler details some of the most interesting and rewarding moments of his career:

Although my resignation from the Environmental Protection Agency in 2003 (as a result of the Bush Administration's adoption of a wetland assessment method that considered natural wetlands as sources of pollution, accelerating their loss in the western Everglades) was traumatic for many reasons, not the least of which my wife's concern for how we would pay our bills, I was immensely gratified by the outpouring of concern and support from the environmental community. Not only did I receive letters and phone calls from hundreds of colleagues expressing support for my ethical action, I received emails and letters from many emminent scientists and national environmental leaders. Robert Kennedy Jr. even asked to interview me on Air America (NPS said no).

Personally, the thousands of acres of wetlands that I prevented from being destroyed in Southwest Florida while working as a wetlands scientist is very rewarding to me. While it could be seen as some vindication that I so strongly opposed the unbridled development (loss of wetlands) in southwest Florida that is now causing such problems in the housing market, the Florida state legislature just recently passed a law further limiting government oversight over protections of wetlands and associated development.

On a more positive note, this year Congress finally assigned the National Park Service, not the Corps of Engineers, to be the lead on a critical component of the largest environmental restoration project in the world, and I have been assigned the role of project manager. The NPS and U.S. Department of the Interior have given this project the highest priority, and I have been told by Washington that I cannot fail to deliver. It is exciting and gratifying to finally be in the position that I have worked so hard to achieve.

collect and sort samples. Tim Schowalter, for instance, usually hires several high school students each summer.

"I hire both college and high school students," Tim explains. "These students learn to sort and weigh samples. They also learn to use different software programs for recording information. I try to get each student out in the field once or twice, to get them excited. I also give each student an overview of the proposal and the methods involved, so that they can see the significance of the study."

Though he tries to give each student some field experience, Tim concedes that the students he hires spend the majority of their time measuring and sorting data. He believes this is a fairly accurate reflection of a scientist's life. "Science is mostly grunt work," he explains, "and only about 5 percent 'Eureka!' factor."

WHO WILL HIRE ME?

Approximately 75 percent of land and water conservation jobs are in the public sector. This includes the federal government, the largest employer. The U.S. Fish and Wildlife Service, the National Park Service, the Bureau of Land Management, and the U.S. Geological Survey are among the federal agencies that manage U.S. conservation. The Environmental Protection Agency also employs ecologists. Other public sector opportunities are with states, regions, and towns. Opportunities in the private sector can be found with timber companies, utilities, and consulting firms. Some ecologists work as teachers at high schools or colleges.

Smaller percentages of ecologists work for consulting firms, state or local governments, or environmental nonprofit organizations. A small number of ecologists work for private industry. Ecologists who work for private industry help companies achieve their business objectives in ways that are least disruptive to surrounding ecosystems. They also help comply with environmental regulations. Most companies employ only one or two ecologists, though, so these positions can be difficult to find.

WHERE CAN I GO FROM HERE?

Opportunities for advancement are limited for individuals who have only a bachelor's or master's degree. Those who earn doctoral degrees, however, may advance in many ways. Ecologists who conduct research can gain recognition for their work by publishing reports and articles in scientific journals. Highly visible ecologists may accept public speaking engagements, which can significantly augment their income. Those who work for universities or colleges also can advance by serving on committees or assuming administrative responsibilities. Some ecologists become department chairs. These positions require considerable administrative work but offer higher salaries. Ecologists who work for smaller academic institutions also can advance by seeking positions within larger or more prestigious institutions.

Within government positions, ecologists may advance by assuming positions of greater responsibility, such as supervisory or branch chief positions. In these positions individuals must manage staff personnel and other scientists. Supervisory positions usually entail significant administrative work. Individuals in these positions may find themselves spending more time hiring and managing employees, conducting performance reviews, and completing the paperwork than they devote to actual science.

Senior ecologists within the government are, however, able to influence legislation, inform government officials, and educate the public.

As in government and academia, ecologists in industry advance by assuming more responsibility. Most large companies employ very few ecologists, however, so management opportunities may be quite limited. After gaining experience by working within private industry for a length of time, some ecologists choose to become consultants. Ecologists who are able to develop a large and varied clientele can significantly increase their income and gain prominence in the field.

WHAT ARE THE SALARY RANGES?

Ecologists' salaries vary greatly depending on the individual's level of education, place of employment, and years of experience. A few generalizations are possible, however. Ecologists who have doctoral degrees typically earn more than those who have less education. Ecologists who work for private industry usually earn higher salaries than those in academia or governmental positions. Those who

work for nonprofit environmental agencies earn the lowest salaries of all.

Salaries for environmental scientists and specialists (a group that includes ecologists) ranged from less than $36,310 to $102,610 or more annually in 2008, according to the U.S. Department of Labor. The median annual income was $59,750. Ecologists employed by the federal government earned average salaries of $85,770.

Ecologists earn a variety of benefits depending on the employer. These usually include health insurance, retirement or 401(k) plans, and paid vacation days.

WHAT IS THE JOB OUTLOOK?

Employment in ecological-related careers is expected to increase about as fast as the average for all occupations through 2016, according to the U.S. Department of Labor. Environmental concerns are fueling growth in this field, as nations around the world become more aware of the dangers posed by pollutants, pesticides, greenhouse gasses, uninhibited population growth, and global warming and climate change. People who have the interdisciplinary skills to help communities and countries find practical ways to protect or repair ecosystems will find ecology a challenging and rewarding profession.

"I think ecologists will continue to have good employment opportunities in academia, state and federal land management agencies, and conservation organizations," predicts Tim Schowalter. "Public attention to the quality of the environment will increase, rather than decrease, although it has been apparent that people are not eager to pay the increased costs of protecting environmental quality. Hopefully, this will change, or the costs of alternative energy will decline. Effects of climate change also are a major ecological focus. What are the drivers of global change? Models connecting fossil fuel combustion with atmospheric change, global warming, melting of ice caps, sea level rise, and changes in sea currents indicate unprecedented positive feedback that contributes to further warming. Is this reversible, or what plans are needed to adjust to a changing environment? However, the current financial downturn has resulted in hiring freezes at all levels of government, and private organizations also are proceeding cautiously."

Tim also considers agricultural security to be an important issue for ecologists. "Organic (or low-pesticide) food is expensive to produce," he says, "and invasive species invariably restrict options available to manage food production and quality. Whereas biological controls can be used to control some agricultural pests when economic thresholds are not too low, the serious effects of some invasive pests (e.g., some we are working on can kill entire crops over large areas—effectively eliminating some crops if hard pesticides are not used) are not amenable to such soft control methods. Much ecological research now is being focused on the threats of invasive species and how to control these with minimum environmental damage."

Forensic Scientists

SUMMARY

Definition
Forensic scientists apply natural science principles and methods to the analysis, identification, and classification of physical evidence relating to criminal (or suspected criminal) cases. Many work in laboratories, where they subject evidence to tests and then record the results. They may travel to crime scenes to collect evidence and record the physical facts of the site. Forensic scientists may also be called upon to testify as expert witnesses and to present scientific findings in court.

Alternative Job Titles
Forensic experts

Salary Range
$30,000 to $75,000 to $300,000+

Educational Requirements
Varies by specialty

Certification or Licensing
Required for certain positions

Employment Outlook
Faster than the average

High School Subjects
Biology
Chemistry

Personal Interests
Science

"The most rewarding thing that has happened to me as a forensic nurse is to receive a letter or thank-you card from family members who have lost a loved one," says Bobbi Jo O'Neal, the deputy coroner and forensic nurse death investigator in the Charleston County Coroner's Office in Charleston, South Carolina. "Knowing that I help them obtain justice for their loved one, helped them through their grief process, and helped answer their questions is reward enough."

WHAT DOES A FORENSIC SCIENTIST DO?

"*Forensic scientist*" is an umbrella phrase for a wide range of specialists who combine knowledge of forensic science with expertise in a secondary field such as computer science, anthropology, chemistry, engineering, nursing, or dentistry. The following paragraphs provide a summary of the major specialties in the field.

Computer forensics specialists search for evidence stored on computers of illegal activities such as credit card fraud, identity theft, child pornography, terrorism, stealing trade secrets from a company or government agency, and illegally gaining access to, or "hacking," individual, corporate, or government computer systems.

Criminalists apply scientific principles and methods to the classification, analysis, identification, and individualization of physical evidence relating to criminal (or suspected criminal) cases. They do much of their work in laboratories, where they subject evidence to tests and then record the results. Criminalists are often called upon to testify as expert witnesses and to present scientific findings in court.

Fingerprint analysts collect, catalog, and compare fingerprints of suspected criminals with records to determine if the people who left the fingerprints at the scene of a crime were involved in previous crimes. They may also try to match the fingerprints of unknown corpses with fingerprint records to establish their identity. Fingerprints and impressions left by the palms of the hand and soles and toes of the feet that have been left on an object or surface and collected from the surface or object are known as latent prints. They are usually invisible to the human eye and must be processed to make them visible. Fingerprints purposely obtained from a person, such as someone who has been arrested, are known as ten-prints (meaning prints from all 10 fingers).

Fire investigators analyze the cause, origin, and circumstances of fires involving loss of life and considerable property damage. Their scientific report must be

---

To Be a Successful Forensic Scientist, You Should...

- have an aptitude for scientific investigation
- be curious
- have a logical mind
- have patience and persistence
- have a good memory
- have excellent communication skills
- be able to work as a member of a team
- be willing to continue to learn throughout your career
- be emotionally stable in order to work at sometimes grisly or disturbing death scenes

---

supportable by court testimony. Some fire investigators prepare investigation reports, interrogate witnesses, and arrest and seek prosecution of arsonists. These latter workers are known as *fire marshals.*

Forensic anthropologists examine and identify bones and skeletal remains for the purposes of homicide, scientific, archaeological, or judicial investigations. Forensic anthropology is a branch of physical, or biological, anthropology.

Ballistics is the study of projectiles in flight. *Forensic ballistics experts* analyze firearms that may have been used in a crime and bullets, bullet paths, and bullet impacts. Since no two firearms create the same marks on fired bullets or cartridges, ballistics experts can analyze these differences to determine if a firearm was used to commit a crime.

Forensic biologists analyze biological materials, such as blood, saliva, and other bodily fluids, bones, hair, nails, skin, and other bodily tissue. They may also work with nonhuman-based biological samples, such as those from plants or animals. It is the responsibility of the forensic biologist to analyze the biological material using various laboratory procedures and document their findings so they can be presented as evidence in legal proceedings.

Forensic botanists draw on their knowledge of plant anatomy, structure, and environments to analyze plant samples found at crime scenes. It is the responsibility of forensic botanists to analyze the plant samples through various laboratory procedures and document their findings so they can be presented as evidence in legal proceedings. They use such laboratory equipment as microscopes to do so.

Forensic chemists conduct tests on evidence from crime scenes, such as paint chips, hair, fire debris, or glass fragments, either to identify unknown substances or to match the evidence against materials found on potential suspects. Forensic chemists also play a major role in the fight against trafficking of illegal drugs; they work to identify new substances that appear on the market, and they may also be called in to assist in the dangerous task of cleaning up illegal drug labs. These spe-

cialists are often known as *forensic drug chemists* or *forensic drug analysts.*

Forensic engineers study materials, devices, structures, and products that do not work as they were designed or fail to work completely. They have backgrounds in many different engineering disciplines.

Forensic entomologists use their knowledge of insects—such as where they live, their life cycle, and their behaviors—to interpret evidence in legal matters. In a criminal case, for example, a forensic entomologist can often determine the general time, location, and perhaps the likely cause of death by using insect evidence gathered from and around a murder victim. In a civil case, forensic entomologists might be called on to use their skills to determine when and where an insect infestation began and how far it has progressed, useful in cases where someone is trying to determine who is responsible for the problem and therefore liable for any damaged incurred.

Forensic nursing is a relatively new and expanding field of nursing that combines nursing skills with investigative skills. *Forensic nurses* use a combination of skills to meet multiple purposes, often serving not only as nurses, but also as crime solvers and advocates for victims. They can specialize in forensic nurse death investigation, sexual assault investigation, forensic nursing psychiatry, legal nurse consulting, and other areas. They are employed in a variety of settings. They may work in hospitals (particularly in emergency rooms) or other health care facilities, correctional institutions, the offices of medical examiners and coroners, psychiatric facilities, insurance agencies, social service agencies . . . the list goes on. In general, anywhere that a registered nurse might work is a setting in which the skills of a forensic nurse will likely be of use, especially if it is a place where victims or suspects in a crime or accident may be investigated or treated. In addition to performing general nursing duties, forensic nurses are likely to be involved with additional tasks related to investigations of accidents or crimes. These duties include observing the victims of (and sometimes the scene of) an accident or crime for potential evidence—forensic nurses are generally better trained than other nurses to spot signs of abuse or trauma. They may also examine suspected perpetrators of crimes. A forensic nurse must carefully collect, document, and preserve any evidence they find for any future legal proceedings. Many forensic nurses are called on to provide testimony in court.

Forensic odontologists, also referred to as *forensic dentists,* work with medical examiners or police investigators, examining and evaluating dental evidence to identify partial human remains that often cannot be identified any other way. Forensic dentists are frequently called in for their identification skills after natural disasters such as Hurricane Katrina that result in numerous fatalities. Another important part of the forensic dentist's job is to assess and try to determine the source of bite-mark injuries. Forensic odontologists can also be of service in dental malpractice or dental insurance fraud investigations, and they must be certain enough of their conclusions to testify about them in court if necessary.

Forensic pathologists examine the deceased (usually those who die unexpectedly, suddenly, or violently) to determine cause and manner of death.

Forensic toxicologists detect and identify the presence of poisons or legal or illegal drugs in an individual's body.

Questioned document examiners study a wide variety of handwritten or machine-generated documents to determine if they are authentic or if they have been altered in any manner. The examination of documents is important in the fight against many types of white-collar crime, including forgery, counterfeiting, fraud, and the enormous and still-growing problem of identity theft. The examiner may be called on to present expert testimony in court to demonstrate the basis and reasons for his/her opinion.

Forensic scientists usually perform the analysis portion of their work in clean, quiet, air-conditioned laboratories, and some are frequently required to travel to crime scenes to collect evidence or study the site to understand more fully the evidence collected by detectives. When gathering evidence and recognizing it, forensic scientists need to be able to concentrate, sometimes at crowded, noisy crime scenes. For this reason, forensic scientists must be adaptable and able to work in a variety of environments, including dangerous or unpleasant places (e.g., side of road, rail yard, etc.).

Many crime scenes are grisly and may be extremely distressing for beginning workers and even for more seasoned professionals. In addition, forensic scientists who work with human remains will regularly view corpses, and, more

of tools, cameras, and chemicals. In order not to risk contaminating evidence, they must follow strict procedures (both in and out of the laboratory) for collecting and testing evidence; these procedures can be extremely time-consuming and thus require a great deal of patience. Forensic scientists also need to be able to arrive at and present their findings impartially. In large labs, they often work as part of a team under the direction of a senior technologist. They may experience periodic eyestrain and minimal exposure to chemicals, but little heavy physical work is involved.

WHAT IS IT LIKE TO BE A FORENSIC SCIENTIST?

Ryan Kubasiak is a computer forensics specialist for the New York State Police Computer Crime Unit. "The decision to enter digital forensics was easy for me," he recalls. "Throughout high school, computer programming was my passion. I continued into college by getting a degree in computer science. Parallel to my desires in the computer realm, law enforcement is a part of my family as well. My father, stepfather, and brother are all New York State Troopers. I also wanted this to be my career path. The New York State Police Computer Crime Unit allowed me to combine both passions.

"My duties specifically are in the laboratory," Ryan continues. "I am responsible for the acquisition, archiving, and analysis of digital evidence. As a part of this, courtroom testimony for grand jury and trial is included. Testimony in cases happens often in grand jury. Trials don't happen as often. During the course of a year, I par-

often than not, these corpses may have been mutilated in some way or be in varying degrees of decomposition. Individuals interested in this field need to develop the detachment and objectivity necessary to view corpses and extract specimens for testing and analysis.

Simulating the precise conditions of a crime site is often crucial, so forensic scientists often return to the site so that they can perform tests or functions outside of the controlled environment of their lab. When traveling to the scene of a crime, forensic scientists may have to carry cases

ticipate in numerous court proceedings of some type. There are suppression hearings, Huntley hearings, federal sentencing testimony, etc. The environment for each of these are similar in demeanor, but different in who might be in attendance. For instance, in grand jury, there is no judge, only a prosecutor and the jurors to listen to testimony. Key to any presentation is understanding the material that I am speaking about. When I testify, I am speaking to a diverse audience (jurors, judge, prosecutor, and defense counsel). I only have one chance to explain my testimony, so I need to understand my topic well enough to present it in a manner that everyone can take in the technology I am attempting to express."

Ryan is also responsible for serving as the system administration of his unit's forensic network. "Along with my supervisor," he explains, "I maintain servers, the network, fiber, workstations and laptop computers. These duties also include the upkeep of installed software and writing of standard operating procedures for applications and equipment.

"One of the key benefits of my position is the technology I get to deal with. I am able to learn about multiple operating systems, several hardware platforms, and some of the coolest gadgets. Because this technology is submitted to our laboratory for analysis, I have the opportunity to become very familiar with items that I may not otherwise get my hands on in my personal life. One of the downfalls of my position is the cost involved with the multitude of training that is required to stay current with all of this technology. Each digital examiner must constantly learn and train on the latest offerings, and this becomes very expensive quickly."

Ryan says that the most rewarding moment of his career came the day he was followed out of a courtroom by the father of a homicide victim. "He walked up to me and shook my hand, thanking me for the testimony I gave in the case," he recalls. "The defendant ultimately was sentenced to 25 years to life in a state prison in large part from digital evidence of a calculated homicide. My job, as with any other member of the New York State Police, is to 'protect and serve' and on that day, I felt like I had done my job for that family."

Bobbi Jo O'Neal is the deputy coroner and forensic nurse death investigator in the Charleston County Coroner's Office in Charleston, South Carolina. She is also the author of *Investigating Infant Deaths* (Boca Raton, Fla.: CRC Press, 2006). "I investigate deaths which occur in my community and ensure that the correct cause and manner of death are determined," Bobbi Jo explains. "My responsibilities are to determine who the deceased person is (which can be very difficult in some situations), notify their next-of-kin of the death, determine if an autopsy needs to be completed or not, and investigate the circumstance surrounding the death. As a nurse not only am I able to help determine what happened to the decedent, but I am also able to help their family with the grief process, and then provide my community with education to try to prevent some types of deaths from occurring.

"As a forensic nurse death investigator," Bobbi Jo continues, "my days are never the same as I never know what might happen from day to day or minute to minute. My call begins at 8:30 A.M., and I will remain on-call for 48 hours. A day may look something like this:

"8:45 A.M.: While driving to my office my pager goes off notifying me that there has been a traffic-related fatality on the highway. I obtain directions from the police dispatchers and drive to the scene. Since traffic is backed-up due to the accident I have to turn on my blue lights and sirens to be able to drive down the median to get to the accident location. Once there I am briefed by the law enforcement agency that has jurisdiction. I then do a walk-through and photograph the accident. When all agencies are ready I instruct our rescue squad to assist me in removing the deceased individual from the driver's seat of the car. Once removed from the car I examine the body to determine what injuries, if any, caused the death and evaluate the individual's personal effects in order to determine who the deceased individual is.

"10:00 A.M.: The body is then transported to the morgue for further investigation and an autopsy if needed. In this case, I don't see any injuries and decide to interview witnesses who saw the accident. A witness driving behind this driver reports that the driver was driving really slow and then slowly drove off the side of the road before the vehicle came to rest near a fence.

"10:30 A.M.: After interviewing the witness, I then try to determine where the individual's family may be located and try to find them to make them aware of the death of their loved one.

"1:15 P.M.: After hours of searching for the family I find a family member at his work. I enter his work area and ask to speak with him in a quiet area and inform him of the accident that has occurred.

During my time with [members of] the family I learn that the individual had a lot of medical problems and was complaining of chest pain during the night. This individual left his home around 7:45 and was driving himself to his doctor's office. I assist the family in getting to their home and answer their questions.

"3:00 P.M.: I return to my office. I then call the forensic pathologist to provide them with the information they need prior to an autopsy, which is scheduled for the next morning.

"4:30 P.M.: I receive a call from a local hospice agency that an expected death has occurred at a residence. I call the agency representative and gather needed information prior to contacting the funeral home to let them know they can go remove the body and begin preparations for the funeral. Even though I don't have to respond to this death I do have to fill out paperwork and complete a case report on this death that was reported to us.

"4:45 P.M.: I make phone calls to families who are awaiting results of laboratory tests and open the mail to reveal that I have been delivered a subpoena to testify in a homicide case the next week. I try to do some paperwork before leaving the office at 5:30 to go home.

"6:15 P.M.: After arriving home, my pager goes off again notifying me of a death that may be the result of a drug overdose. I get something quick to eat and head out again.

"9:30 P.M.: After investigating the scene and the body, transporting the body, and interviewing family members and witnesses I finally arrive back home. My pager goes off again as the media is calling and wanting me to release the name of the gentleman who was in the car accident earlier in the day. I return those phone calls and crash in bed to get some rest.

"3:00 A.M.: My pager goes off . . . again. This time there is a death that occurred in an emergency room at a local hospital. The staff is required to notify us when that happens. I gather the needed information and determine that it is a natural death and direct the hospital staff to release the body to the funeral home.

"3:30 A.M.: I try to go back to sleep.

"7:30 A.M.: The alarm goes off as I have to get up and attend the autopsy for the gentleman in the car accident from the day prior. The autopsy revealed that he did not sustain any injuries and that he suffered a heart attack. Although he was in a car, the death will be ruled due to natural causes.

"10:00 A.M.: I leave the autopsy room and my pager goes off . . . again."

DO I HAVE WHAT IT TAKES TO BE A FORENSIC SCIENTIST?

To be successful in this field, you should have an aptitude for scientific investigation, an inquiring and logical mind, and the ability to make precise measurements and observations. Patience and persistence are important qualities, as is a good memory. Forensic scientists must constantly bear in mind that the accuracy of their lab investigations can have great consequences for others.

Louis Maucieri, a forensic training consultant in Sacramento, California, says that the most important personal and professional attributes for forensic scientists are "enjoying teaching, having the ability to speak to a jury, answering only

Key Skills for Forensic Nurses

Bobbi Jo O'Neal details the most important personal and professional skills for forensic nurses:

Important personal skills include being observant, inquisitive, persistent, and honest. Professionally, forensic nurses need to be able to interview effectively and must have strong anatomy, physiology, and pharmacology knowledge to name just a few important traits.

the question asked, waiting to consider a question before you answer, a willingness to keep training, and emotional control for being in stressful situations."

HOW DO I BECOME A FORENSIC SCIENTIST?
Education
High School

In high school you can begin to prepare for careers in forensic science by taking a heavy concentration of science courses, including chemistry, biology, physiology, and physics. Computer skills are also important. A basic grounding in spoken and written communications will be useful because forensic scientists must write very detailed reports and are sometimes called on to present their findings in court.

"High school students interested in this field are well advised to take courses in biology and chemistry—through quantitative analysis and organic," advises Louis Maucieri. "When in college, join a regional forensic association. The California Association of Criminalists has a plethora of educational and career information available."

Postsecondary Training

Educational requirements vary greatly by specialty. For example, the career of fire investigator requires at least some postsecondary training, although a bachelor's degree or higher is required for top jobs. A bachelor's degree is required to work in many forensic science careers—such as forensic engineering, forensic botany, and forensic biology. The career of forensic anthropologist requires a doctorate. Forensic pathologists, forensic nurses, and forensic odontologists require a professional degree.

Advice for Aspiring Forensic Nurses

Bobbi Jo O'Neal offers the following advice to young people who want to become forensic nurses:

First off, forensic nurses must be registered nurses with lots of experience in a variety of settings. I always recommend that new nurses work in either an emergency room or in an intensive care unit for a few years to learn as much about injury assessment as possible. The other thing that new young students need to learn is how to network with other people and agencies and learn as much as possible from others who have worked in the area of forensics. There is a lot about forensics that cannot be taught in a book or in a class, they are things that you have to learn through experience. Always seek out a mentor who can teach you via their experience.

A number of universities and community colleges in the United States offer programs in forensic science, odontology, toxicology, pathology, and various aspects of crime lab work. These courses are often spread throughout the school, in the anatomy, physiology, chemistry, or biology departments, or they may be grouped together as part of the criminal justice department. Additionally, some colleges may have separate forensic science departments. Visit the Web sites of the American Academy of Forensic Sciences (http://www.aafs.org) and the Council on Forensic Science Education (http://www.criminology.fsu.edu/COFSE/default.html) for lists of colleges and universities that offer classes and programs in forensic science.

Certification or Licensing

Certification and licensing requirements for forensic scientists vary greatly by specialty. Contact the professional association in your field of interest for more information. See the sidebar on pages 71–72 for a list of organizations.

Internships and Volunteerships

Internships are an excellent way to learn more about the demands of a career in forensic science while you are still in school. Colleges typically require you to participate in an internship as part of your educational program. Internships may be available at a crime lab, government agency, or other related employers. It will be difficult to locate volunteer opportunities, especially as a high school student. One way to gain an introduction to this field is to participate in summer educational programs at colleges

Forensic Science Professional Associations

Academy of Forensic Nursing Science
http://www.academyofforensicnursing
science.com

American Academy of Forensic Sciences
http://www.aafs.org

American Association of Legal Nurse
Consultants
http://www.aalnc.org

American Board of Criminalistics
http://www.criminalistics.com

American Board of Forensic
Anthropology
http://www.theabfa.org

American Board of Forensic Document
Examiners
http://www.abfde.org

American Board of Forensic
Entomology
http://www.forensicentomologist.org

American Board of Forensic
Odontology
http://www.abfo.org

American Board of Forensic Toxicology
http://www.abft.org

American Board of Pathology
http://www.abpath.org

American College of Forensic Examiners
http://www.acfei.com

American Society for Investigative
Pathology
http://www.asip.org

American Society of Forensic
Odontology
http://www.asfo.org

American Society of Questioned
Document Examiners
http://www.asqde.org

Association of Firearm and Tool Mark
Examiners
http://www.afte.org

Association of Forensic DNA Analysts
and Administrators
http://www.afdaa.org

California Association of Criminalists
http://www.cacnews.org

Computer Security Institute
http://www.gocsi.com

International Association for
Identification
http://www.theiai.org

International Association of Arson
Investigators
http://www.firearson.com

International Association of Bloodstain
Pattern Analysts
http://www.iabpa.org

International Association of Bomb
Technicians and Investigators
http://www.iabti.org

International Association of Computer
Investigative Specialists
http://www.iacis.com

International Association of Forensic
Nurses
http://www.iafn.org

International Association of Forensic
Toxicologists
http://www.tiaft.org

(continued on next page)

(continued from previous page)

International High Technology Crime Investigation Association
http://www.htcia.org

International Organization on Computer Evidence
http://www.ioce.org

International Society for Forensic Genetics
http://www.isfg.org

International Society of Forensic Computer Examiners
http://www.isfce.com

National Academy of Forensic Engineers
http://www.nafe.org

National Association of Medical Examiners
http://www.thename.org

Society of Forensic Engineers and Scientists
http://forensic-society.org

Society of Forensic Toxicologists
http://www.soft-tox.org

and universities. See "Get Involved" in Section 4 for a list of these programs.

WHO WILL HIRE ME?

Forensic scientists are typically employed by large police departments or state law enforcement agencies nationwide. However, individuals in certain disciplines are often self-employed or work in the private sector. For example, forensic engineers may be employed by large corporations, small firms, or government agencies. Forensic anthropologists may work within a university or college, teaching related courses, conducting research, and consulting on cases submitted by law enforcement agencies. They may also be employed by the federal government (including the FBI and the military) or a medical examiner's office. Many forensic science concentrations also offer part-time or consulting opportunities, depending on your level of education and experience.

Crime labs are maintained by the federal government and by state and local governments. Applications should be made directly to the personnel department of the government agency supporting the lab. Civil service appointments usually require applicants to take an examination. Such appointments are usually widely advertised well in advance of the application date. Those working for the FBI or other law enforcement agencies usually undergo background checks, which examine their character, previous employers, and family and friends.

WHERE CAN I GO FROM HERE?

In a large crime laboratory, forensic scientists may advance to a position as project leader or being in charge of all aspects of one particular investigation. Some forensic scientists may advance to become directors of crime labs. Others

Forensic Scientist Profile: Randy Stone

Randy Stone is a computer forensics specialist and detective for the Wichita Police Department in Wichita, Kansas. He discussed his career with the editors of *What Can I Do Now? Science.*

Q. What made you want to enter this career?

A. About 12 or 13 years ago, I was assigned to the undercover narcotics section. Several times we encountered computers during the investigation of drug crimes and it became evident that we didn't have a way of adequately investigating cases involving computers or recovering evidence from them. I didn't originally start out planning on doing computer forensics, but it developed into a niche within the police department that provided a very specialized investigative capability. From that, our unit has developed to the point where we have some of the highest-trained and highest-certified examiners in the state.

Q. What are your main and secondary job duties?

A. We utilize a definition of computer forensics of "the acquisition, searching, and analysis of digital evidence in a forensically sound manner." Our primary duty is to conduct forensic examinations of computers to recover evidence. It is similar to doing an autopsy on a computer. We typically make a copy of the media, and then search it for the evidence in the case. Once the media has been searched, we have to analyze the results to determine what role the computer and its contents had in the commission of the crime and how this proves the guilt or innocence of the suspect. Additionally, we assist in writing and executing search warrants and conduct training for citizens, businesses, and other law enforcement officers on the topics of computer crime, computer forensics, and Internet safety.

Q. Could you detail your work on the BTK serial killer investigation?

A. My participation in the BTK investigation related to several different areas and together helped demonstrate the need for a computer forensic examiner to have a wide base of knowledge. I began initially by assisting with the building of a network at the first command post used by the BTK Task Force. This consisted of installing hardware and configuring software for network communication. Next, I was involved with tracing emails sent to the tip line. Some of the emails received were suspicious and needed followup to identify the sender. This relied on investigative skills, the creation of legal documents such as affidavits and subpoenas, and additional follow-up. I also monitored several chat rooms and discussion boards on the Internet in an undercover capacity. Finally, when BTK sent in a floppy disk and later with computers seized during warrants, I conducted forensic analysis of media seized during the case. BTK sent us a floppy disk as a means of communication and it was from this floppy disk that we were able to identify Dennis Rader as the BTK suspect. On the floppy disk he had included a Word document. Within this document was

(continued on next page)

(continued from previous page)

metadata identifying that the software that created the file was registered to a church and that the last person who had saved the file was named Dennis. From these two items of information, we were able to locate Dennis Rader as affiliated with the church. The rest of the investigation was traditional police work. [For more on the BTK serial killer investigation, visit http://www.kansas.com/news/special_packages/btk.]

Q. What are some of the pros and cons about work in your profession?

A. One of the biggest pros of this career is the opportunity to get involved in almost any kind of case. We have worked everything from murder and arson, to burglary and auto theft, to child exploitation. Each one has the opportunity to have some kind of digital evidence associated with it, ranging from emails to cell phones to computers. The two biggest cons are related to each other and are the cost of providing computer forensic capabilities and a shortage of positions. Unfortunately, providing equipment, initial training, sustainment training, and progressive training is pretty expensive. A department can expect to spend about $20,000 in equipment and training the first couple of years per detective in order to do a good job at computer forensic investigations.

The department should then plan on several thousand dollars per year after that for training and replacement equipment. This prices competent computer forensics out of the reach of many small and mid-size departments. Some departments choose to attempt computer forensics without adequate resources, which can be dangerous because it can result in well-intentioned but low-quality investigations and a potential for improper charging and convictions.

Another con would be the lack of continuity among states on computer crime statutes. In the 11 years I have been doing computer forensic investigations, the Kansas law on computer crime has changed once, even though the capacity and variety of computer crimes has grown exponentially. A state has to adapt the state statutes on computer crime at a pace that keeps up with the ability to commit computer crime in order to protect its citizens and their property.

Q. What is the future employment outlook for your field?

A. There are two sides of the employment outlook for computer forensics: civil and government.

Computer forensics is used a lot in the e-discovery process on the civil side. Many of these positions are filled with retired law enforcement. Frequently, a detective will get training through his department and spend a

become college professors or publish books or magazine articles about their specialty.

Crucial to advancement is further education. Forensic scientists need to be familiar with scientific procedures such as gas chromatography, ultraviolet and infrared spectrophotometry, mass spectroscopy, electrophoresis, polarizing microscopy, light microscopy, and conventional and isoelectric focusing; knowledge of these analytical techniques

few years getting experience. He will then retire or quit law enforcement, going to work as a civilian doing e-discovery or training and frequently working for several times his government salary.

On the government side, there is a need for computer forensics in the investigation of cases involving the Department of Justice and Department of Defense at the national level along with investigations at the state and local levels. Many of these federal positions are contracted out to civilian companies to provide contractors to fill computer forensic positions. There can be good money in these positions, but most expect the contractor to arrive in the position already possessing skills, certifications, and experience. Many of these people gained experience through either a law enforcement agency or the military. At the state and local levels, within a law enforcement agency, there can be a strong competition for positions. Our department has a little more than 700 positions, but only two computer forensic detectives. To get one of these two positions, an officer has to spend years on patrol, get promoted to detective, wait until one of the two positions becomes available, and then compete for the position. Then the department has to find the money to train the new examiner.

Several branches of the military have units that specialize in computer security and this can be a good place to get exposure and experience. The army has an active duty unit with the 1st IO Command and several reserve units within the ARIOC that do computer security missions. The air force and air guard have aggressor squadrons and intel units that have a large emphasis on computer and network security. These units can provide training and experience, but obviously require a commitment of at least several years and may have a competitive process to join the units.

Q. What advice would you give to high school students who are interested in becoming a computer forensics specialist?

A. A person who wants to get involved in computer forensics still needs to have a broad background and [base of knowledge] in computer and network security. To focus just on computer forensics can result in a person being too specialized and not being able to work within the bigger picture. Because of the need for competent computer forensic examinations and the liability involved with network and computer security, employers will typically want to hire the most qualified person they can find. This results in a strong competition for a small number of positions, so a student needs to excel in as many areas as he can in order to be competitive for a computer forensics position.

and procedures is taught or more fully explored at the master's and doctorate levels. Other, more specific areas of forensics, such as DNA analysis, require advanced degrees in molecular biology and genetics.

WHAT ARE THE SALARY RANGES?

Earnings for forensic scientists vary with the employer, geographic location, specialty, and educational and skill levels.

Starting salaries range from $30,000 to $50,000. Salaries for those with experience and advanced degrees range from $75,000 to more than $300,000 a year.

Benefits for full-time workers include vacation and sick time, health, and sometimes dental, insurance, and pension or 401(k) plans.

WHAT IS THE JOB OUTLOOK?

Overall employment for forensic scientists is expected to be good during the next decade. Population growth, a rising crime rate, and the greater emphasis on scientific methodology in crime investigation have increased the need for trained scientists. Forensic scientists who are employed by state and local public safety departments should experience especially strong employment opportunities, although some government agencies may be under pressure to reduce staff because of budget problems. Forensic scientists with advanced degrees and training will enjoy the best employment prospects.

Employment predictions will vary by professional specialty. Although most career fields are growing, some fields such as forensic anthropology and forensic entomology employ only a small number of professionals. Aspiring forensic scientists should contact professional associations in their chosen specialty for more information on employment trends.

Bobbi Jo O'Neal predicts that employment for forensic nurses will be very strong in coming years. "Violence is a health care problem and it will take health care professionals to help stop violence," she explains. "More forensic nurses will be needed to help assess and document injuries, to investigate the causes of those injuries, and to develop ways to help prevent violence in their community."

Genetic Scientists

SUMMARY

Definition
Genetic scientists study heredity. They study plants and animals, including humans, to learn how characteristics are passed from one generation to the next. Some specialties involve manipulating or altering particular genetic characteristics to better understand how genetic systems work. Others involve seeing patients who have, or are at risk for having, a genetic disease. Together, their work adds to the body of knowledge and helps decrease morbidity (the rate of disease) and mortality (or illness and death) from genetic disease.

Alternative Job Titles
Genetic specialists
Geneticists

Salary Range
$27,026 to $75,000 to $134,770+

Educational Requirements
Bachelor's degree; advanced degree required for certain positions

Certification or Licensing
Recommended (certification)
Required for certain positions (licensing)

Employment Outlook
Faster than the average

High School Subjects
Biology
Chemistry
Mathematics
Psychology

Personal Interests
Science

Karen Powell, a certified genetic counselor, once saw a patient who had an amniocentesis (genetic testing of her pregnancy) because of some concerns seen on an ultrasound. "Ultimately," she recalls, "the test came back indicating that her pregnancy was affected with Down syndrome. She came back into clinic and we discussed the diagnosis. I was able to support her through the difficult time after the diagnoses and while she was learning more about Down syndrome. After a couple years, this patient came back for her second pregnancy and we were able to provide her with news that her current pregnancy was not affected with Down syndrome! At this time she revealed to me how much my support had meant to her and helped her cope. This was 12 to 13 years ago, and I still think about this patient and how rewarding it was to learn how much my support meant to her."

WHAT DOES A GENETIC SCIENTIST DO?

The goal of *genetic scientists* is to increase knowledge in order to do a variety of things, such as understand and treat disease; decrease the risk for morbidity and mortality from genetic disease; counsel families at risk of having children with genetic disorders; and breed new crops and livestock, among other things. These goals can be obtained in a laboratory or clinical setting. Many genetic scientists spend their time in a laboratory isolating particular genes in tissue samples and conducting experiments to find out for which characteristics those genes are responsible. They work with chemicals, heat, light, and such instruments as microscopes, computers, electron microscopes, and other technical equipment. Besides having excellent mathematical and analytical skills, which will help them design and carry out experiments and analyze results, genetic scientists must also develop good writing and teaching techniques. They must be able to communicate their research results to students in classroom settings and to colleagues through published papers. Other genetic scientists see patients in a clinical setting. Patients with physical changes or developmental concerns may be seen by a *clinical geneticist* or *genetic counselor*. Clinical geneticists will provide patients with a physical examination, looking for subtle differences that may indicate a specific genetic condition. Genetic counselors discuss the results of the physical exam, genetic testing options, and the implications of the genetic testing and condition to the individual and family. Genetic testing, performed by *laboratory geneticists*, can provide answers to physical or developmental concerns that are identified by the clinical geneticists.

Profound academic and technological advances made over the last two decades have brought about rapid progress in the field. Some of the many specialty areas for geneticists are described in the following paragraphs.

Research geneticists typically complete a Ph.D. program, carrying out original research under a faculty member's direction. After earning their Ph.D.'s, most graduates conduct research for two to four years as postdoctoral fellows. Following this training, they are then qualified to hold faculty positions at academic institutions or to join the staff of research institutes or biotechnology firms.

Laboratory geneticists apply modern genetic technology to agriculture, police work, pharmaceutical development, and clinical medicine. They typically have a master's degree and are part of a staff of scientists trained in molecular biology, cytogenetics, biochemical genetics, immunogenetics, and related disciplines.

Some genetic scientists specialize as *genetic counselors*. Genetic counselors are health professionals with a master's degree specializing in medical genetics and counseling. They work as a valuable part of a health care team, giving information and support to families affected by birth defects or genetic disorders, individuals who themselves have genetic conditions and couples concerned about having a child with a genetic condition. Genetic counselors identify family members who are at risk for disease by generating family medical histories and obtaining and interpreting information about genetic conditions. They discuss how genetic testing can detect possible gene changes and the likelihood of a genetic disease occurring in other family members, including children. Genetic counselors go through available options with their patients, serving as patient advocates and making referrals to community or state support services. Some genetic counselors serve in administrative roles, while others conduct research activities related to the field of medical genetics and genetic counseling.

Clinical geneticists are generally medical doctors, having received an MD degree and completed a pediatric, internal medicine, family medicine or obstetric residency, followed by a genetics fellowship or residency. Many clinical geneticists work at university medical centers or large hospitals, while some have private practices or work in biotechnology companies. Generally, this job involves recognizing genetic disorders and birth defects in patients, arranging the proper medical management, and helping the patient and family understand and cope with the diagnosis. Some clinical geneticists work primarily with infants and children, while others may specialize in the genetic problems of babies still in the womb. They may also work with adult patients with inherited forms of heart disease, cancer, or neurological disease. An important role for the clinical geneticist is being the link between the research geneticists who are constantly advancing the field and the patients who stand to benefit from their discoveries.

Cytogenetic technologists prepare, analyze, and examine chromosome structure. Living cells are first treated with a special stain that reveals stripes of light and dark regions along the length of each chromosome. Because the stripes are highly specific for a particular chromosome, stripe patterns help differentiate chromosomes from one another, making any abnormalities in structure easily seen. Chromosome analysis may be performed on just about any living tissue, but for clinical work, it usually is performed on amniotic fluid (fluid surrounding the fetus), chorionic villi (fetal placenta), blood, saliva samples, buccal smears (cells from the inside of the cheek), bone marrow, and miscarriages.

Molecular geneticists study and analyze cellular DNA to identify genetic abnormalities. The majority of their work focuses on three areas: prenatal diagnosis (examining fetal cells for possible abnormalities), carrier testing (examining cells to determine if an individual is at risk from a single gene disorder), and confirmation of diagnosis (testing samples provided by other health care professionals to confirm or contradict a diagnosis).

Genetic engineers experiment with altering, splicing, and rearranging genes for specific results. This research has resulted in the discovery and production of insulin and interferon, two medical breakthroughs that can treat diseases like diabetes and leukemia. Genetic engineering successes have also been seen in agricultural science. Agricultural triumphs like hybrid corn, disease-resistant grains, and higher quality livestock are all products of the principles of recombinant DNA and cloning.

Another specialty area for genetic scientists is population genetics. *Population geneticists* look at allele frequency within populations and how they change during immigration, emigration, and through evolution. Population geneticists can look at genetic changes that occur spontaneously in human populations or are introduced purposely in farm animals and crops to produce a marketable result.

Genetic scientists work in both laboratories and in clinical settings. Those who work in laboratories spend much of their time designing and conducting research experiments. While most of these experiments will take many hours and yield few publishable results, they can result in patents and significant royalties, with the goal of reducing the morbidity and mortality from genetic disease. Even small discoveries in the genetics field add to biological knowledge and can lead to disease treatments. Genetic scientists also spend considerable time writing reports about their experiments, lecturing or teaching about their research, and preparing grant proposals to federal or private agencies to secure funding to support their research. Because federal grants are extremely competitive, only the best-written and most scientifically up-to-date proposals will receive funding. Therefore, genetic scientists must keep improving their skills and knowledge throughout their careers to keep up with new developments in the field and to advance their own research. Usually, geneticists work as part of a research team, consisting of graduate students and laboratory personnel, which cooperate on various aspects of their experiments. They may work from nine to five, although they may be required to work late into the night and on weekends during critical periods of an experiment. They may also work extra hours to complete research projects, to write reports of findings, or to read the latest developments in their specialty.

Other genetic scientists (such as genetic counselors and clinical geneticists) work in clinical settings such as university medical centers, large hospitals, and private practice and frequently interact with patients. They translate technical information about inherited health disorders into language that can be understood by the average person. They explain health disorders, the available options for test-

Genetic Scientist Profile: Dr. Harry Orr

Dr. Harry Orr is the director of the Institute of Human Genetics (http://www.med. umn.edu/ihg) and the Tulloch Professor of Genetics at the University of Minnesota. He discussed his career with the editors of *What Can I Do Now? Science.*

Q. How long have you worked in the field? Why did you decide to become a genetic scientist?

A. I have been doing genetics for about 30 years. I started during my postdoctoral fellowship, coming to genetics via molecular biology and the HLA/histocompatibility system. Prior to that I was a biochemist/neuroscientist.

Q. How did you train for this field?

A. Besides the usual undergraduate and graduate courses dealing with genetics and molecular biology, training was pretty much on the job—postdoc and as a junior faculty member.

Q. Can you provide a brief overview of the Institute of Human Genetics and your typical responsibilities?

A. The Institute of Human Genetics (IHG) is charged by the dean of the medical school to bridge basic and clinical genetics. There are about 12 core faculty located in IHG space with about half coming from a basic science department (Genetics & Cell Biology, Neuroscience) and half from a clinical department (Neurology, Pediatrics, Medicine). I still spend the largest portion of my time overseeing the research in my lab (60 percent). As IHG director I interact with faculty helping to move their research forward. Currently this largely deals with funding issues—national and local. I also interact with administration (the dean), ensuring that genetics is at the table when strategic plans are being discussed. Other efforts are directed at faculty recruiting and retention.

Q. What do you like most and least about being a genetic scientist?

A. I like the clarity and linear thought process of genetics. I came into genetics via molecular biology so I also like the ability to manipulate a biological system using molecular genetic and genetic approaches. Dislikes are those that face all academic researchers these days—funding issues; regulatory matters and the time it takes to deal with that process; administrators with little knowledge of or interest in learning about research and what it takes to be successful.

Q. What are the most important skills for genetic scientists?

A. Again, they are really no different than skills required to be successful in any other research/academic area. On the research side it is important to focus and focus on the important questions—not to get bogged down in relatively unimportant details. One also needs to admit when you are wrong and be able to move on. Being able to deal with rejection is a must. Grants are not always funded and papers may be rejected.

Q. What is one of the most interesting or rewarding things that has happened to you while working in the field?

A. Easy—the spinocerebellar ataxia type 1 (SCA1) story. [Visit http://www.ataxia.org for more information.]

(continued on next page)

(continued from previous page)

Cloning the gene was challenging in the days before the genome project. Taking the project from isolating the gene to making a model of the disease in mice to identifying a potential therapeutic target has been very rewarding. Most important has been the great collaboration from almost day one with Huda Zoghbi [a professor at Baylor College of Medicine]. It is always good to have fun and have a colleague and friend to share it with. Interacting with patients and families has also been very inspiring. These are brave and gutsy people.

ing for or treatment of these disorders, and the risks associated with each option. They also help patients come to terms with the emotional and psychological aspects of having an inherited disorder or disease.

WHAT IS IT LIKE TO BE A GENETIC SCIENTIST?

Karen Powell is a certified genetic counselor and the project coordinator of The Genomedical Connection (http://www.genomedical.com) at the University of North Carolina at Greensboro. "I always knew that I wanted to work in the health care field," she says. "When I went to college, I became interested in genetics, and started learning how I could be involved in both the health care and genetics fields. I found a summer job in a genetics lab and soon realized that, while I was interested in genetics, I did not want to work in a lab. An adviser directed me to the genetic counselors on campus. I made an appointment with one genetic counselor who became a mentor to me. She provided me with literature about a career in genetic counseling, and let me borrow educational materials that she would provide to patients. She invited me to participate in the genetics clinic's weekly meetings, and eventually I was able to see a patient or two with her. That exposure helped influence my decision to apply for graduate programs in genetic counseling. I started my genetic counseling graduate program in 1992 and completed it in 1994.

"When I started working as a genetic counselor, I saw patients in a prenatal, pediatric, and adult clinical setting," she continues. "In 2004 I moved into a nonclinical genetic counseling position with a project called The Genomedical Connection. The Genomedical Connection is a project whose intent is to develop a model for preventative medicine that can be used in primary care by collecting and utilizing the family health history of patients. This means that we have created a program/protocol that will be used by family medicine or internal medicine physicians who have agreed to participate in our project. Physicians will use this protocol to determine if they can identify more patients than they have in the past who would benefit from either

1) increased screening and counseling how making lifestyle changes can help prevent certain diseases, or 2) a referral to a genetic specialist for discussion of genetic testing. We are looking specifically at breast and ovarian cancer, colon cancer, and blood clotting diseases called thrombophilias. If they find that they are identifying more people at risk for these diseases, we will offer this program to other providers in our community. If it is successful at a whole community level, we will then expand it further. My position in this project is to help educate our community on how to collect and use their family health history." Karen's day-to-day activities can vary from providing outreach to community members through presentations or health fairs to writing newsletters or articles for community members through different venues or gathering opinions of community members through the use of focus groups or other measures. She also helps educate health care providers in her area.

"The dichotomy of genetic counseling is that the thing you dislike the most can also be the most rewarding," Karen explains. "Thinking back to the days when I saw patients, the thing I liked least about my job was giving bad news. This could mean telling parents that their unborn child had Down syndrome, or telling parents searching for a reason why their young child had developmental problems that we could not find the answers to their questions. It could also mean telling someone they inherited the gene for Huntington disease, and therefore will eventually get the disease. However, some of these times were also the most

rewarding. Providing support and education to the parents whose pregnancy was affected with Down syndrome or the person who found out that they inherited the gene change for Huntington disease could also be incredibly rewarding."

DO I HAVE WHAT IT TAKES TO BE A GENETIC SCIENTIST?

Successful genetic scientists need to have good analytical skills. They must be able to evaluate results and draw conclusions from measurable criteria. They should also be able to work with abstract theories and ideas and in cooperation with others. Genetic scientists need both written and oral communication skills in order to share research and clinical information. Important personal qualities include patience, determination, and attention to detail.

Genetic counselors must have mature judgment and strong communication skills to work with people coping with highly emotional issues. They must be able to establish trust quickly and have the right mix of objectivity (the ability to be neutral) and sensitivity to do their work well. Karen Powell says that important skills for genetic counselors include "knowing how to find resources that will help patients make informed decisions; being able to communicate scientific information in a way that a person without a science background can understand—both written and verbal; feeling comfortable talking with patients about difficult or uncomfortable topics, and; keeping up to date in a fast-paced field. While, many of these skills can be learned in a graduate program, a person who wants to become a genetic counselor *must* be empathetic and have a desire to help people navigate through the emotions and issues that arise from learning about their risk for a genetic disease. The latter things cannot be learned in graduate school."

HOW DO I BECOME A GENETIC SCIENTIST?
Education

High School

If you are interested in becoming a genetic scientist, you should study math, chemistry, and physics in high school, along with biology. English, writing, and computer studies are helpful for developing communication skills.

Postsecondary Training

In college, students wishing to become a genetic scientist typically major in biology or genetics, taking math, chemistry, and physics courses. However, you could also major in any one of the physical sciences with a minor in biology and still enter graduate school in the field of genetics. Laboratory geneticists, including molecular geneticists, cytogeneticists, biochemical geneticists, and others, require a doctoral degree and postdoctorate training. Clinical geneticists usually earn an MD degree, which requires being admitted to medical school, then completing a three- to five-year residency in a medical specialty followed by an additional two to three years of specialized training in genetics.

There are also career options for those with bachelor's or master's of science degrees, particularly in the rapidly growing biotechnology field, which is using genetics to produce everything from medicines to microchips. This industry needs well-trained research technicians who typically have a bachelor's of science degree in biology with a molecular or biochemistry emphasis. The federal government also has a need for research technicians and hires college graduates and those with master's degrees to work in hospitals and U.S. Department of Agriculture laboratories. Cytogenetic technologists generally need a bachelor's of science degree.

Genetic counselors usually hold master's degrees.

"Training to become a genetic counselor involves graduating from a genetic counseling graduate program that has been accredited by the American Board of Genetic Counseling," says Karen Powell. A list of these programs can be found at http://www.nsgc.org/career/training program.cfm. Karen earned a master's degree from the University of Minnesota in Minneapolis. "The training included course work, clinical rotations through different genetics clinics, and a 'Plan B' project, similar to a thesis," she recalls. "The clinical rotations allowed me to see patients in different settings. This included seeing patients in a prenatal, pediatric, and adult clinical setting. More recently, a few genetics companies or laboratories have started offering internships—some of which provide a stipend. The number of internships is generally limited, but they offer an experience similar to the clinical rotation and are usually offered during the summer when students do not have academic obligations. Exposure to a variety of patients is crucial because students need to keep a log of the type of cases they see in order to be eligible to sit for a certification exam."

Certification or Licensing

Licensing and/or certification may be necessary, depending on the specialty that is chosen. Molecular geneticists, cytogeneticists, biochemical geneticists, and clinical geneticists may obtain certification through the American Board of Medical Genetics while genetic counselors are certified by the American Board of Genetic Counseling. Additionally, clinical geneticists must be licensed to practice medicine, and some states now require genetic counselors to obtain a license. Some genetic laboratories require staff to have specific training and certification in cytogenetic or medical technology, while others hire people with relevant BS or MS degrees as long as they show an aptitude for the work.

Internships and Volunteerships

Most college programs will require that you participate in an internship with a government agency or private organization that employs genetic scientists. Schools with degree programs that require an internship usually will have a partnership set up with local industry or government. What are the benefits of internships? Internships will offer you an opportunity to make valuable contacts as well as learn more about the field from experienced genetic scientists. If they cannot land an

internship, college students may also be able to land a volunteer opportunity or a research assistantship with a genetics-related employer.

WHO WILL HIRE ME?

Genetic scientists work for a variety of employers, including biotechnology firms, government agencies, universities, medical centers, research centers, and agricultural stations and farms. Government agencies that employ genetic scientists include the Department of Agriculture, the National Institutes of Health, the Fish and Wildlife Service, and several others.

Because this career is so broad with many varied specialties within it, methods of entry also vary, depending on the specialty area you choose. Opportunities exist for paid and unpaid internships at a number of science laboratories. Job seekers can get leads from their professors or fellow students. You could join a team of researchers as a laboratory aide or technician.

Federal agencies often come to college campuses to recruit graduates. If you are interested in a job with the federal government, visit http://www.fedjobs.gov, or you can look up federal job openings in the biweekly *Federal Jobs Digest* to apply directly to the federal agency or department you are interested in. The *Federal Jobs Digest* is available online (http://www.jobsfed.com), by subscription, and at your local library.

If you would like to work at a college or university after completing an advanced degree, you may wish to continue your

Nontraditional Roles for Genetic Counselors

- diagnostic laboratories
- health consulting
- Internet companies and Web sites
- pharmaceutical industry
- public health
- research

Source: National Society of Genetic Counselors

education through a postdoctoral fellowship, assisting a prominent scientist with research. Joining a professional organization, such as the American Society of Human Genetics, the American College of Medical Genetics, or the National Society of Genetic Counselors can also provide you with the network to find open positions. Colleges and universities advertise open positions in professional journals and in the *Chronicle of Higher Education,* which is available online (http://chronicle.com) and at public libraries. You should also consult the human resources departments of pharmaceutical and biotechnology companies for employment opportunities in those industries.

WHERE CAN I GO FROM HERE?

At colleges and universities, starting professors and researchers are hired at the assistant professor level. With additional years of experience and an impressive level of published research and teaching, they can advance to the position of associate professor and then to full professor. Many times, individuals go through the process to obtain tenure. Similar years of experience lead to promotion in private industry and government agencies. Promotion usually involves an increase in salary as well as more job duties and greater work prominence.

WHAT ARE THE SALARY RANGES?

Genetic scientists with a bachelor's degree who are hired by the federal government typically start at the GS-5 salary level. This salary was $27,026 in 2009. For those with a master's degree, who qualified to start at the GS-7 or GS-9 levels, the beginning salary was $33,477 and $40,949, respectively. Doctoral degree holders who qualified to start at the GS-11 level earned $49,544. The average salary for genetic scientists working in private industry is approximately $75,000, with biotechnology firms offering even higher salaries. Universities, which generally hire only geneticists with doctoral degrees, offer starting salaries ranging from less than $33,000 for new assistant professors to $123,000 or more for full professors, according to the U.S. Department of Labor. Salaries for all medical scientists ranged from less than $39,870 to $134,770 or more in 2008.

In 2008 the National Society of Genetic Counselors conducted a survey of 2,130 members who were employed full time. It found that the average mean salary for respondents was $63,483. Salaries at the 25th percentile were $52,000, and at the 90th percentile, $85,000.

Benefits for genetic scientists depend on the employer; however, they usually include such items as health insurance, retirement or 401(k) plans, and paid sick and vacation days.

WHAT IS THE JOB OUTLOOK?

Employment for medical scientists (a category that includes the career of genetic scientist) will grow faster than the average for all occupations through 2016, according to the U.S. Department of Labor. Interest in genetic research has exploded in the past decade, with breakthrough discoveries bringing greater attention to the decreasing morbidity and mortality of genetic disease.

As the need to understand human and animal biology and genetics grows, demand for scientists will continue to increase. Rapidly growing specialty areas include the fields of genetic counseling and medical genetics, and genomic medicine (the use of genetic information to improve health outcomes). The world of criminal investigation is increasingly using genetics to determine guilt and innocence, drawing on genetic test results to identify culprits from a tiny drop of blood. Genetics is also being used in food testing to detect contamination by disease-causing organisms.

Geologists

SUMMARY

Definition
Geologists study the processes, makeup, and history of the earth.

Alternative Job Titles
Geological scientists
Geoscientists

Salary Range
$40,786 to $79,160 to $155,430+

Educational Requirements
Bachelor's degree

Certification or Licensing
Voluntary (certification)
Required by certain states (licensing)

Employment Outlook
Much faster than the average

High School Subjects
Earth science
Geography

Personal Interests
Camping/hiking
Science

"The things I like least about being a geologist," says Jennifer Bauer, "are the few days that are very hot and filled with ticks, snakes, and poison ivy. But even those days beat the days we spend in long meetings in the office, debating mapping methods for hours. The things I like most about being a geologist are being outside learning new things about the land where I live and working with other geologists. Overall, they are a very fun, intelligent, and creative group of people who are very willing to share what they know, and learn from each other."

WHAT DOES A GEOLOGIST DO?

Geologists study all aspects of the earth, including its origin, history, composition, and structure. Along more practical lines, geologists may, through the use of theoretical knowledge and research data, locate groundwater, oil, minerals, and other natural resources. They play an increasingly important role in studying, preserving, and cleaning up the environment. Geologists working to protect the environment may design and monitor waste disposal sites, preserve water supplies, and reclaim contaminated land and water to comply with federal environmental regulations. Geologists also advise construction companies and government agencies on the suitability of locations being considered for buildings, highways, and other structures. They also prepare geological reports, maps, and diagrams.

Geologists use a wide variety of laboratory instruments, including X-ray diffractometers, which determine the crystal structure of minerals, and petrographic microscopes for the study of rock and sediment samples.

Geologists often specialize in one of the following disciplines.

Marine geologists study the oceans, including the seabed and subsurface features.

Paleontologists specialize in the study of the earth's rock formations, including remains of plant and animal life, in order to understand the earth's evolution and estimate its age.

Geochronologists are geoscientists who use radioactive dating and other techniques to estimate the age of rock and other samples from an exploration site.

Petroleum geologists attempt to locate natural gas and oil deposits through exploratory testing and study of the data obtained. They recommend the acquisition of new properties and the retention or release of properties already owned by their companies. They also estimate oil reserves and assist petroleum engineers in determining exact production procedures.

Closely related to petroleum geologists are *economic geologists,* who search for new resources of minerals and fuels.

Engineering geologists are responsible for the application of geological knowledge to problems arising in the construction of roads, buildings, bridges, dams, and other structures.

Mineralogists are interested in the classification of minerals composing

To Be a Successful Geologist, You Should...

- be able to work well with others
- have knowledge of computers and data processing techniques
- have strong oral and written communication skills
- be able to think independently and creatively
- have physical stamina if involved in fieldwork

rocks and mineral deposits. To this end, they examine and analyze the physical and chemical properties of minerals and precious stones to develop data and theories on their origin, occurrence, and possible uses in industry and commerce.

Petrologists study the origin and composition of igneous, metamorphic, and sedimentary rocks.

Stratigraphers study the distribution and relative arrangement of sedimentary rock layers. This enables them to understand evolutionary changes in fossils and plants, which leads to an understanding of successive changes in the distribution of land and sea.

Closely related to stratigraphers are *sedimentologists,* who determine processes and products involved in sedimentary rock formations.

Geohydrologists, also known as *hydrogeologists,* study the nature and

Good Advice

● ● ● ● ● ● ●

Jennifer Bauer provides the following tips for young people who want to become geologists:

- Take as many science classes as you can: chemistry, physics, earth science, hydrogeology, math, and some engineering courses if your school offers them.

- Look into getting your geologist license as soon as you get your degree (http://www.asbog.org).

- Take some business courses if you would like to own your own firm at some point.

- Contact geology professionals out in the working world so that you can have a mentor or someone to answer questions for you. One of the best ways to meet geology professionals is to contact a professional society, such as the Association of Environmental & Engineering Geologists (http://www.aegweb.org), the American Association of Petroleum Geologists (http://www.aapg.org), or any other member societies of the American Geological Institute (http://www.agiweb.org). Many of these professionals will be more than willing to mentor you and help you on your geology career path. Plus, many of these professionals are potential employers after graduation.

- A few more general suggestions: pay attention to detail; learn to visualize things in your mind, such as layers under the earth's surface, or 3-D images; and be passionate about whatever you choose to do.

distribution of water within the earth and are often involved in environmental impact studies.

Geomorphologists study the form of the earth's surface and the processes, such as erosion and glaciation, which bring about changes.

Glacial geologists study the physical properties and movement of ice sheets and glaciers.

The geologist is far from limited in a choice of work, but a basic knowledge of all sciences is essential in each of these specializations. An increasing number of scientists combine geology with detailed knowledge in another field. *Geochemists,* for example, are concerned with the chemical composition of, and the changes in, minerals and rocks, while *planetary geologists* apply their knowledge of geology to interpret surface conditions on other planets and the moon.

Some geologists spend most of their time in a laboratory or office, working a regular 40-hour week in pleasant conditions; others divide their time between fieldwork and office or laboratory work. Those who work in the field often travel to remote sites by helicopter or four-wheel drive vehicle and cover large areas on foot. They may camp for extended periods of time in primitive conditions with the members of the geological team as their only companions. Exploration geologists often work overseas or in remote areas, and job relocation is not unusual. Marine geologists may spend considerable time at sea.

WHAT IS IT LIKE TO BE A GEOLOGIST?

Jennifer Bauer is a geologist with the North Carolina Geological Survey (NCGS) in Swannanoa, North Carolina. She has worked in the field for eight years. "The NCGS is a section of the Division of Land Resources in the Department of Environmental and Natural Resources," she explains. "Its mission is 'to provide unbiased and technically accurate applied earth science information to address societal needs. This includes geologic maps, mineral resource and geochemical information, topographic maps and digital products, and earth science education initiatives.'" Jennifer is on the Landslide Hazard Mapping team, and she and her coworkers make landslide hazard maps for the counties of Western North Carolina. "These maps," she says, "are in digital format so that county planning boards, emergency management, and the public can zoom around on the computer to find the property or area in which they are interested. These maps show people where we've mapped landslides and landslide deposits, hazard zones where landslides might start, and areas where landslides might travel. They are intended for public safety, to identify areas that might need attention in emergency situations, and to make people aware of areas where they need to take extra precautions if they are going to build."

Jennifer typically works from 8 A.M. to 5 P.M., but she says that her hours can vary depending on fieldwork, conferences, and deadlines. "My typical responsibilities are identifying landslides remotely from air photos or digital elevation models (DEMs); field verifying these features; collecting soil, rock, and groundwater data; inputting data into the database and geographic information system (GIS); analyzing data for input into the computer models; final map preparation; interacting with the public and answering questions about our maps; and presenting our work to the public and peers in the geology community."

There are two different components of Jennifer's job—office days and field days. "Both are extremely important to the mapping process," she says. "We start the process bringing up several different vintages of aerial photographs, ranging from 1940 to the present, on the computer, and looking through them for what might be landslides. We mark any locations we think need to be checked in the field. We also use DEMs, or digital topography, to identify areas that have the geomorphology, or 'look' of a landslide deposit. We circle these locations as well."

After Jennifer and her coworkers complete the initial office work to define areas in the field that they feel need to be visited, they begin fieldwork. "A day in the field," she says, "can vary from driving to remote parts of the county meeting various land owners and field verifying features that we have identified back in the office, to spending the day hiking to the top of a ridge to find a landslide initiation zone, or area where the landslide started. These days are the most fun and rewarding. While at the initiation zone, we collect information about the slope, soil, rocks, groundwater, and vegetation."

When Jennifer returns to the office, she and her coworkers input all of the information they have collected into a database and into a geographic information system. "The data is then analyzed," she says, "and then goes into our computer models that predict the zones where landslides might start or travel down slope. Then we just have to make the maps."

Dorian Kuper is the co-owner of Kuper Consulting, a geological consulting firm in Portland, Oregon. She has worked in the field since 1978. "I took an earth science class in high school in Phoenix, where I grew up, and we went on several field trips and I enjoyed geology," she explains when asked why she entered the field. "I also grew up around my grandparents' cattle ranch in northern Arizona, so I was an outdoor tomboy! I love to ride horses and seeing the geology in that way at a young age excited me."

Dorian's husband is also a geologist, and they are partners in their two-person firm. "We primarily work for private aggregate mining companies," she explains, "securing mine permits and designing mine plans and reclamation plans for their sites. A day in our firm can [include] being in the field either drilling or trenching a site for potential aggregate resources (sand and gravel, or basalt rock in this part of the world—Oregon)—usually 10-hour days of logging the drill core as drilling occurs, mapping the geologic units in the field, depending on exposures, and securing samples of the rock for testing. For every day in the field, there is typically a day in the office reviewing the geologic logs, drawing geologic cross sections, geologic maps, and preparing technical reports on a specific job site. We are unique in that we do not have any employees, so our work schedule depends on how busy the work is. Meeting with clients, coordinating other consultants (noise, air, groundwater, traffic, wetlands, and wildlife) is typical. We manage the various consultants for our clients to prepare an environmental impact statement-like technical report, presenting impacts, or lack thereof, of a proposed mine site on the land. And we work with the various consultants to 'think out of the box' and create reclamation plans, which will provide a beneficial use for the property once mining is completed."

Dorian says that "collecting overdue invoices that clients haven't paid" is her least favorite part of the job. "The best part—being outside in the elements, mapping the geology and untangling difficult geologic conditions, and figuring out what works best for our clients needs. I also enjoy solving problems."

DO I HAVE WHAT IT TAKES TO BE A GEOLOGIST?

To be a successful geologist, you should have a familiarity with computer modeling and data processing, as well as have good interpersonal, organizational, and oral and written communication skills. You should also be able to think independently and creatively. Physical stamina is needed for those involved in fieldwork. Geologists who own their own businesses should have skills in business administration.

HOW DO I BECOME A GEOLOGIST?

Education

"I love the outdoors and enjoy learning about the earth and the environment I live in," Jennifer Bauer comments in response to being asked why she entered the field. "My freshman year of college I took an introductory geology class and was instantly intrigued by all of the processes that occur on earth. The next semester I decided to take another geology class, the Geology of National Parks, and saw that the geology department was offering a spring break field trip to eastern California. During this field trip, I got a firsthand look at what geologists do, and for the first time realized that there were careers out there that allowed scientists to work outside and do research at the same time. It was after that trip that I decided being a geologist would be a great career for me."

High School

Because you will need a college degree in order to find work in this profession, you should take a college preparatory curriculum while in high school. Such a curriculum will include computer science, history, English, and geography classes. Science and math classes are also important to take, particularly earth science, chemistry, and physics. Math classes should include algebra, trigonometry, statistics, and calculus if possible.

An Interesting Experience

Jennifer Bauer details one of her most interesting experiences as a geologist:

One of the most interesting things I've seen while working for the North Carolina Geological Survey is the initiation zone of a landslide that traveled 2.25 miles from near the top of the ridge down to the river in the bottom of a valley. This landslide that was triggered by back-to-back hurricanes released a slurry of mud, boulders, and trees down the stream, killing four people and an unborn baby, and destroying 16 houses on its way down. It was hard for me to imagine that amount of soil coming loose from the hillside where only bare rock is now exposed. I saw 20-foot long boulders that had been moved by the muddy slurry screaming down the hill at 30+ miles per hour. Seeing the destruction left by the landslide helped me to realize the power and unpredictability of nature, and made me want to learn even more about it.

Postsecondary Training

A bachelor's degree is the minimum requirement for entry into lower-level geology jobs, but a master's degree is usually necessary for beginning positions in research, teaching, and exploration. A person with a strong background in physics, chemistry, mathematics, or computer science may also qualify for some geology jobs. For those wishing to make significant advancements in research and for teaching at the college level, a doctoral degree is required. Those interested in the geological profession should have an aptitude not only for geology but also for physics, chemistry, and mathematics.

A number of colleges, universities, and institutions of technology offer degrees in geology. Programs in geophysical technology, geophysical engineering, geophysical prospecting, and engineering geology also offer related training for beginning geologists.

Traditional geoscience courses emphasize classical geologic methods and concepts. Mineralogy, petrology, paleontology, stratigraphy, and structural geology are important courses for undergraduates. Students interested in environmental and regulatory fields should take courses in hydrology, hazardous waste management, environmental legislation, chemistry, fluid mechanics, and geologic logging. A field school course is important for learning field mapping methods and applying what is learned in the classroom.

In addition, students should take courses in related sciences, mathematics, English composition, and computer science. Students seeking graduate degrees in geology should concentrate on advanced courses in geology, placing major emphasis on their particular fields.

Certification or Licensing

The American Institute of Professional Geologists (AIPG) grants the certified professional geologist (CPG) designation to geologists who have earned a bachelor's degree or higher in the geological sciences and have eight years of professional experience (applicants with a master's degree need only seven years of professional experience and those with

a Ph.D., five years). Candidates must also undergo peer review by three professional geologists (two of whom must be CPGs) and pay an application fee.

The institute also offers the member designation to geologists who are registered in various states and are not seeking AIPG certification. Applicants must have at least a bachelor's degree in the geological sciences with at least 30 semester hours of geology, be licensed by the state they wish to work in, undergo peer review, and pay an application fee.

More than 30 states require geologists to be registered or licensed. Most of these states require applicants (who have earned a bachelor's degree in the geological sciences) to pass a two-part exam, the Fundamentals of Geology and Practice of Geology, a standardized written exam developed by the National Association of State Boards of Geology.

Internships and Volunteerships

You will most likely participate in an internship at a government agency, private geologic consulting firm, or other employer as part of your college education. Participation in an internship is key to landing a position in the field. Many geologists get their first jobs directly from their internship assignments, and it is important to choose your internships carefully to make sure that they offer many opportunities for hands-on experience and interaction with skilled geologists.

Dorian Kuper advises students to "volunteer where possible and work for free (intern) or at least go out in the field with geologists working for firms to see what

Geologist Profile: Duane Kreuger

Duane Kreuger is a registered geologist and the environmental group manager for Geotechnology Inc. He supervises a group of 13 geologists, engineers, and scientists and manages several environmental projects. Duane discussed his career with the editors of *What Can I Do Now? Science*.

Q. Can you tell us a little about Geotechnology Inc.?

A. Geotechnology is a 25-year-old geotechnical, environmental, materials testing, geophysics, and drilling firm with 120 employees headquartered in St. Louis, Missouri.

Q. How long have you worked in the field? Why did you decide to become a geologist?

A. I have been employed at Geotechnology for 17 years and worked the first seven to eight years in the field. I became a geologist because I always loved the outdoors and was curious about the earth.

Q. What do you like most about being a geologist?

A. Working outside and trying to understand the subsurface from limited amounts of information (soil and water samples, etc.).

Q. What are the most important personal and professional skills for geologists?

A. Personal: Develop your ability to contemplate the big picture and to understand things you can't readily see. Professional: Learn how various disciplines interact and how they contribute to a project. Learn to communicate, collaborate, and work with a variety of professionals such as engineers, groundwater scientists, geophysicists, laboratories, and drillers.

Q. What is one of the most interesting or rewarding things that has happened to you while working in the field?

A. A few times while drilling along major rivers (like the Mississippi) we found old pieces of trees while soil sampling very deep (at 80 to 100 feet), which must have been deposited thousands or tens of thousands of years ago.

Q. What is the employment outlook for geologists?

A. Good. I think the petroleum industry will need geologists well into the future. And the environmental field seems to still be going strong, as we continually are finding new man-made messes that need to be cleaned up.

---

really goes on during a day in the life of a geologist. The more exposure someone has, the more apt that person will retain that knowledge and apply it once hired. Plus, it looks good on a resume. The other idea if they don't have summer field classes behind them is to take a summer field class. It can be expensive but it should be a requirement in all geology-degreed schools, but this isn't always the case. When someone is first coming out of school, I look to see if that is on their resume. If not, it makes me wonder how serious a student in geology is, if they haven't learned the basics in a six-week field class. I want to know that person understands the basics of geology before they are hired."

WHO WILL HIRE ME?

Approximately 31,000 geoscientists (including geologists) are employed in the United States. The majority of geologists are employed in private industry. Some work for oil and gas extraction and mining companies, primarily in exploration. The rest work for business services, environmental and geotechnical consulting firms, or are self-employed as consultants to industry and government. The federal government employs geologists in the Department of the Interior (in the U.S. Geological Survey or the Bureau of Reclamation) and in the Departments of Defense, Agriculture, and Commerce. Geologists also work for state agencies, nonprofit research organizations, and museums. Many geologists hold faculty positions at colleges and universities and most of these combine their teaching with research.

After completing sufficient educational requirements, preferably a master's degree or doctorate, the geologist may look for work in various areas, including private industry and government. For those who wish to teach at the college level, a doctorate is required. College graduates may also take government civil service examinations or possibly find work on state geological surveys, which are sometimes based on civil service competition.

Geologists often begin their careers in field exploration or as research assistants in laboratories. As they gain experience, they are given more difficult assignments and may be promoted to supervisory positions, such as project leader or program manager.

Jennifer Bauer landed her first geology job by answering an ad in the newspaper for a geologist at an engineering consulting firm. "While I was interviewed, I tried to show that, although I was not familiar with the task I was applying for, I was willing and capable of learning," she recalls. "I showed enthusiasm for learning new things, and ended up getting the job. After being hired, I realized that there was going to be a lot of on-the-job training, but the people I worked with were willing to teach me, and I caught on quickly. I started out behind a drill rig, logging soil and rock for subsurface investigations for the North Carolina Department of Transportation bridge projects. I was introduced to the engineering properties of soil and rock, things I was not taught in school. Although not always fun, I think that all geologists need some behind-the-rig experience, to become familiar with long, sweaty hours, and constructing cross-sections of the soil below the surface in real time."

WHERE CAN I GO FROM HERE?

Geologist with a bachelor's degree will have a very difficult time advancing to higher-level positions. Continued formal training and work experience are necessary, especially as competition for these positions increases. A doctorate is essential for most college or university teaching positions and is preferred for much research work.

WHAT ARE THE SALARY RANGES?

Graduates with a bachelor's degree in the geological sciences earned starting salaries of about $40,786 in 2007, according to the National Association of Colleges and Employers.

The median annual salary for geoscientists was $79,160 in 2008, according to the U.S. Department of Labor. Salaries ranged from less than $41,700 to more than $155,430. In the federal government, the average salary for geologists in managerial, supervisory, and nonsupervisory positions was $91,030 a year in 2008.

Although the petroleum, mineral, and mining industries offer higher salaries, competition for these jobs is strong and there is less job security than in other areas. In addition, college and university teachers can earn additional income through research, writing, and consulting. Salaries for foreign assignments may be significantly higher than those in the United States.

Benefits for full-time workers include vacation and sick time, health, and sometimes dental, insurance, and pension or 401(k) plans. Self-employed geologists must provide their own benefits.

WHAT IS THE JOB OUTLOOK?

Employment of geologists is expected to grow much faster than the average for

A Great Experience

Geologist Dorian Kuper details one of the most interesting experiences of her career:

Since 1987, about every three years we attend the International Conference and Field Trip on Landslides (ICFL), which is sponsored by the International Landslide Research Group and of which I am president. It is an opportunity to travel to a foreign country to see how they are dealing with geohazards—primarily landslides, rockfalls, mass movements, and impacts to the urban environment. There are usually 40 geologists and engineers representing countries such as Norway, Germany, Austria, Italy, Spain, Poland, Czech Republic, Slovakia, Switzerland, Japan, United States, and others. The ICFL has been to Australia, New Zealand, Tasmania, Switzerland, Austria, Italy, Spain, Czech and Slovak Republics, Poland, England, and Japan. This is a 10-day field trip where not only do we travel to various engineering geologic problem sites but also give advice to those countries that are having problems related to engineering geology. As a result, we have numerous discussions, solutions, and remedial measures thrown out. We are also exposed to the local countryside fare and customs that most tourists would never experience. It is very rewarding in that we learn as much from each other as does the host country. Graduate students are usually involved, as we visit sites that are under investigation and where the professors who are working on the problems have students working with them. So it gives us an opportunity to meet foreign students.

all occupations through 2016, according to the *Occupational Outlook Handbook*. Opportunities in the field are expected to be good because a large number of geologists are expected to retire from the field during the next decade.

"Right now there are a lot of job opportunities for geologists," says Jennifer Bauer, "with the recent emphasis on the environment (cleaning things up), energy (finding new sources of petroleum), and increased construction (engineering geology). In addition, the number of students majoring in geology has been decreasing while the number of retiring professional geologists is increasing."

Additionally, in response to the curtailed petroleum activity in the late 1980s and 1990s, the number of graduates in geology and geophysics, especially petroleum geology, dropped considerably in the last decade. Relative stability has now returned to the petroleum industry, increasing the need for qualified geoscientists. With improved technology and greater demand for energy resources, job opportunities are expected to be good, especially for those with a master's degree and those familiar with computer modeling and the global positioning system. Geologists who are able to speak a foreign language and who are willing to work overseas will also have strong employment prospects. In addition to the oil and gas industries, geologists will be able to find jobs in environmental monitoring, protection, and reclamation.

Meteorologists

SUMMARY

Definition
Meteorologists study weather conditions and forecast weather changes. By using numerical forecasting models and analyzing weather maps covering large geographic areas and related charts, like upper-air maps and soundings, they can predict the movement of fronts, precipitation, and pressure areas. They forecast such data as temperature, winds, precipitation, cloud cover, and flying conditions.

Alternative Job Titles
Atmospheric scientists

Salary Range
$35,572 to $81,290 to $1,000,000+

Educational Requirements
Bachelor's degree; advanced degree required for top positions

Certification or Licensing
Recommended

Employment Outlook
About as fast as the average

High School Subjects
Geography
Physics

Personal Interests
Science

"All of my responsibilities are challenging, and never the same from one day to the next or from one case to the next," says Dr. John Scala, a private weather consultant and a broadcast meteorologist at WGAL-TV (NBC). "The opportunity to observe, diagnose, and learn is ever present, which makes that aspect of this career path the most interesting. My career contains moments of great fulfillment when my words of caution or warning help save lives. I receive great satisfaction when my knowledge can be used to better understand a sequence of events or identify the weather conditions that led to an accident."

WHAT DOES A METEOROLOGIST DO?

Although most people think of weather forecasting when they think of meteorology, meteorologists do many other kinds of work. They research subjects ranging from radioactive fallout to the dynamics of hurricanes. They study the ozone levels in the stratosphere. Some teach in colleges and universities. A few

To Be a Successful Meteorologist, You Should...

- be organized
- have strong technical skills
- be able to work well with others
- have comprehensive knowledge of meteorology
- have strong communication skills, especially if you work in broadcasting
- be able to work well under pressure in order to meet deadlines and plot severe weather systems
- be willing to work a variety of shifts, including nights and weekends

meteorologists work in radio and televised weather forecasting programs. Networks usually hire their own staff of meteorologists.

Meteorologists generally specialize in one branch of this rapidly developing science; however, the lines of specialization are not clearly drawn and meteorologists often work in more than one area of specialization. The largest group of specialists are called *operational meteorologists,* the technical name for *weather forecasters,* who interpret current weather information, such as air pressure, temperature, humidity, and wind velocity, reported by observers, weather satellites, weather radar, and remote sensors in many parts of the world. They use this data to make short- and long-range forecasts for given regions. Operational meteorologists also use Doppler radar, which detects rotational patterns in violent thunderstorms, in order to better predict tornadoes, thunderstorms, and flash floods, as well as their direction and intensity.

Other specialists include *climatologists,* who study past records to discover weather patterns for a given region. The climatologist compiles, makes statistical analyses of, and interprets data on temperature, sunlight, rainfall, humidity, and wind for a particular area over a long period of time for use in weather forecasting, aviation, agriculture, commerce, and public health.

Dynamic meteorologists study the physical laws related to air currents. *Physical meteorologists* study the physical nature of the atmosphere including its chemical composition and electrical, acoustical, and optical properties. *Environmental meteorologists* study air pollution, global warming, ozone depletion, water shortages, and other environmental problems and write impact statements about their findings. *Industrial meteorologists* work in a variety of private industries, focusing their expertise on such problems as smoke control and air pollution. *Synoptic meteorologists* study large-scale patterns responsible for the daily weather as well as find new ways to forecast weather events by using mathematical models and computers. *Flight meteorologists* fly in aircraft to study hurricanes and other weather phenomena.

The tools used by meteorologists include weather balloons, instrumented aircraft, radar, satellites, and computers. Instrumented aircraft are high-performance airplanes designed to sample and observe many kinds of weather. Radar is used to detect a variety of precipitation types, and the motions within clouds that may lead to violent weather. Doppler radar can measure wind speed and direction. It has become the best tool for the short-term prediction of severe weather. Satellites use advanced remote sensing to measure temperature, wind, and other characteristics of the atmosphere at many levels. The entire surface of the earth can be observed with satellites.

The introduction of computers has changed research and forecasting of weather. The fastest computers are used in atmospheric research, as well as large-scale weather forecasting. Computers are used to produce detailed simulations of upcoming weather.

Weather stations operate 24 hours a day, seven days a week. This means that some meteorologists, often on a rotating basis, work evenings and weekends. Although most of these weather stations are at airports located near cities, a number of weather stations are located in isolated and remote areas. One of the most remote meteorological posts is in the Antarctic. However, it provides some of the most interesting and relevant data in meteorology. In these places, the life of a meteorologist can be quiet and lonely. Operational meteorologists often work overtime during weather emergencies such as hurricanes. Meteorologists who work in college and university settings enjoy the same working conditions as other professors.

WHAT IS IT LIKE TO BE A METEOROLOGIST?

Michael Vescio is the meteorologist in charge of the National Weather Service Forecast Office in Pendleton, Oregon. He has been in this position for about six and a half years and employed by the National Weather Service a little more than 19 years. He has been a meteorologist since 1988. Michael is also the president of the National Weather Association. "I knew at a very early age that I wanted to become a meteorologist and never veered from that path," he recalls. "When I was seven years old a severe storm hit my hometown and lasted several hours during the night. We had a creek that ran near our backyard, and it kept rising. Eventually it rose high enough to flood our basement with several feet of water. That storm really scared me and from that point on I guess you could say I was obsessed with the weather and wanted to know everything about it. I read tons of books and got more and more interested as time went on."

Michael's main job is to manage and lead the Pendleton, Oregon, National Weather Service Forecast Office. "We have a staff of 25 professional meteorologists, electronics technicians, hydrometeorological technicians, and support staff," he says. "Our office is open around the clock and we never close. We provide warning and forecast services for a large portion of central and northeast Oregon and southeast Washington. My job focus varies from day to day depending on what issues arise from an operation of this size. It is never boring. The part that I enjoy the most is when I can bring new tools to the operational staff to help them do their job more efficiently and effectively." Michael also fills in on the forecast desk about 20 percent of the time, which varies depending on the office's staffing level. "I have always been a forecaster at heart," he says, "so it is nice to keep my skills sharp and stay familiar with the ever changing technology on the operational floor. When not filling in on a shift, my typical work hours are Monday–Friday from 8 A.M. to 4:30 P.M."

Michael says that one of his most rewarding experiences as a meteorologist came when he served as the lead forecaster at the National Weather Service's Storm Prediction Center from 1995 to 2000. "In this position," he recalls, "I was responsible for issuing the tornado and severe thunderstorm watches for the contiguous United States. The watch helps people get ready for the severe storms that are anticipated to develop during the next one to two hours. It was a very challenging job with a lot of pressure on significant severe weather days. This job was very rewarding in that you set the tone for the local National Weather Service offices and the public."

Dr. John Scala is a private weather consultant and a broadcast meteorologist at WGAL-TV (NBC) in Lancaster, Pennsylvania. He is also the past president of the National Weather Association. Dr. Scala has been a meteorologist since 1990. "Science was my primary interest in high school," he recalls. "I pursued a double major in college, biology and geology, but it wasn't until I began my graduate studies that I decided to pursue atmospheric science as a career path. I was always fascinated by storms but failed to consider weather as a subject of study until I completed my postsecondary education. I took a weather forecasting class while working on my master's degree and became hooked. The interdisciplinary nature of my undergraduate and graduate coursework provided an excellent background for my environmental and ultimately meteorological studies. My focus in the field of meteorology did change over the past 19 years but my fascination with severe weather, particularly from a forecasting and diagnostic perspective, remains unchallenged."

Dr. Scala's work responsibilities are a bit unusual since he holds more than one job. "I work part time at the local NBC TV station as a broadcast meteorologist," he explains. "I am responsible for the on-air forecast as part of the regularly scheduled newscasts as well as Web updates and radio forecasts. I provide updates during periods of severe weather and work with the National Weather Service to assess storm damage. I often serve as the station scientist, answering a variety of questions that arrive via email or by phone. I am also employed as a forensic scientist outside of my television responsibilities. This work requires me to investigate past weather and prepare reports that are used in criminal and civil litigation. My 'expert' opinion is cited in the adjudication of these cases when weather plays a critical role in an accident, personal injury, storm-related damage, or questionable death. My shift schedule at the television station may occur almost anytime during the day and any day of the week. My work as a forensic scientist does not follow any formal hours. I am contacted for information or requested to participate in a case that usually carries with it a hearing or court date. Most jobs in the field of meteorology are not 9 to 5, 40 hours per week. And why should they be? The atmosphere is a 24/7 proposition!"

DO I HAVE WHAT IT TAKES TO BE A METEOROLOGIST?

Meteorologists must be able to work well under pressure in order to meet deadlines and plot severe weather systems. "Operational forecasting will always contain a time constraint and a certain degree of stress, particularly during rapidly changing weather conditions," says Dr. Scala. "These attributes of a broadcast meteorologist's job coexist on a daily basis and they require an adjustment in thinking and demeanor to attain an acceptable level of comfort. Additionally, the forecast will always be in error in someone's eyes, and some [people] are more than willing to convey that message."

Meteorologists must be able to communicate complex theories and events, orally and in writing. They must be able to absorb pertinent information quickly and pass it on to coworkers and the public in a clear, calm manner. Meteorologists who work in broadcasting must have especially good communication skills in order to deal with the pressure and deadlines of the newsroom and convey information to the public.

Meteorologists must also have strong technical skills. "Things have changed since I entered the job market two decades ago," says Michael Vescio. "The

meteorologist today needs to have considerable technical savvy to go along with their meteorological background. The technology that is used to assist the meteorologist is changing very rapidly and continuously and is becoming very sophisticated. Entry-level meteorologists need to be comfortable with new and emerging technology and with change in general. Also, a meteorologist's job is customer focused and people new to the field must now be ready to interact more directly with their customer base."

HOW DO I BECOME A METEOROLOGIST?
Education
High School

You can best prepare for a college major in meteorology by taking high school courses in mathematics, geography, computer science, physics, and chemistry. Excelling in English and speech classes is essential because you must be able to describe complex weather events and patterns in a clear and concise way.

Postsecondary Training

Although some beginners in meteorological work have majored in subjects related to meteorology, the usual minimum requirement for work in this field is a bachelor's degree in meteorology. For entry-level positions in the federal government, you must have a bachelor's degree (not necessarily in meteorology) with at least 24 semester hours of meteorology courses, six hours of atmospheric dynamics and thermodynamics, six hours

Meteorologist Profile: Jill Hasling

Jill Hasling is a certified consulting meteorologist, president of the Weather Research Center, and executive director of the John C. Freeman Weather Museum in Houston, Texas. She discussed her career with the editors of *What Can I Do Now? Science*.

Q. How long have you been a meteorologist? Why did you decide to enter this career?

A. I graduated from the University of St. Thomas in 1975. I worked as a meteorological technician during my final year of school. My father [Dr. John C. Freeman] was a meteorologist and I was working for him so my education did not stop when I graduated. I received [the] certified consulting meteorologist [designation] from the American Meteorological Society in 1991 and became the first woman member of the National Council of Industrial Meteorologists in 1992.

Q. How did you train for this field? Did you participate in any internships or similar experiences? If so, please detail.

A. At the time I went to school, you did not hear of many internships. Also, there were not many women in the field. Since I was working as a meteorological technician and programmer while I went to school I was getting on-the-job training. My first programs dealt with modeling different layers in the atmosphere and numerical weather predication. My father was my mentor and I continued to train under him until he died in 2004. He had a passion for meteorology.

Q. What are your main and secondary job duties?

A. My main duty is president and researcher at the Weather Research Center (WRC). My secondary job is training meteorologists in the art of marine and tropical weather forecasting worldwide. My typical day starts around 7 A.M. and can go as late as 7 P.M. but usually ends around 5 P.M. When I am on the forecast schedule my day starts at 4 A.M.

At the Weather Research Center, the forecasting shift starts at 4 A.M. and lasts until 4 P.M. The shift begins with making 300 detailed marine site-specific forecasts for the Gulf of Mexico and monitoring the Indian Ocean and the West Pacific for signs of tropical development. The Gulf of Mexico forecasts are updated in the afternoon and forecasts for the Indian Ocean, West Pacific, and Mediterranean are prepared. The forecaster begins by reviewing the current and past observations, radar, and satellite and then reviews the model data from various global models. The forecaster then uses the WRC Marine Weather Forecast Model to forecast the winds, waves, and swells for the next seven days.

Q. What is one of the most interesting or rewarding things that has happened to you while working in this field?

A. Working with my father for 30 years was the most rewarding thing in my career. I learned something new every day and enjoyed trying to keep up with him. His love for meteorology was contagious. I was so fortunate to have this opportunity and continue to learn something new in meteorology each day.

Visit http://www.wxresearch.com for more information on the John C. Freeman Weather Museum and the Weather Research Center.

in the analysis and prediction of weather systems, three hours of physical meteorology, and two hours of remote sensing of the atmosphere or instrumentation, among other courses. Other required courses include calculus, physics, and other physical science courses, such as statistics, computer science, chemistry, physical oceanography, and physical climatology. Advanced graduate training in meteorology and related areas is required for research and teaching positions, as well as for other high-level positions in meteorology. Doctorates are quite common among high-level personnel.

Because the armed forces require the services of so many meteorologists, they have programs to send recently commissioned, new college graduates to civilian universities for intensive work in meteorology.

Certification or Licensing

The American Meteorological Society (http://www.ametsoc.org) provides the following certification designations: certified broadcast meteorologist and certified consulting meteorologist. The National Weather Association (http://www.nwas.org) offers the Weathercaster Seal of Approval. Contact these organizations for information on certification requirements.

Internships and Volunteerships

You will most likely participate in an internship as part of your college education. Internships allow you to learn more about the field, work closely with meteorology professionals, and make valuable networking contacts. The American Meteorological Society offers a listing

---

Rewarding Experiences

Dr. John Scala recalls some of his most rewarding experiences as a meteorologist:

I received several emails from viewers thanking me for my thoughtful and reassuring words during a recent tornado warning. It is the station's policy to break into regular programming to cover a tornado warning live in its entirety. There is great satisfaction knowing that my efforts helped someone make an informed and correct decision during a threatening weather situation. I also enjoy speaking one-on-one or in a group setting where the time constraint is lifted and I can indulge my passion for public education. I can pursue the same outcome in a courtroom setting as well.

---

of internship opportunities for college students at its Web site (http://www.ametsoc.org/amsstudentinfo/internships.html).

There are several ways that you can explore volunteer opportunities in meteorology. Each year, for example, the federal government's National Weather Service accepts a limited number of student volunteers, mostly college students but also a few high school students. Some universities offer credit for a college student's volunteer work in connection with meteorology courses.

WHO WILL HIRE ME?

The American Meteorological Society has more than 14,000 members. The federal government is the largest employer of meteorologists. Most of its civilian meteorologists work for the National Oceanic and Atmospheric Administration's National Weather Service forecast offices across the country. The remainder of the meteorologists work mainly in research and development or management. Additionally, several hundred civilian meteorologists are employed by the Department of Defense. Many opportunities are also available in the armed forces and in educational settings. There are hundreds of meteorologists teaching at institutions of higher education.

Other meteorologists work for private weather consulting firms, engineering service firms, commercial airlines, radio and television stations, computer and data processing services, and companies that design and manufacture meteorological instruments and aircraft and missiles.

You can enter the field of meteorology in a number of ways. For example, new graduates may find positions through career services offices at the colleges and universities where they have studied. National Weather Service volunteers may receive permanent positions as meteorologists upon completing their formal training. Members of the armed forces who have done work in meteorology often assume positions in meteorology when they return to civilian life. In fact, the armed forces give preference in the employment of civilian meteorologists to former military personnel with appropriate experience. Individuals interested in teaching and research careers generally assume these positions upon receiving their doctorates in meteorology or related subjects.

Other federal employers of meteorologists include the Department of Defense, the National Aeronautics and Space Administration, and the Department of Agriculture.

WHERE CAN I GO FROM HERE?

Meteorologists employed by the National Weather Service advance according to civil service regulations. After meeting certain experience and education

Continuing to Learn

• • • • • • • • • • •

Dr. John Scala details the importance of continuing to learn throughout one's career as a meteorologist:

My formal education ended with the awarding of my Ph.D. in 1990. However, the education and training to be a meteorologist remains an ongoing process. Technological advances combined with an improved understanding of the atmosphere and its role in regulating the earth's weather system necessitates a continual effort to gain knowledge.

The science of meteorology would pass me by if I did not work to remain current in the field. This pursuit is accomplished through reading, research, and interaction with colleagues. Of course, a fundamental knowledge of the atmosphere was acquired through my years of study as a student. For example, I learned to launch a radiosonde, take observations, record and analyze data, and work with a cloud model in graduate school. I gained experience as a flight scientist, forecaster, and storm analyst during my participation in several field experiments following completion of my studies.

Today's curriculum offers opportunities, even at the undergraduate level, to engage in operational forecasting, data sampling and analysis, even exposure to numerical modeling that were not available to me. Additional experiences gained through internships and participation in undergraduate research is similar to what I acquired in the years after my formal schooling ceased. Consequently, students of today's programs in meteorology and atmospheric science are offered the opportunity to train in specific areas of the science prior to graduation, a key advantage in today's highly competitive employment market. Nonetheless, the learning never ends, regardless of how it began.

requirements, they advance to classifications that carry more pay and, often, more responsibility. Opportunities available to meteorologists employed by airlines are more limited. A few of these workers, however, do advance to such positions as flight dispatcher and to administrative and supervisory positions. A few meteorologists go into business for themselves by establishing their own weather consulting services. Meteorologists who are employed in teaching and research in colleges and universities advance through academic promotions or by assuming administrative positions in the university setting.

WHAT ARE THE SALARY RANGES?

Median annual earnings of atmospheric scientists in 2008 were $81,290, according to the U.S. Department of Labor. Salaries ranged from less than $38,990 to more than $127,100. The average salary for meteorologists employed by the federal government was about $89,950 in 2008. In the federal government, entry-level meteorologists with a bachelor's degree and no experience received starting salaries of $35,572 in 2007.

In broadcast meteorology, salaries vary greatly. Television weathercasters earn salaries that range from $16,000 to $1,000,000 or more.

Benefits for meteorologists depend on the employer; however, they usually include such items as health insurance, retirement or 401(k) plans, and paid vacation days.

WHAT IS THE JOB OUTLOOK?

Employment for meteorologists should grow about as fast as the average for all careers through 2016, according to the U.S. Department of Labor. The National Weather Service (NWS) has hired all the meteorologists it needs to staff its recently upgraded weather forecast offices. The agency has no plans to build more offices or increase the number of meteorologists in existing offices for many years. Employment at other federal government agencies, such as the Department of Defense, is expected to decline.

Opportunities for atmospheric scientists in private industry, however, are expected to be better than in the federal government through 2016. Private weather consulting firms are able to provide more detailed information than the NWS to weather-sensitive industries, such as farmers, commodity investors, radio and television stations, and utilities, transportation, and construction firms.

Employment should be fair for broadcast meteorologists. This field is highly competitive, and the best opportunities will be available to those with certification and strong broadcasting skills.

Michael Vescio says that the employment outlook for meteorologists is very competitive. "There are many colleges and universities offering degree programs in meteorology and the job market is tight," he explains. "I certainly would not want to discourage people from becoming a meteorologist, but if this is your path you need to position yourself to stand out in the crowd. Excelling in school; belonging to professional societies; volunteering at NWS offices, TV stations, or private companies; or going on and getting that higher-level degree will help you to land that highly sought after job."

"Students seeking a career in meteorology must be aware of the highly competitive nature of the job market," advises Dr. Scala. "Our educational institutions are graduating twice as many students in the field as there are opportunities for employment. This reality necessitates a rethinking of where graduates should be looking for jobs. Keys to successful employment include experience prior to graduation in some form (internships, part-time employment, government-funded opportunities for participation in field projects and research), a willingness to consider nontraditional fields of work (for example, utilities, airlines, insurance), and a desire to set yourself apart from the rest of the field. Good jobs will always exist for exceptional people."

Physicists

SUMMARY

Definition
Physics is a science that deals with the interaction of energy and matter. Physicists study the behavior and structure of matter, the ways that energy is generated and transferred, and the relationships between matter and energy.

Alternative Job Titles
Scientists

Salary Range
$57,160 to $102,890 to $159,400+

Educational Requirements
Bachelor's degree; advanced degree required for top positions

Certification or Licensing
Required (elementary and high school teachers only)

Employment Outlook
About as fast as the average

High School Subjects
Mathematics
Physics

Personal Interests
Science

A career as a physicist is filled with the joy of discovery. Sometimes these discoveries can also help other scientists in their research. Astrophysicist Lisa Kewley recounts one such experience: "While I was working with a very large spectroscopic dataset (45,000 galaxies!), I noticed that the galaxies with actively feeding supermassive black holes divided into two types based on their emission-line properties. No one had ever seen this before, and it helped solve a long-standing mystery about the types of galaxies that harbor active black holes. I used this data to develop a new classification scheme that is now used by many astrophysicists in their own work. It was very rewarding to learn so much about these galaxies and to develop a scheme that is so useful to many people."

WHAT DOES A PHYSICIST DO?

Physics is the most comprehensive of the natural sciences because it includes the behavior of all kinds of matter from the smallest particles to the largest galaxies.

Basic, or pure, physics is a study of the behavior of the universe and is organized into a series of related laws. Basic physics can be studied from two points of view, experimental and theoretical. A physicist may work from one or both of these points of view. The *experimental physicist* performs experiments to gather information. The results of the experiments may support or contradict existing theories or establish new ideas where no theories existed before.

The *theoretical physicist* constructs theories to explain experimental results. If the theories are to stand the test of time, they must also predict the results of future experiments. Both the experimental physicist and the theoretical physicist try to extend the limits of what is known.

Not all physicists focus on testing or developing new theories. *Applied physicists* develop useful devices and procedures and may hold alternative job titles. Various types of engineers, such as electrical and mechanical engineers, are trained in physics. Applied physics and engineering have led to the development of such devices as television sets, airplanes, washing machines, satellites, elevators, computer chips, digital communication devices, and global positioning technology.

Physicists rely heavily on mathematics. Mathematical statements are more precise than statements in words alone. Moreover, the results of experiments can be accurately compared with the various theories only when mathematical techniques are used.

The various laws of physics attempt to explain the behavior of nature in a simple and general way. Even the most accepted laws of physics, however, are subject to change. Physicists continually subject the laws of physics to new tests to see if,

To Be a Successful Physicist, You Should...

- have good computer programming and mathematical skills
- be detail oriented and precise
- have patience and perseverance
- be self-motivated
- be able to work alone or on research teams

under new conditions, they still hold true. If they do not hold true, changes must be made in the laws, or entirely new theories must be proposed.

At the beginning of the 20th century, the laws of physics were tested extensively and found to be too narrow to explain many of the new discoveries. A new body of theories was needed. The older body of laws is called classical physics; the new is called modern physics.

Classical physics is usually divided into several branches, each of which deals with a group of related phenomena. Mechanics is the study of forces and their effect on matter. Hydromechanics studies the mechanics of liquids and gases. Optics is the study of the behavior of light. Physicists in this field study such things as lasers, liquid crystal displays, or light-emitting diodes. Thermodynamics is the study of heat. Acoustics is the study of sound, such as in recording studio acoustics, underwater sound waves, and electroacoustical devices such as loudspeakers. The study of electricity and magnetism also forms a branch of classical physics. Research in this area includes microwave propagation, the magnetic properties of matter, and electrical devices for science and industry.

Modern physics is also broken up into various fields of study. Atomic physics is the study of the structure of atoms and the behavior of electrons, one of the kinds of particles that make up the atom. Nuclear physics is the study of the nucleus, or center, of the atom and of the forces that hold the nucleus together. High-energy physics, or particle physics, is the study of the production of subatomic particles from other particles and energy. The characteristics of these various particles are studied using particle accelerators, popularly called atom smashers.

Solid-state physics is the study of the behavior of solids, particularly crystalline solids. Cryogenic, or low-temperature, techniques are often used in research into the solid state. Research in solid-state physics has produced transistors, integrated circuits, and masers that have improved computers, radios, televisions, and navigation and guidance systems for satellites. Plasma physics is the study of the properties of highly ionized gases. Physicists in this field are concerned with the generation of thermonuclear power.

Although biology and geology are separate sciences in their own right, the concepts of physics can also be applied directly to them. Where this application has been made, a new series of sciences has developed. To separate them from their parent sciences, they are known by such names as biophysics (the physics of living things) and geophysics (the physics of the earth).

Biophysicists apply physical principles to biological problems. They study the mechanics, heat, light, radiation, sound, electricity, and energetics of living cells and organisms and do research in the areas of vision, hearing, brain function, nerve conduction, muscle reflex, and damaged cells and tissues.

Geophysicists are concerned with matter and energy and how they interact. They study the physical properties and structure of the earth, from its interior to its upper atmosphere, including land surfaces, subsurfaces, and bodies of water.

Similarly, the sciences of chemistry and physics sometimes overlap in subject matter as well as in viewpoint and procedure, creating physical chemistry. *Physical chemists* study the physical characteristics of atoms and molecules.

In astrophysics, *astrophysicists* use the principles of physics to study the solar system, stars, galaxies, and the universe. How did the universe begin? How is the universe changing? These are the types of questions astrophysicists try to answer through research and experimentation. To do their work, astrophysicists need access to large, expensive equipment, such as radio telescopes, spectrometers, and specialized computers. This equipment is generally available only at universities with large astronomy departments and government observatories; therefore, most astrophysicists are employed by colleges or the government. A primary duty of most astrophysicists is making and recording observations. What they observe and the questions they are trying to answer may vary, but the process is much the same across the profession. They work in observatories, using telescopes and other equipment to view celestial bodies. They record their observations on charts, or more often today, into computer programs that help them analyze the data.

Most physicists are engaged in research, and some combine their research with teaching at the university level. Some physicists are employed in industries, such as petroleum, communications, manufacturing, and medicine.

Most physicists work a 40-hour week under pleasant circumstances. Laboratories are usually well equipped, clean, well lighted, temperature controlled, and functional. Adequate safety measures are taken when there is any sort of physical hazard involved in the work. Often, groups of scientists work together as a team so closely that their association may last over a period of many years.

Physicists who teach at the high school, college, or university level have the added benefit of the academic calendar, which gives them ample time away from teaching and meeting with students in order to pursue their own research, studies, or travel.

WHAT IS IT LIKE TO BE A PHYSICIST?

Dr. Brian Schwartz is the vice president for research and sponsored programs and professor of physics at The Graduate Center of the City University of New York. "I decided to become a scientist (actually a mathematician) while in high school," he recalls. "I was very good in science, but much better in mathematics. While in college, I realized that being a first-rate mathematician required a certain steady and isolated commitment to research. I was fairly outgoing for a scientist and did not want to devote my life to abstract mathematical research. I made a compromise and decided to study theoretical physics, which has a large mathematical component yet in many instances deals with real-world phenomena, and one can often work with experimental data.

"I have worked professionally in the field since 1963," Dr. Schwartz continues, "the year I received my Ph.D. in physics from Brown University. I followed a traditional academic path taking a postdoctoral appointment at Rutgers University for two years and then went to the Massachusetts Institute of Technology (MIT) as a researcher in the Francis Bitter Magnet Laboratory and as a faculty member in the physics department. After 12 years at MIT, I took the position of dean of the School of Science at Brooklyn College as an administrator and as a researcher. In the late 1980s I took a position within the professional society of physicists, the American Physical Society (APS). At the APS I had a number of responsibilities in education, minority and women's issues, science-related politics, and communication of science to the public. By the late 1990s, I was second in command at the APS as the associate executive officer. In 1999 I joined The Graduate Center of the City University of New York as the vice president for research and sponsored programs and a professor of physics. In this position I am responsible for promoting research in all fields of graduate study."

Dr. Schwartz's research specialty is in the field of theoretical condensed matter physics with a subspecialty in the fields of superconductivity and magnetism. "Superconductivity," he explains, "is a very low temperature phenomenon in which below a certain transition temperature, the material loses all its resistance to the flow of current (moving electrons). How and why this happens puzzled the theoretical physics community for nearly 50 years after the initial discovery of superconductivity in 1911. Professor Leon Cooper, the physicist who was my thesis adviser, was one of three physicists (the others were John Bardeen and J. Robert Schrieffer) who developed the theory of superconductivity in 1957. They won the Nobel Prize in Physics for the theory of superconductivity."

Dr. Schwartz says that a typical workweek has many components. "I am an administrator, which occupies at least 40 percent of my time," he explains. "I also work with graduate students in the recently established New Media Lab at The Graduate Center. My students have conducted research within the New Media Lab on such problems as the physics of traffic, the motion of superconducting vortices (swirls of current), and the nature of the algorithms of google-like searches for different networks. In each case, in addition to presenting the theory, the students had to develop visualizations and simulations for their solutions to the problems. The New Media Lab has excellent facilities for these types of presentations."

Dr. Schwartz says that there is little that he dislikes about the field of phys-

ics, although he wishes that some physicists were better communicators. "What concerns me is that too often scientists are relatively poor communicators and thus they are seen in character as 'mad' scientists. Physicists have access to powerful knowledge, such as the development of nuclear weapons, and thus have a responsibility to work toward the control and positive use of their science. This is true of most of the sciences—especially the new discoveries in biology, which have many ethical implications. What I like most about being a physicist is the ability to look at some parts of the world and understand the physics behind day-to-day phenomena such as forces, motion, electricity, light, etc. It is a pleasure to understand why and how things move, the how and why of rainbows, how computer chips are made and work, and more esoteric physics like the big bang, black holes, and the world of particle physics."

Dr. Lisa Kewley is an assistant professor of astronomy at the University of Hawaii. She has been an astrophysicist for eight years. In 2008 Dr. Kewley received the Newton Lacy Pierce Prize from the American Astronomical Society, which is "awarded annually for outstanding achievement, over the past five years, in observational astronomical research based on measurements of radiation from an astronomical object," and an Early CAREER Award from the National Science Foundation. "I decided to become an astrophysicist when I was in high school," Dr. Kewley recalls. "My junior year physics teacher loved astronomy and most of our practical experiments were astronomy based. We went on an astronomy camp in the countryside where we looked through telescopes. I saw the moons of Jupiter and beautiful star clusters. I started reading astronomy magazines and books, and I became fascinated with the field of astrophysics, especially galaxies and black holes."

Dr. Kewley's research focuses on how the amount of oxygen in galaxies changes with time. "By looking at galaxies at different distances from us," she explains, "I can look back in time to when the universe was very young. The light from distant galaxies takes so long to reach us that it was first emitted many billions of years ago." Dr. Kewley also researches galaxy collisions. "Huge amounts of new stars form in galaxy collisions and many colliding galaxies have supermassive black holes at their center which are actively feeding from the surrounding dust and gas. I am trying to understand how a galaxy collision affects the star formation and black hole feeding in galaxies."

As an astrophysicist, Dr. Kewley is responsible for a variety of tasks. "In a typical workday," she says, "I check the latest research papers that are submitted every day on the Web (at http://arxiv.org/archive/astro-ph). I meet with one to two of my Ph.D. students to give them comments on their latest results. I then do some of my own research, which involves measuring the intensity of emission lines in galaxy spectra. I do this using a special astronomy package on my computer called IRAF. I do calculations of the amount of star formation, emis-sion from gas surrounding supermassive black holes, and the amount of oxygen in galaxies based on the intensity of the lines that I measured from the spectra. I use IDL, a mathematical language, to write programs that do these calculations and make plots of the results. Sometimes I run theoretical models of star formations to help interpret the results. If my results are ready for publication, I will spend most of my day writing a paper. It is very satisfying to complete a project through to a paper that is accepted in an astrophysics journal.

"A few nights per semester," Dr. Kewley continues, "I observe on the Keck or Subaru telescopes on Mauna Kea. I stay up all night in a control room that is filled with computers. The data is taken onto charge-coupled devices (CCDs), which are like very large digital cameras; so the data is taken in digital form. We use the computers to tell the telescope what to look at, and we also use the computers to view the data as it is coming in."

Dr. Kewley says that the least favorite part of her job is data reduction. "When galaxy data comes through the telescope," she explains, "it is contaminated by emission or absorption from our atmosphere, reflections from within the telescope, and noise from the electronics from the telescope instrumentation and CCD. Removing this junk is called data reduction and it can be tedious and difficult sometimes. What I like most about my career is having the freedom to research whatever I find the most interesting. I look forward to going to work each day because I am excited by what I will find (or what my students will find)."

DO I HAVE WHAT IT TAKES TO BE A PHYSICIST?

Physicists are detail oriented and precise. They must have patience and perseverance and be self-motivated. Physicists should be able to work alone or on research teams. Dr. Kewley says that the most important traits for physicists are computer programming and mathematical skills.

HOW DO I BECOME A PHYSICIST?

Education

High School

Take college preparatory courses to prepare for college and a career as a physicist. You should take as much mathematics as is offered in your school as well as explore as many of the sciences as possible. English skills are important, as you must write up your results, communicate with other scientists, and lecture on your findings. In addition, get as much experience as possible working with computers.

Postsecondary Training

Physicists may have one, two, or three degrees. Physicists at the doctoral level command the jobs with the greatest responsibility, such as jobs in basic research and development. Those at the master's level often work in manufacturing or applied research. Those with a bachelor's degree face the most competition and generally work as technicians in engineering, software development, or other scientific areas. Dr. Kewley earned her Ph.D. from The Australian National University. She then participated in a fellowship at the Harvard-Smithsonian Center for Astrophysics and a Hubble Fellowship at the University of Hawaii.

Some employers are attracted to those with a broad scientific background. With a bachelor's degree in physics or a related science, you may be hired with the intention of being trained on the job in a specialty area. As you develop competency in the special field, you may then consider returning to graduate school to concentrate your study in this particular field.

In addition, some teaching opportunities are available to those with bachelor's degrees at the primary and secondary school level. However, in order to teach at the college level (and even at some secondary schools), you will need an advanced degree. While a master's degree may be acceptable to teach at a junior college, most universities require that professors have their doctorates. Those with a master's degree may obtain a job as an assistant in a physics department in a university while working toward a Ph.D. in physics.

More than 760 colleges and universities offer a bachelor's degree in physics, and about 255 schools offer master's and doctoral programs. The American Institute of Physics and American Physical Society provide lists of graduate institutions at their Web sites; see "Look to the Pros" in Section 4 for more information.

Certification or Licensing

Those who plan to teach at the elementary or secondary school level may be able to obtain a teaching position with a bachelor's degree if they also meet the certification requirements for teaching (established by the department of education in each state).

Physics Education for the Masses

Dr. Brian Schwartz has a strong interest in educating high school students, college students who are not majoring in science, and the general public about the wonders of physics. He has developed many programs over the years to teach people about physics, including Science & the Arts. One of his recent programs was titled Science as Performance: A Proactive Strategy to Communicate and Educate Through Theatre, Music, and Dance. Dr. Schwartz provides an overview of this interesting program in the paragraphs below:

I've always had a strong interest in communicating science to non-science majors in college (and high school), and to the general public. The Science as Performance program is based upon the presupposition that communicating the excitement of and developments in science, technology, engineering, and mathematics (STEM) to the public is a challenge, especially to new audiences that often are not particularly interested in science and are hard to reach. The concept of learning about and developing an interest in science through the series Science & the Arts (http://web.gc.cuny.edu/sciart) has been developed and tested at The Graduate Center for more than nine years. A primary target audience for Science & the Arts is the general public of all backgrounds, especially those segments of the public—adults and non-science college students and pre-college students—who often are difficult to reach by means of standard techniques such as [the television show] NOVA, science museums, and science lectures. We have shown that the performing (and visual) arts are able to make the sciences accessible, relevant, and exciting to diverse audiences in ways

that provide both excellent scientific content and significant artistic and entertainment values.

I started communication programs to the public in a major way when I was chosen as the national director of the centennial celebration of the American Physical Society. The event was held in Atlanta in March 1999 and featured many science and art public programs (http://web.gc.cuny.edu/sciart/festival), including the first citywide physics festival. The festival included a public lecture by Stephen Hawking entitled "The Universe in a Nutshell" before 6,000 Atlanta citizens. In venues throughout Atlanta, new science communication events played to huge and appreciative audiences. The presentations included "The Physics of Star Trek," "The Science of Ballet" (with participation by the Atlanta Ballet), "The Physics of Brass Instruments" (with virtuoso performances), the "Physics of Art and Fractals" (at the High Museum), "The Science of Baseball," "The Science of Beer," and the world premiere of a science-based play entitled Schrödinger's Girlfriend.

As a lasting centennial memento I produced a unique wall chart and Web site for a timeline entitled, A Century of Physics (http://timeline.aps.org). The timeline depicts the major events in physics (as well as medicine, technology, art, architecture, and relevant artifacts) over the last century and is being used by high school teachers, students, and the public. To date, more than 21,000 copies of the 11-panel, 23-foot long timeline have been distributed free of charge to schools, museums, and libraries throughout the United States and abroad. Lucent Technologies, the National Science Foundation, the Department of Energy,

(continued on next page)

(continued from previous page)

the IBM Corporation, and UPS were among the supporters of the timeline project.

In March 2000, when I was newly appointed vice president for research, I organized a full day symposium at The Graduate Center entitled Creating Copenhagen, prior to the opening of the play *Copenhagen* on Broadway. The symposium consisted of three, approximately two-hour sessions. The first, devoted to the sciences, related to the times and subject matter of the play. The second focused on the personalities of the play's main characters as discussed by two elder statesmen of science—Hans Bethe (Cornell) and John Wheeler (Princeton)—and noted historians of science. The third featured the playwright Michael Frayn and the director Michael Blakemore. The symposium attracted overflow audiences and received broad coverage in the press. The audience was diverse, ranging from humanists, to scientists, to artists. The broad coverage of the symposium included the scientific press, the theatrical press, and the popular press. This symposium represented a new way of communicating science to the public and has been the basis of a worldwide movement of a new paradigm of combining the sciences and the performing arts to communicate with the public.

In the fall of 2008 I worked with the Alfred P. Sloan Foundation, Matthew Goldstein, the chancellor of the City University of New York, and Peter Gelb, the general manager of the Metropolitan Opera, to develop 10 public outreach programs at The Graduate Center related to the performances of the opera *Doctor Atomic* at the Met. You can see examples of the programs at the Web site (http://web.gc.cuny.edu/sciart), in the *New York Times* interviews of veteran scientists of the Manhattan Project, and in the building and dropping of the atomic bomb at http://www.nytimes.com/interactive/2008/10/28/science/28manhattan project.html?ref=science.

Because different states have different certification requirements, undergraduates should research the requirements for the state in which they hope to teach.

Internships and Volunteerships

Many postsecondary institutions require that their degree students fulfill an internship. Intended to provide students with hands-on work experience, the internship experience also grants students the opportunity to network and gain a deeper insight into the various career paths in physics. If an internship is required, it usually lasts from four to 12 months, or roughly somewhere between one and two semesters. Schools are usually instrumental in locating internships, but placing cold calls or writing query letters to companies or government agencies you have already carefully researched can also be an effective way of locating a quality internship. Internships required by the school are usually non-paying; students are often compensated in the form of credit toward semester hours. The American Physical Society also provides listings of summer internships at its Web site, http://www.aps.org. Internships were recently offered at Los Alamos National Laboratory, National Renewable Energy Laboratories, and Sandia National Laboratories.

Other students gain experience by participating in an undergraduate research assistantship. Volunteer opportunities are also sometimes available, and can help aspiring physicists make valuable contacts in the field.

WHO WILL HIRE ME?

Approximately 17,000 physicists work in the United States, most of them in industry, in research and development laboratories, and in teaching. Twenty-one percent of all physicists work for the federal government, mostly in the Department of Defense. Other government physicists work in the Departments of Energy, Health and Human Services, and Commerce and for the National Aeronautics and Space Administration. Those working in industry jobs may hold a job title other than physicist, such as computer programmer, engineer, or systems developer.

The career services office of the college or university from which you obtain a degree will often have listings of jobs available. In addition, many industries send personnel interviewers to college campuses with physics programs to seek out and talk to students who are about to receive degrees. Students should also attend industry, career, and science fairs to find out about job openings and interview opportunities.

Those who are interested in teaching in public schools should apply to several school systems in which they may want to work. Some of the larger school systems also send personnel interviewers to campuses to talk with students who are about

Good Advice

Dr. Lisa Kewley offers the following advice to young people who want to pursue careers in physics:

There are lots of interesting and exciting jobs in physics and it is definitely worth the study to get there. Take every opportunity to get experience doing research and to talk to scientists for tips on pursuing careers in physics. You can get some research experience in your high school with science fair projects, or you could do a project that involves interviewing local scientists about their jobs. If you live near a college with an interesting physics program, email the coordinator of the program and ask if you could have a tour or talk with some of the physicists there. Many departments are very happy to talk with high school students about their work. When you are in college, try to get an undergraduate research assistantship with one of the professors to get more experience with research. Many physics departments and institutes have summer research programs for undergraduate college students, and this is a great way to get research experience and get paid for it, too.

to receive degrees in science and who also have acquired the necessary courses in education.

Teaching jobs in universities are often obtained either through the contacts of the student's own faculty members in the degree program or through the career services office of the university.

Jobs with government agencies require individuals to first pass a civil service examination. For more information on federal employment, check out the USAJOBS Web site (http://www.usajobs.opm.gov).

WHERE CAN I GO FROM HERE?

High school physics teachers can advance in salary and responsibility as they acquire experience. Their advancement is also likely to be facilitated by the attaining of advanced degrees. The college or university teacher can advance from assistant to full professor and perhaps to head of the department. Higher rank also carries with it additional income and responsibilities.

The research physicist employed by a university advances by handling more responsibility for planning and conducting research programs. Salaries should also increase with experience in research over a period of years.

Physicists in federal government agencies advance in rank and salary as they gain experience. They may reach top positions in which they are asked to make decisions vital to the defense effort or to the safety and welfare of the country.

Scientists employed by industry are usually the highest paid in the profession and with experience can advance to research director positions.

WHAT ARE THE SALARY RANGES?

The median salary for physicists was $102,890 in 2008, according to the U.S. Department of Labor. Salaries ranged from less than $57,160 to $159,400 or more. Physicists employed by the fed-eral government had mean earnings of $108,020 in 2008.

As highly trained and respected scientists, physicists usually receive excellent benefits packages, including health plans, vacation and sick leave, and other benefits.

WHAT IS THE JOB OUTLOOK?

Employment for physicists should grow about as fast as the average for all occupations through 2016, according to the *Occupational Outlook Handbook*. Although increases in government research, particularly in the Departments of Defense and Energy, as well as in physics-related research in the private sector, will create more opportunities for physicists, there will be stiff competition among Ph.D. holders for basic positions. The need to replace retiring workers will account for almost all new job openings.

Private industry budgets for research and development will continue to grow, but many laboratories are expected to reduce their physics-based research to focus on product and software development and applied or manufacturing research. Opportunities will exist for physicists who work with information technology, computer technology, semiconductor technology, and other applied sciences.

Job candidates with doctoral degrees have the best outlook for finding work. Graduates with bachelor's degrees are generally underqualified for most physicist jobs. They may find better employment opportunities as engineers, technicians, or computer specialists. With a suitable background in education, they may teach physics at the high school level.

"The employment prospects for a physicist who has a good command of science and can also communicate well is quite good," says Dr. Schwartz. "We live in a increasingly technological society (Internet, cell phones, lasers, in vitro fertilization, climate change, etc.), and the understanding of mathematics and science is playing a larger role in required employment skills. The outlook for a Ph.D. physicist interested in basic research in an academic environment will be somewhat limited due to tight budgets. More opportunities will exist in applied sciences and in the application of quantitative techniques to solving societal problems. Having a physics background for the undergraduate degree combined with an advanced degree in another field like medicine, business, law, or politics would be advantageous in the employment marketplace."

Science Technicians

SUMMARY

Definition
Science technicians help scientists, engineers, and researchers solve problems and invent new processes and products.

Alternative Job Titles
Life science technicians
Physical science technicians
Science assistants

Salary Range
$22,000 to $52,960 to $97,000+

Educational Requirements
Required for certain positions

Certification or Licensing
Required for certain positions

Employment Outlook
About as fast as the average

High School Subjects
Computer science
Mathematics
Science

Personal Interests
Computers
Figuring out how things work
Science

"When I step back to survey what I have accomplished in this job," says Elizabeth Hale, a physical science technician for the National Park Service, "there is a real sense of satisfaction. My maps are used by park visitors to learn about and enjoy this park. The park's data is accessible and organized, and I have improved its reliability since I started working here. I have also been in a position to help a number of interns get valuable work experience and training. I think any job is rewarding that puts you in a position to make a meaningful contribution. The National Parks are a legacy that America passes down through its generations."

WHAT DOES A SCIENCE TECHNICIAN DO?

The following paragraphs provide an overview of the most popular specialties for *science technicians*.

Agricultural technicians assist engineers, scientists, and conservationists in food, plant, soil, and animal research, production, and processing. Agricultural technicians can choose to specialize in one of four areas: food science, plant science, soil science, or animal science. The type of work performed varies according to the specialization.

Agribusiness technicians combine their agriculture and business backgrounds to manage or offer management consulting services to farms and agricultural businesses.

Biological technicians assist biological scientists, often working on teams in laboratory experiments. They may work with lab animals, analyze organic substances (such as food or blood), record data, and use lab equipment such as microscopes and centrifuges. Many biological scientists work in medical research—helping to find a cure for AIDS or multiple sclerosis or develop medicines.

Chemical technicians conduct physical tests, chemical analyses, and instrumental analyses for research, product development, quality control, and establishing standards. They work in research, new product development, quality control, or criminal investigation. Those in research and development often work in pairs or small groups with Ph.D. chemists and chemical engineers to develop chemicals, synthesize compounds, or develop new processes. Technicians who perform quality control tests often work together in groups under supervision. They make samples of new products or collect soil, water, or air samples. They study their compositions or test certain properties. Other technicians conduct physical tests on samples to determine such things as strength and flexibility, or they may characterize the physical properties of gases, liquids, and solids and describe their reactions to changes of temperature and pressure.

Engineering technicians assist engineers, scientists, and other workers in a variety of tasks. They are highly trained workers with strong backgrounds in a specialized technological field, such as aerospace, civil, materials, and many other types of engineering. In short, engineering technicians can be found supporting engineers and other workers in any engineering discipline that comes to mind. They bridge the gap between the engineers who design the products, structures, and machines, and those who implement them.

Environmental technicians, also known as *pollution control technicians,* conduct tests and field investigations to obtain soil samples and other data. Their research is used by engineers, scientists, and others who help clean up, monitor, control, or prevent pollution. An environmental technician usually specializes in air, water, or soil pollution. A small number specialize in noise pollution. Although work differs by employer and specialty, technicians generally collect samples for laboratory analysis, using specialized instruments and equipment; monitor pollution control devices and systems, such as smokestack air "scrubbers"; and perform various other tests and investigations to evaluate pollution problems. They follow strict procedures in collecting and recording data in order to meet the requirements of environmental laws. In general, environmental technicians do not operate the equipment and systems designed to prevent pollution or remove pollutants. Instead, they test environmental conditions. In addition, some analyze and report on their findings.

Forensic science technicians, also known as *forensic technicians,* help forensic scientists to analyze, identify, and classify physical evidence relating to criminal cases. They may work in laboratories or they may travel to crime scenes to collect evidence. Forensic technicians work in many different areas of crime scene investigation and forensic science. One technician may work only with cadavers in a morgue, another may work only in a lab analyzing evidence, another may investigate and photograph crime scenes, and another may analyze fingerprints. Some forensics technicians assist in a number of different areas of investigation, including crime scene and lab work. Some technicians assist criminalists, and use instruments of science and engineering to examine physical evidence. They use spectroscopes, microscopes, gas chromatographs, infrared and ultraviolet light, microphotography, and other lab measuring and testing equipment to analyze fibers, fabric, dust, soils, paint chips, glass fragments, fire accelerants, paper and ink, and other substances in order to identify their composition and origin. They analyze poisons, drugs, and other substances found in bodies by examining tissue samples, stomach contents, and blood samples. They analyze and classify blood, blood alcohol, semen, hair, fingernails, teeth, human and animal bones and tissue, and other biological specimens. Using samples of the genetic material DNA, they can match a person with a sample of body tissue. They study documents to determine whether they are forged or genuine. They also examine the physical properties of firearms, bullets, and explosives.

Forestry technicians help plan, supervise, and conduct operations necessary to maintain and protect the country's forests. They also manage forests and wildlife areas, control fires, insects, and disease and limit the depletion of forest resources. The day-to-day duties of a forestry technician are based on a range of activities for managing and harvesting the nation's forest resources. They plant trees to replenish forest reserves that have become depleted through harvesting, fire, or disease. They care for maturing trees by spraying them with pesticides (if disease infested), by thinning to ensure the best growth of the forest, and by protecting them from fire and other dangers. They inventory (or scale) trees to determine the amount of lumber to be gained through harvesting. They then harvest forests and assist in the marketing of the lumber. And finally, they recondition the harvested forest and plant new trees, beginning the cycle anew.

Geological technicians assist geologists and engineers by gathering, plotting, and storing samples and technical data. Geological technicians work in the field of the geosciences. Geosciences are the sciences dealing with the earth, including geology, geophysics, and geochemistry. Usually, they work under the supervision of a geologist or geoscientist who is trained to study the earth's physical makeup and history. Often, geoscientists specialize in one area of study. Among these specialties are environmental geology, the study of how pollution, waste, and hazardous material affect the earth and its features; geophysics, the study of the earth's interior and magnetic, electric, and gravitational fields; hydrology, the investigation of the movement and quality of surface water; petroleum geology, the exploration and production of crude oil and natural gas; and seismology, the study of earthquakes and the forces that cause them.

Hydrologic technicians are concerned with weather patterns, precipitation, and water supply. They study the properties, distribution, and circulation of waters on or beneath the earth's surface as well as in the atmosphere. Hydrologic technicians also assist hydrologists in the study of precipitation, including the form, intensity, and rate at which it penetrates the soil. They also research how precipitation moves through the earth and returns to the ocean and atmosphere. Hydrologic technicians collect, analyze, and interpret hydrologic data to assess the availability and quality of water, including lakes, streams, groundwater supply, and more.

Seismic technicians help seismologists gather data so they can better understand and predict earthquakes and other vibrations of the earth. Seismic technicians use seismographs and other geophysical instruments to collect and analyze data.

Nuclear technicians, also known as *radiation protection technicians*, monitor radiation levels, protect workers, and decontaminate radioactive areas. They work under the supervision of nuclear scientists, engineers, or power plant managers and are trained in the applications of nuclear and radiation physics to detect, measure, and identify different kinds of nuclear radiation. They know federal regulations and permissible levels of radiation. Technicians who control nuclear reactors are known as *nuclear reactor operators.* They are responsible for the continuous and safe operation of a nuclear reactor. The nuclear reactor operator (NRO) can be thought of as the nuclear station's driver, in that the NRO controls all of the machines that are used to generate power at the station. He or she is responsible for making sure that the station continues running safely and continuously. Most nuclear power plants consist of more than one nuclear reactor unit. Each NRO is responsible for only one of the units.

Petroleum technicians assist in the exploration of petroleum fields and in the production of oil and gas. They test potential sources, drill test wells, improve drilling technology, collect petroleum from producing wells, and deliver oil to pipelines. Petroleum technicians are a subcareer of geological technicians.

Soil conservation technicians develop conservation plans for landowners, such as farmers and ranchers, that help preserve the earth's natural resources: soil, water, wildlife, and forests. Soil conservation technicians work with soil conservationists to help preserve and protect the earth's natural resources. They devise plans to control land and water erosion, reforest lands, and improve and preserve wildlife habitat that adhere to government conservation regulations. Soil conservation technicians assist landowners in conserving woodlands, pastures, and rangeland. They typically work with farmers and ranchers, but recreational landowners often request help, as do home owners. With their knowledge of conservation practices and engineering and agricultural science, soil technicians

To Be a Successful Science Technician, You Should...

- work with accuracy and precision
- have excellent communication skills
- be punctual
- be able to follow instructions
- have a detail-oriented personality
- be willing to continue to learn throughout your career
- be able to work independently and as part of a team
- have scientific aptitude
- be willing to work irregular hours when necessary

know best how to minimize the damage that we humans may cause to the land.

WHAT IS IT LIKE TO BE A SCIENCE TECHNICIAN?

Elizabeth Hale is a physical science technician for the National Park Service. She is employed at Oregon Caves National Monument (http://www.nps.gov/orca) in Cave Junction, Oregon. "My interest in the national parks led me to this job," she explains. "I worked in Yosemite National Park two summers during college. I also took advantage of a student hiring program in the National Park Service called

STEP, which stands for Student Temporary Employment Program. I worked at Mammoth Cave National Park as a STEP hire, giving cave tours while I was still a college student. I became interested in resource management in the national parks and took a Student Conservation Association internship after college. I built up the necessary experience I needed to get hired as a physical science technician."

A typical workweek for Elizabeth usually runs 40 hours. "The responsibilities of a physical science technician can vary quite a bit depending on where you work," she explains. "My job focuses on cave management, so my responsibilities include cave cleanup and restoration, environmental monitoring in the cave, and data management. Here are some examples of how my work day can be spent: going into the cave to download data from data loggers; training employees to conduct scientific monitoring; summarizing and validating data sets; designing project proposals for funding; producing maps from geographic information systems (GIS) data; writing standard operating procedures so that essential duties are conducted the right way each time; organizing a volunteer cave cleanup; and spending time on the computer maintaining files and datasets in good order."

Elizabeth says that there are many pros to working as a physical science technician. "My job offers opportunity to use intelligence and creativity on a weekly basis," she says. "I appreciate being able to spend a portion of my time outdoors or in

Science Technician Profile: Vincent Villena

Vincent Villena is a forensic technician II in the Toxicology Unit at the Kern County Regional Criminalistics Laboratory in Bakersfield, California. He discussed his career with the editors of *What Can I Do Now? Science.*

Q. What made you want to enter this career?

A. I developed my passion for science, specifically chemistry, in high school. I knew that I wanted to pursue a career that involved the application of chemical science. I had a little detour on [the path to] my chemistry career when I joined the Marine Corps immediately after high school. However, I took night classes while I was in the service and managed to achieve an associate's degree. Science classes were unavailable in night school and I worked as a corrections officer in the military; I figured it was only appropriate to take a criminal justice degree. This inspired me to search for a career that combined both fields and, hence, forensic science.

Q. How did you train for this field?

A. The position, forensic technician, requires a baccalaureate degree in a physical or natural science, forensic science, or a closely related laboratory science. Course work for chemistry (toxicology or drugs unit) must include 24 semester hours of chemistry including course work in quantitative analysis, organic and inorganic chemistry, as well as a course in statistics. Course work for biology (DNA) must include a minimum of 12 semester hours of biochemistry, genetics, and molecular biol-ogy (molecular genetics, recombinant DNA technology), or other subjects that provide a basic understanding of the foundation of forensic DNA analysis, as well as statistics and/or population genetics as it applies to forensic DNA analysis. Course work must satisfy DNA Advisory Board [requirements].

In high school I took advanced chemistry. I graduated from San Jose State University with a bachelor's of science degree in justice studies with a concentration in chemical forensics.

Q. What are your main and secondary job duties as a forensic technician?

A. I am currently assigned to our Toxicology Unit. We perform analyses from pre-employment drug screening to law enforcement of drugs-of-abuse. My primary duty is performing confirmation analyses of drugs-of-abuse. This entails extraction of drug metabolites from a given specimen, e.g. blood, urine, saliva, etc. Among the other duties I have in the lab are drug screening, coroner sample analyses for glucose, electrolyte panel, and carbon monoxide, forensic alcohol analyses, special case analyses, and research. Of course, one cannot leave out regular laboratory tasks, such as inventory, sample login, and instrument maintenance.

Q. What are some of the pros and cons of work as a forensic technician?

A. Pros: Compared to other private laboratory work, there is a wide array of tasks bestowed upon a forensic scientist. Other than lab work, we also testify

(continued on next page)

(continued from previous page)

our results in court, attend continuous education seminars, conduct research, and respond to crime scenes.

Cons: In our lab, a forensic technician cannot go on crime scene responses; only criminalists may join crime scene units. A consequence of being in a crime scene unit, however, is [that] you are placed on-call 24/7 for two weeks at a time.

Q. What are the most important personal and professional qualities for forensic technicians?

A. Personal motivation is important in this field. Science and law enforcement are both fields that constantly change. A forensic scientist has to keep himself or herself up to date with the latest information. This requires initiative and self-development. In addition, this career requires genuine integrity since it deals not only with your own career but also with other people's lives. All tests performed have to be unbiased and always accurate. There is no room for complacency.

the cave. For some people, the remoteness of national park jobs can become an issue. Many national park jobs are far away from big cities and amenities. At my particular site, we lost our telecommunications for over half a year, and cell phone coverage is spotty. For some people, the lack of phones and Internet was a real challenge, but I actually did not mind. When you work in the national parks, there is not a lot to complain about. You get to experience the best natural areas in the country more intimately than most."

DO I HAVE WHAT IT TAKES TO BE A SCIENCE TECHNICIAN?

Science technicians must be able to express their ideas clearly in speech and in writing. Good communication skills are important for a technician in the writing and presenting of reports and plans. These skills are also important for working alongside other technicians and professionals, people who are often from many different backgrounds. Many tasks assigned to science technicians require patience and methodical, persistent work. Other important skills include organizational ability, a detail-oriented personality, punctuality, and the ability to follow instructions.

Many science technician positions require outdoor work. Technicians in these positions must enjoy working outdoors in all weather and not mind getting dirty on the job.

Technicians should be willing to continue to learn throughout their careers in order to improve their skills and stay up to date with changing technology and other advances in the field. Individuals planning to advance beyond the technician's level should be willing to and capable of pursuing some form of higher education.

HOW DO I BECOME A SCIENCE TECHNICIAN?

Education

High School

In high school, take courses in mathematics, science, computer science, English, and speech to give yourself a good general preparation for the field. If you've already picked a particular career path, it is a good idea to take classes in this area. For example, if you want to become a chemical technician, you should take classes in chemistry. If you want to work as an environmental technician, then take classes in environmental science, botany, zoology, and ecology. If you think a career as a forensic technician is in your future, you should take forensic science, chemistry, and related classes.

You might find it valuable to participate in the extracurricular science clubs at your school. Science contests are another fun way to apply principles learned in classes to a special project. You may work alone or on a team in competitions that are held within your own school, across the state, or even nationally.

Postsecondary Training

Most science technician positions require an associate's degree or a certificate in applied science or science-related technology. Biological technicians and forensic science technicians need a bachelor's degree. Many college programs incorporate an internship with a local employer into their curriculum. Some technicians enter the field with only a high school diploma and receive extensive on-the-job training before eventually earning a two-year degree.

Elizabeth Hale offers the following advice to aspiring physical science technicians: "At a minimum you should get a bachelor's of science degree with a major in a physical or environmental science. Some training in GIS is helpful. If a career in the National Park Service interests you, check out the Student Temporary Employment Program and the Student Career Experience Program while you are in college. You can begin to get on-the-job experience through these programs while you are still a student. Also, check out the internships offered by the Student Conservation Association. Additionally, the national parks offer many opportunities to volunteer."

Certification or Licensing

Certification and licensing requirements vary by science technician profession. Certification is highly recommended for certain professions, while it may not be available in others. The following paragraphs provide a basic overview of certification and licensing requirements for the major specialties in the field. Check with the professional associations in your particular specialty for complete details.

Many engineering technicians choose to become certified by the National Institute for Certification in Engineering Technologies. To become certified, you must combine a specific amount of job-related experience with a written examination. Certifications are offered at several levels of expertise. Electronics engineering technicians may obtain voluntary certification from the International Society

Salaries for Science Technicians, 2008

Agricultural and food science technicians: $22,190 to $53,880+

Biological technicians: $24,530 to $62,260+

Chemical technicians: $26,170 to $64,650+

Environmental science and protection technicians, including health: $25,830 to $64,580+

Forensic science technicians: $30,990 to $80,330+

Forestry and conservation technicians: $22,540 to $51,810+

Geological and petroleum technicians: $26,630 to $97,380+

Life and physical science technicians, all other: $22,720 to $67,310+

Nuclear technicians: $40,310 to $93,350+

Source: U.S. Department of Labor

sional Environmental Practice offers the qualified environmental professional and the environmental professional intern certifications.

The International Association for Identification offers the voluntary crime scene certification for forensic science technicians. The certification consists of a tri-level program: Level I: certified crime scene investigator, Level II: certified crime scene analyst, and Level III: certified senior crime scene analyst. To attain the first level, applicants must have at least one year of experience in the field, have completed at least 48 hours of approved instruction in crime scene-related courses within the past five years, and pass a written test. Applicants for the upper levels must meet more stringent experience and educational requirements. Certification is also available in several other categories including bloodstain pattern examiner, footwear, forensic art, forensic photography, latent print certification, and tenprint fingerprint.

In some states, forestry technicians need to be licensed to perform certain duties. For example, those working with pesticides or chemicals must be trained and licensed in their use. Technicians who make surveys of land for legal public property records are also required to hold a license.

Nuclear reactor operators are required to be licensed, based on examinations given by the Nuclear Regulatory Commission.

The Soil Science Society of America and the American Society of Agronomy offer voluntary certification in the fol-

of Certified Electronics Technicians and the Electronics Technicians Association International.

Certification or licensing is required for some positions in pollution control, especially those in which sanitation, public health, a public water supply, or a sewage treatment system is involved. For example, the Institute of Profes-

lowing areas: crop advisory, agronomy, and soil science/classification. In order to be accepted into a program, applicants must meet certain levels of education and experience.

Internships and Volunteerships

Some two-year college programs require students to complete internships before granting degrees. Some large corporations offer internship programs, and professional associations are excellent resources for information on internship opportunities. Contacting companies or organizations directly and inquiring about internships would be a good idea. Completing an internship assures employers that you have hands-on experience and will make you a more desirable candidate.

Volunteer opportunities are especially plentiful for technicians who specialize in environmental fields. Many nonprofit groups sponsor activities and field trips, and volunteers are frequently needed to help ecologists, foresters, geologists, or geoscientists working in the field. Many government agencies offer volunteer opportunities. It will be more difficult to gain direct volunteer experience in non-environmental fields such as forensic science or the nuclear industry.

WHO WILL HIRE ME?

There are approximately 267,000 science technicians employed in the United States. They work for government agencies, as well as in the private sector. Some workers are self-employed consultants who advise private industry owners and government agencies. The following paragraphs detail top employers for science technicians by occupational specialty.

Biological technicians are employed by pharmaceutical companies, hospitals, biotechnology companies, and laboratories. Government employers include the U.S. Department of Interior, the U.S. Fish and Wildlife Service, the National Oceanic and Atmospheric Administration, the U.S. Department of Health and Human Services, the U.S. Public Health Service, the Environmental Protection Agency, and the Department of Agriculture, among others.

Chemical technicians can find employment wherever chemistry is involved: in industrial laboratories, in government agencies such as the Department of Health and Human Services and the Department of Agriculture, and at colleges and universities. They can work in almost any field of chemical activity, such as industrial manufacturing of all kinds, pharmaceuticals, food, and production of chemicals.

Engineering technicians work in manufacturing; in professional, scientific, and technical service industries; and for government agencies at all levels.

Many environmental technicians work for government agencies that monitor the environment, such as the U.S. Environmental Protection Agency (EPA), and the Departments of Agriculture, Energy, and Interior. Others work for the National Park Service. Water pollution technicians may be employed by manufacturers that produce wastewater, municipal wastewater treatment facilities, private firms hired to monitor or control pollutants in water or wastewater, and government regulatory agencies responsible for protecting water quality. Air pollution technicians work for government agencies such as regional EPA offices. They also work for private manufacturers producing airborne pollutants, research facilities, pollution control equipment manufacturers, and other employers. Soil pollution technicians may work for federal or state departments of agriculture and EPA offices. They also work for private agricultural groups that monitor soil quality for pesticide levels. Noise pollution technicians are employed by private companies and by government agencies such as the Occupational Safety and Health Administration.

Forensic science technicians are typically employed by large police departments or state law enforcement agencies nationwide. However, individuals in certain disciplines are often self-employed or work in the private sector.

About half of all forestry technician positions are found with the federal, state, or local government. In the federal government, most jobs are in the U.S. Department of Agriculture's Forest Service or the Department of Interior's Bureau of Land Management. Opportunities in the federal government also exist with the Natural Resources Conservation Service, the National Park Service, and the U.S. Army Corps of Engineers. State governments also employ forestry technicians to provide services to private forestland owners and to manage state forest lands. In many states, the Cooperative Extension Service and the Department of Natural Resources have forestry positions. County and municipal governments may also have forestry positions. There are also a number of employment opportunities in the private sector. Technicians work with companies that manage forestlands for lumber, pulpwood, and other products. Companies that use forest products and suppliers of forestry equipment and materials also hire forestry technicians. Other employers include private estates, tree service companies, and forestry consulting firms.

Geological technicians are employed by major oil and gas companies. Environmental consulting and environmental engineering firms may also be a source of employment in the private sector. With these firms, geological technicians assist in creating environmental impact studies. The federal government hires geologists and may employ geological technicians in the Department of the Interior (specifically in the U.S. Geological Survey and the Bureau of Reclamation) and in the Departments of Defense, Agriculture, and Commerce. State agencies, nonprofit research organizations, and state-funded museums are also possible sources of employment for geological technicians.

There are slightly more than 100 commercial nuclear power plants operating at more than 60 sites in the United States, according to the Nuclear Energy Institute. In addition, there are approximately 36 reactors used for research and training at educational and other institutions, according to the Nuclear Regulatory Commission. Nuclear reactor operators, naturally, work at nuclear power plants and are employed by utility or energy companies, universities, and other institutions operating these facilities. Nearly half of all nuclear technicians are employed by utilities. Others work in research at colleges and universities and in other settings.

Soil science technicians work for private agencies and firms such as banks and loan agencies, mining or steel companies, and public utilities companies. At the federal level, most soil science technicians work for the Natural Resources Conservation Service, the Bureau of Land Management, the Forest Service, and the Bureau of Reclamation. Others work for agencies at the state and county level.

Petroleum technicians work in the crude petroleum and natural gas industry for major oil and natural gas companies and independent producers. The oil and gas field services industry, which includes drilling contractors, logging companies,

Key Skills

Elizabeth Hale details the most important personal and professional skills for physical science technicians:

- Background in science: You need to understand the fundamentals of physical and environmental science. You need to know the scientific method and be able to read scientific papers. You need to be able to take accurate measurements and collect reliable data.

- Communication skills: Giving PowerPoint presentations and writing standard operating procedures and reports are part of the job. You must be able to communicate your results. You also need the communication skills necessary to collaborate with others on projects and gather information.

- Resourcefulness: You need to know how to find information and solve problems. As a physical science technician, it is your job to work out the details. You are not expected to know everything, but you are expected to be able to find it out. You need to be able to use help manuals and talk to specialists.

- Computer and technology skills: You need to know how to use a computer and other digital devices, which may include meters and global positioning system units. At the most basic level, you will need to be able to use spreadsheets and databases to work with data. Skill in geographic information systems is becoming increasingly important.

- Teachability: You need to be able to learn! You will always be learning because scientific knowledge is always increasing, technology is always advancing, and new ways of doing things always come about. You may be asked to take on a project that requires you to learn new skills in order to accomplish it. Being able to teach yourself something new through reading and tutorials is a very useful skill.

- Curiosity: You should be interested in the outcome of your projects. What you find out should cause you to ask more questions, and you should be motivated to find ways to answer them.

and well servicing contractors, is the other major source of employment.

WHERE CAN I GO FROM HERE?

As science technicians remain with a company, they become more valuable to the employer. Opportunities for advancement are available if you are willing to accept greater responsibilities either by specializing in a specific field, taking on more technically complex assignments, or by assuming supervisory duties. Some technicians advance by moving into technical sales or customer relations. Others pursue advanced education to become scientists or engineers.

WHAT ARE THE SALARY RANGES?

Because of their many work situations and conditions, science technicians' salaries vary widely. Salaries also vary according to geographic location, experience, and education. The U.S. Department of Labor reports the following mean annual earnings for science technicians in 2008 by specialty: agricultural and food science technicians, $36,470; biological technicians, $40,900; chemical technicians, $43,710; environmental science and protection technicians, including health $43,180; forensic science technicians, $52,960; forest and conservation technicians, $35,320; geological and petroleum technicians, $57,080; and nuclear technicians, $66,910. Salaries for science technicians ranged from less than $22,000 to $97,000 or more. In general, technicians working in remote areas and under severe weather conditions usually receive higher rates of pay, as do technicians who work at large companies and companies with unions.

Benefits for science technicians depend on the employer; however, they usually include such items as health insurance, retirement or 401(k) plans, and paid vacation days.

WHAT IS THE JOB OUTLOOK?

According to the *Occupational Outlook Handbook,* employment of science technicians is expected to increase about as fast as the average for all careers through 2016. The employment outlook varies by occupational specialty. For example, employment for chemical technicians is expected to grow more slowly than the average, while little change is expected in the employment of forestry and conservation technicians. Faster than average employment growth is predicted for biological technicians. Employment for forensic science technicians and environmental science and protection technicians is expected to grow much faster than the average for all careers.

Technicians are gaining more respect from employers. In the past they have been considered assistants to the "real" scientists, but their status is changing to one of valued, highly trained specialists who are indispensable in the workforce.

SECTION 3

Do It Yourself

So you're thinking about a career in science—good choice! Not only are careers in science exciting and rewarding, they also offer many varied opportunities for employment. Although many science careers require a college education, there are many science-related activities for people your age. Read on for some suggestions.

❏ READ BOOKS AND PERIODICALS

Your school and local libraries are great places to begin learning about science. They are loaded with books, periodicals, DVDs, and other resources that provide information on science-related topics, including how to have a successful career as a scientist; renowned scientists such as Linus Pauling, E. O. Wilson, Lise Meitner, Stephen Hawking, George Washington Carver, and Marie Curie; career options (such as astronomer, genetic scientist, and science technician); and almost any other topic imaginable. For a list of books and periodicals about science, check out "Read a Book" in Section 4.

❏ SURF THE WEB

The Internet offers a wealth of information about science—from biographies of famous scientists and career information, to lists of museums and science-related books, to information on college science programs and much more. To help get you started, we've prepared a list of what we think are some of the best science-related sites on the Web. Check out "Surf the Web" in Section 4 for more info.

❏ TAKE HIGH SCHOOL CLASSES

Most, if not all, high schools offer courses devoted to the major branches of science. Take as many of theses classes as possible as an introduction to the field. If you are interested or excel in a particular area, such as biology or astronomy, you may decide to pursue higher-level instruction. The science department at Fort Myers High School in Florida, for example, offers a diverse selection of classes ranging from basic freshmen courses such as Biology 101, Earth Science 101, and Chemistry 101 to Advanced Placement courses and higher-level classes in marine science, anatomy and physiology, physics, and environmental science.

Other nonscience-based classes also can provide important training. Take as many math and computer classes as possible, as these subjects will help you to calculate scientific formulas and solve problems. Also, sign up for speech classes to help you develop your oral communication skills, which you will use frequently as a scientist. You should also take English and as many writing-intensive courses as possible. Being able to convey your thoughts on paper is important; scientists must be able to document and prepare their research in written format to share with their colleagues and the general public.

Don't forget to work closely with your high school counselor throughout your high school years to make sure you are taking your required classes and electives in the proper sequence.

❏ LEARN ABOUT THE TOOLS OF THE TRADE

Scientists rely on a variety of tools and equipment to help them conduct experiments and research. It is a good idea to try to learn about and use as many of these tools as possible. Following are a few of the most common tools used by scientists.

A *microscope* is an optical instrument that uses a combination of lenses to magnify an image. Scientists use microscopes to view prepared slides of items too small to see with the naked eye.

A *telescope* is a sophisticated scientific tool that gathers visible light via lenses and/or mirrors to allow direct observation or photographic recording of a distant item. Scientists use telescopes to study remote objects and phenomena such as faraway planets and constellations. The most common type of telescope is the optical telescope.

Scientists use *glass test tubes, beakers,* and other containers to measure, mix, and store chemicals and other materials during experiments. Other laboratory tools include *tweezers* and *clamps* to hold items, *rubber gloves* for handling hazardous materials, and *heating and cooling sources* to help create chemical reactions.

Other tools are specially designed to assist workers in a particular career specialty, but may be used by professionals in other fields, too. When visiting a site, geologists rely on special tools that are strong enough to break through hard rock and packed earth, as well as small precision instruments to collect tiny samples. They use *steel-tipped geologi-*

cal hammers and *picks, mallets* made of wood or rubber, as well as *steel chisels* to separate rock samples from their resting places. *Trowels* are used to help separate rock samples from dirt. *Brushes* are used to clear dust from rocks and other objects. Sometimes geologists use *sieves* to separate very small samples from sediment.

Meteorologists use a variety of specially designed tools to help them study and observe weather. They use *thermometers* to measure air temperature and *barometers* to measure air pressure. Relative humidity is measured with a *psychrometer.* Changing wind speeds can be tracked using an *anemometer.* Meteorologists use *weather balloons* to study the weather at high altitudes or during fierce storms. They also use *weather satellites* to monitor and record weather developments over a large area, along with *computer software* to analyze and interpret these changes over a period of time.

❏ JOIN AN ASSOCIATION

Professional associations provide their members with the opportunity to learn the latest industry news and developments, continuing education, and a forum in which to discuss and share ideas with other science professionals. Many of these associations offer membership to college students, while others, such as the American Institute of Professional Geologists and the Sierra Student Coalition, offer membership categories for high school students or people who are simply interested in the field. Check out "Look to the Pros" in Section 4 for more information on associations that offer student membership.

❏ MAKE THE MOST OF YOUR SUMMER VACATION

Another good way to learn more about the world of science is to participate in related summer programs at colleges and universities. Summer programs usually consist of classes, seminars, workshops, field trips, and hands-on activities that introduce you to opportunities in biology, forensic science, chemistry, meteorology, astronomy, and other science-related fields. Participating in these programs will allow you to explore different science specialties, meet other young people who are interested in these fields, and interact with faculty members. Summer programs are covered in depth in "Get Involved" in Section 4; check out this chapter for further information.

❏ VISIT A MUSEUM

Museum visits are a great way to learn about science. Since so many cities have museums, particularly those focusing on science and related fields, you will probably find it quite easy to find a science museum in your area! Here are two examples of interesting science museums.

The Arizona Science Center (http://www.azscience.org) is located in downtown Phoenix, Arizona. It houses about 300 permanent hands-on exhibits and plays host to many national traveling exhibits that are designed to educate, inspire, and entertain students of all ages. In its Dorrance Planetarium exhibit, visitors can be fully immersed in the imagery of the galaxy through its state-of-the-art NanoSeam Dome. In a recent exhibit titled How We Live With the Sun, visitors learned about the different ways people can protect themselves from harmful rays, yet utilize the sun's power to heat homes, grow crops effectively, and harness power. In the Forces of Nature exhibit, visitors learned about "everything from the movement of the tectonic plates to the power of wind and sand erosion." Exhibits at science museums change frequently so the possibilities for exploration are endless!

Do you get a buzz when you think about entomology? Then perhaps a visit to Hawaii's Bishop Museum (http://www.bishopmuseum.org) is more your speed. One recent exhibit was called Backyard Monsters: The World of Insects. The exhibit featured robotic insects such as a 12-foot tarantula spider that depicted the insects' graceful, yet quick, movements. Visitors were able to view two Atlas beetles in fight and participate in hands-on activities to learn about bug sounds, the bug populations of the world, insect vision, and how bugs help or harm our environment.

While you will probably take at least one field trip to an area science museum in school, don't think that is your only way to visit. Ask you parents to take you to a science museum in your town, or perhaps include one on the itinerary of your next family vacation. If all else fails, don't forget to check out science museums online. Most museums have Web sites full of interactive exhibits, games, and trivia. They may also provide information on competitions and internships, volunteer positions, and employment opportunities.

For a searchable database of science museums, visit http://www.aam-us.org/aboutmuseums/directory.cfm.

❏ BECOME A VOLUNTEER

Are you seeking more of an interactive experience during your time at a museum? If so, you may want to consider volunteering. Many museums around the country offer volunteer opportunities for young adults. For example, Chicago's Adler Planetarium encourages teenagers to explore their interest in science by volunteering in a host of roles. You may be assigned to lead educational and interactive activities for planetarium visitors. You would be responsible for leading tours, conducting scientific experiments or crafts designed to compliment a particular exhibit or theme, or leading other hands-on activities. You may be asked to answer questions at an exhibit or information booth, dress in a costume, or lead a story-time session for young visitors. At the planetarium, volunteers must be at least 17 years old, and be able to commit to serving three to 15 hours a week for a full year. For more information on requirements, training available, and other details, visit the Adler Planetarium's Web site, http://www.adlerplanetarium.org/volunteer/teenvolunteer.shtml. To

find science museums in your area, visit http://www.aam-us.org/aboutmuseums/directory.cfm.

❏ PARTICIPATE IN COMPETITIONS

Every year, thousands of middle school and high school students enter science competitions throughout the country. Many of these competitions are sponsored by national laboratories, research companies, computer software companies, and charitable foundations. Competitions are tiered; winners from local contests advance to regional fairs. Those selected as outstanding at this level advance to the state competition, and so forth until only the best science students are remaining to compete at the national level.

One such competition is the Massachusetts State Science & Engineering Fair (http://www.scifair.com), which has been held for more than 60 years. Students hail from public, private, and parochial schools—even a good number of home-schooled children participate in this competition. Science fair projects are done individually, or in student groups, and are critiqued by a panel of judges who listen to a short presentation, read a written report, and view a model or display. Awards include cash, prizes, and college scholarships.

Here's the hardest part: choosing your topic! Past winners at the Massachusetts State Science & Engineering Fair included projects dealing with using garbage as a source of fuel, the effects of colored lighting sources on the health of houseplants, the optimum pH level for mung bean growth, fabric protection against ultraviolet damage, and the effects of bacteria on the DNA of ants. Your topic need not be as difficult or far reaching as these winners; it's more important to find a topic that interests you, or perhaps has some relevance to your life. Try surfing the Web for other ideas. The following Web sites provide a few science fair project ideas to get you started: http://chemistry.about.com/od/sciencefairprojects/a/sciprohigh.htm and http://www.science-ideas.com/high-projects.htm.

❏ TRY SCIENCE ACTIVITIES AT HOME

You don't have to be a full-fledged scientist to engage in scientific activities. There are a number of simple activities you can do at home, using items easily found in your mom's kitchen or pantry. The following paragraphs detail some to try.

Soak some spuds. Slice a potato into two pieces, so each piece has two flat sides. Fill two dishes with water. Put the first slice in a dish; the second in the other dish along with two tablespoons of salt. Now let the potatoes soak for 15 minutes. What do you observe? One potato will be crisp, the other limp. The result is an example of osmosis; the movements of molecules, in this case the salt, from low concentration into high concentration. The potato's natural salt content moved out from the spud into the higher concentration of salt in its surrounding water, thus leaving you with a much limper potato than the other.

Create your own volcanic eruption. For this experiment, you'll need some clay or plaster of paris to build a volcano, a small container (perhaps a baby food jar), baking soda, red food coloring, dishwashing soap, and vinegar. Build your volcano. Inside the center, place the baby food jar filled with a good amount of vinegar and drops of food coloring and dish soap. Carefully spoon the baking soda into the jar. What do you observe? If you've assembled everything correctly, you will see an oozing mess coming out of the volcano. This is actually an example of a chemical reaction taking shape as a physical reaction. The mixture of baking soda and vinegar causes a chemical reaction that creates a different physical form, in this case the ooze. There is no chemical reaction connected with the red food coloring and dishwashing soap—they are strictly for fun and show!

Make some rock candy. For this activity, you'll need a glass jar, water, sugar, and pieces of household string. Place boiling water into the jar. Then add about three cups of sugar into the jar and mix well. Suspend a length of string into the water—you may have to tie one end to a pencil placed over the mouth of the jar. It would also be helpful to tie several knots at the end of the string for the crystals to hold onto—make sure this is the end inside the jar of water. Now wait for your rock candy to grow! What do you observe? Physical changes include evaporation and crystal formation, similar to the way minerals are formed. In nature, when the water in lakebeds or caves evaporates, the mineral deposits are left to form in crystal formation. Also, by putting so much sugar in a small amount of water, you have caused a state of over-saturation, forcing the sugar crystals to creep out of the water and onto the string.

❏ PARTICIPATE IN WORKPLACE VISITS AND JOB SHADOWING

Many laboratories offer tours, educational presentations, and other activities to visitors—what a great way to learn about the work of scientists! Argonne National Laboratory, which is located in Illinois, is one such facility. Part of the U.S. Department of Energy, the lab's mission is to "apply a unique mix of world-class science, engineering, and user facilities to deliver innovative research and technologies." Visitors can spend time in the information center, take guided tours of the scientific and engineering facilities and grounds, and participate in hands-on activities. Younger visitors can view a liquid nitrogen demonstration and learn how different materials behave at sub-zero temperatures; use magnets to levitate objects in the magnet laboratory; or perhaps observe specimen slides using microscopes similar to those used in forensics microscopy.

Students ages 16 years or older can take part in hour-long class demonstrations of calculator-based instruments measuring pH levels, phase changes, or chemical reactions. They may also be able to participate in activities and experiments using Geiger tubes, electro-phoresis, or taxonomic entomology. For more information on how to arrange a tour of the laboratory, visit http://www.anl.gov.

There are other ways to experience the workplace of a scientist besides a tour. One way is to spend the workday with a scientist. Known as job shadowing, you'll follow professionals in the field as they go through their day. To get started, find a laboratory, planetarium, or research site that is close to your home. Then send an inquiry about arranging a job shadowing appointment to the human resource department of the company. They will be able to match you with an appropriate employee and arrange the best day and time. On the day of your appointment, make sure to arrive promptly and dressed appropriately. Be sure to inquire about the company or organization's dress code or required safety wear before your visit. Some departments, especially those that handle chemicals or conduct potentially hazardous experiments, may require their employees to wear long sleeves or protective eyewear. Have any questions you want to ask written down, or perhaps carry a small notebook for jotting down notes, directions, or names of the people you meet during the day. At the end of your visit, thank the person for his or her time, and don't forget to follow up with a written note. If you are unsure of how to locate job-shadowing opportunities, you may want to ask your counselors and teachers for help. They often know of area businesses that are willing to participate in shadowing programs, and may be able to find a match for your intended career.

❏ CONDUCT AN INFORMATION INTERVIEW

Talking with science professionals is an excellent way to learn more about career options, work environments, and the skills you will need for career success. What is an information interview? It is a conversation between you and a science professional (physicist, geological technician, ecologist, etc.) about his or her career. You can conduct an information interview via email, on the telephone, or in person. The person you want to interview typically chooses the format. Here are a few basic questions to ask during an information interview:

- How long have you worked in this field?
- What type of tools do you use in your job?
- What made you want to enter this career?
- How did you train for this field? What classes and major should I take to prepare for this career?
- What are your primary and secondary job duties?
- What are your typical work hours?
- What are the most important personal and professional skills for people in your career?
- What is the employment outlook for your profession?
- What advice would you give to someone who wants to enter the field?
- What has been one of the most rewarding experiences in your career?

Some basic rules to keep in mind during an information interview include dressing appropriately (if conducting the interview in person), being attentive and acting interested during the interview (even if the job doesn't sound as exciting as you thought it would be), respecting time limits established by the worker (if he or she says that they only can give you 20 minutes of their time, don't try to stretch this time limit), and, after you have completed the interview, sending a thank you to the individual for his or her time.

❏ PARTICIPATE IN AN INTERNSHIP

Many private companies and government agencies and laboratories offer internships to students. They can be paid or unpaid. Many offer course credit. The real payoff is the work experience you'll gain by completing an internship. Usually interns work alongside full-time employees, assisting in whatever way possible to get an assignment done. Depending on the company, some interns may be assigned responsibility for an entire project. Many interns use their time to learn more about the industry and decide if it is a good fit for their personality and interests. An internship is also a great way to network for future employment opportunities.

It may be difficult to find internships at the high school level, as most internships are available to college students. Don't let this deter you. Surf the Web, contact companies and government agencies in your area, or perhaps ask your parents and teachers if they know of any available internships. Visit the following Web sites for more information on internships: http://www.high schoolinterns.com, http://www.fastweb. com, and http://www.internweb.com.

SECTION 4

What Can I Do Right Now?

Get Involved: A Directory of Camps, Programs, Competitions, and Other Opportunities

Now that you've read about some of the different science careers, you may be anxious to experience these fields yourself, to find out what they're really like. Or perhaps you already feel certain that a career in science is for you and want to get started right away. Whichever is the case, this section is for you! There are plenty of things you can do right now to learn about science careers while gaining valuable experience. Just as important, you'll get to meet new friends and see new places, too.

The programs listed following this introduction are run by organizations and institutions committed to science and to recruiting young talent into the profession. Many are colleges or universities offering introductory or regular classes, or special workshops, in these areas. Others are professional organizations trying to put the experience and dedication of their members to work for you. The types of opportunities available are listed right after the name of the program or organization, so you can skim through to find the listings that interest you most. Take time to read over the listings and see how each compares to your situation: how committed you are to a science-related field, how much of your money and free time you're willing to devote to these fields, and how the program will help you after high school. These listings are divided into categories, with the type of program printed right after its name or the name of the sponsoring organization.

❏ THE CATEGORIES

Camps

When you see an activity that is classified as a camp, don't automatically start packing your tent and mosquito repellent. Where academic study is involved, the term *camp* often simply means a residential program including both educational and recreational activities. It's sometimes hard to differentiate between such camps and other study programs, but if the sponsoring organization calls it a camp, so do we. Visit the following Web sites for an extended list of camps: http://www.kidscamps.com and http://find.acacamps.org/finding_a_camp.php. A list of summer math camps and programs for students can be found at http://www.ams.org/employment/mathcamps.html.

College Courses/Summer Study

These terms are linked because most college courses offered to students your age must take place in the summer, when you are out of school. At the same time, many summer study programs are sponsored by colleges and universities that want to attract future students and give them a head start in higher education. Summer study of almost any type is a good idea because it keeps your mind and your study skills sharp over the long vacation. Summer study at a college offers any number of additional benefits, including giving you the tools to make a well-informed decision about your future academic career.

Competitions

Competitions are fairly self-explanatory, but you should know that there are only a few in this book because competitions on a regional or national level are relatively rare. What this means, however, is that if you are interested in entering a competition, you shouldn't have much trouble finding one yourself. Your school counselor or teacher can help you start searching in your area.

Conferences

Conferences for high school students are usually difficult to track down because most are for professionals in the field who gather to share new information and ideas with each other. Don't be discouraged, though. A number of professional organizations with student branches or membership options for those who are simply interested in the field offer conferences. Some student branches even run their own conferences. This is an option worth pursuing because conferences focus on some of the most current information available and also give you the chance to meet professionals who can answer your questions and even offer advice.

Employment and Internship Opportunities

As you may already know from experience, employment opportunities for teenagers can be very limited—especially for jobs that require a bachelor's or graduate degree or those that can require a lot of on-the-job experience. While you won't be able to work as a scientist, you can get some experience working as a lab assistant or as a clerk at a laboratory or science-related company or government agency. Another option is to work part time at an after-school job to observe science professionals at work. The key is to take advantage of every opportunity you can to hone your science skills.

Basically, an internship combines the responsibilities of a job (strict schedules, pressing duties, and usually written evaluations by your supervisor) with the uncertainties of a volunteer position (no wages [or only very seldom], no fringe benefits, no guarantee of future employment). That may not sound very enticing, but completing an internship is a great way to prove your maturity, your commitment to a career, and your knowledge and skills to colleges, potential employers, and yourself. Some internships listed here are just formalized volunteer positions; others offer unique responsibilities and opportunities. Choose the kind that works best for you!

Field Experience

This is something of a catch-all category for activities that don't exactly fit the other descriptions. But anything called a field experience in this book is always a good opportunity to get out and explore the work of science professionals.

Membership

When an organization (such as the Astronomical Society of the Pacific) is in this category, it simply means that you are welcome to pay your dues and become a card-carrying member. Formally joining any organization brings the benefits of meeting others who share your interests, finding opportunities to get involved, and keeping up with current events. Depending on how active you are, the contacts you make and the experiences you gain may help when the time comes to apply to colleges or look for a job.

In some organizations, you pay a special student rate and receive benefits similar to regular members. Many organizations, however, are now starting student branches with their own benefits and publications. There are also some organizations that are geared specifically for students. As in any field, make sure you understand exactly what the benefits of membership are before you join.

Finally, don't let membership dues discourage you from contacting these organizations. Some local organizations charge dues as low as $10 because they know that students are perpetually short of funds. When the annual dues are higher, think of the money as an investment in your future and then consider if it is too much to pay.

Seminars

Like conferences, seminars are often classes or informative gatherings for those already working in the field, and are generally sponsored by professional organizations. This means that there aren't all that many seminars for young people. But also like conferences, they are often open to affiliated members. Check with various organizations to see what kind of seminars they offer and if there is some way you can attend.

❏ PROGRAM DESCRIPTIONS

Once you've started to look at the individual listings themselves, you'll find that they contain a lot of information. Naturally, there is a general description of each program, but wherever possible we also have included the following details.

Application Information

Each listing notes how far in advance you'll need to apply for the program or position, but the simple rule is to apply as far in advance as possible. This ensures that you won't miss out on a great opportunity simply because other people got there ahead of you. It also means that you will get a timely decision on your application, so if you are not accepted, you'll still have some time to apply elsewhere. As for the elements that make up your application—essays, recommendations, etc.— we've tried to tell you what's involved, but be sure to contact the program about specific requirements before you submit anything.

Background Information

This includes such information as the date the program or organization was established, the name of the organization that is sponsoring it financially, and the faculty and staff who will be there for you. This can help you—and your family—gauge the quality and reliability of the program.

Classes and Activities

Classes and activities change from year to year, depending on popularity, availability of instructors, and many other factors. Nevertheless, colleges and universities quite consistently offer the same or similar classes, even in their summer sessions. Courses like "Biology 101" and "Astronomy 101," for example, are simply indispensable. So you can look through the listings and see which programs offer foundational courses like these and which offer courses on more variable topics. As for activities, we note when you have access to recreational facilities on campus, and it's usually a given that special social and cultural activities will be arranged for most programs.

Contact Information

Wherever possible, we have given the title of the person whom you should contact instead of the name because people change jobs so frequently. If no title is given and you are telephoning an organization, simply tell the person who answers the phone the name of the program that interests you and he or she will forward your call. If you are writing, include the line "Attention: Summer Study Program" (or whatever is appropriate after "Attention") somewhere on the envelope. This will help to ensure that your letter goes to the person in charge of that program.

Credit

Where academic programs are concerned, we sometimes note that high school or college credit is available to those who have completed them. This means that the program can count toward your high school diploma or a future college degree just like a regular course. Obviously, this can be very useful, but it's important to note that rules about accepting such credit vary from school to school. Before you commit to a program offering high school credit, check with your guidance counselor to see if it is acceptable to your school. As for programs offering college credit, check with your chosen college (if you have one) to see if they will accept it.

Eligibility and Qualifications

The main eligibility requirement to be concerned about is age or grade in school. A term frequently used in relation to grade level is "rising," as in "rising senior": someone who will be a senior when the next school year begins. This is especially important where summer programs are concerned. A number of university-based programs make admissions decisions partly in consideration of GPA, class rank, and standardized test scores. This is mentioned in the listings, but you must contact the program for specific numbers. If you are worried that your GPA or your ACT/SAT scores, for example, aren't good enough, don't let them stop you from applying to programs that consider such things in the admissions process. Often, a fine essay or even an example of your dedication and eagerness can compensate for statistical weaknesses.

Facilities

We tell you where you'll be living, studying, eating, and having fun during these programs, but there isn't enough room to go into all the details. Some of those details can be important: what is and isn't accessible for people with disabilities, whether the site of a summer program has air-conditioning, and how modern the facilities and computer equipment are. You can expect most program brochures and application materials to address these concerns, but if you still have questions about the facilities, just call the program's administration and ask.

Financial Details

While a few of the programs listed here are fully underwritten by collegiate and corporate sponsors, most of them rely on you for at least some of their funding. The 2009 prices and fees are given here, but you should bear in mind that costs rise slightly almost every year. You and your parents must take costs into consideration when choosing a program. We always try to note where financial aid is available, but really, most programs will do their best to ensure that a shortage of funds does not prevent you from taking part.

Residential vs. Commuter Options

Simply put, some programs prefer that participating students live with other participants and staff members, others do not, and still others leave the decision entirely to the students themselves. As a rule, residential programs are suitable for young people who live out of town or even out of state, as well as for local residents. They generally provide a better overview of college life than programs in which you're only on campus for a few hours a day, and they're a way to test how well you cope with living away from home. Commuter programs may be viable only if you live near the program site or if you can stay with relatives who do. Bear in mind that for residential programs especially, the travel between your home and the location of the activity is almost always your responsibility and can significantly increase the cost of participation.

❏ FINALLY . . .

Ultimately, there are three important things to bear in mind concerning all of the programs listed in this section. The first is that things change. Staff members come and go, funding is added or withdrawn, supply and demand determine which programs continue and which terminate. Dates, times, and costs vary widely because of a number of factors. Because of this, the information we give you, although as current and detailed as possible, is just not enough on which to base your final decision. If you are interested in a program, you simply must contact the organization concerned to get the latest and most complete information available or visit its Web site. This has the added benefit of putting you in touch with someone who can deal with your individual questions and problems.

A second important point to keep in mind when considering these programs is that the people who run them provided the information printed here. The editors of this book haven't attended the programs and don't endorse them: we simply give you the information with which to begin your own research. And after all, we can't pass judgment because you're the only one who can decide which programs are right for you.

The final thing to bear in mind is that the programs listed here are just the tip of the iceberg. No book can possibly cover all of the opportunities that are available to you—partly because they are so numerous and are constantly coming and going, but partly because some are waiting to be discovered. For instance, you may be very interested in taking a college course but don't see the college that interests you in the listings. Call its admissions office! Even if the college doesn't have a special program for high school students, it might be able to make some kind of arrangements for you to visit or sit in on a class. Use the ideas behind these listings and take the initiative to turn them into opportunities!

❏ THE PROGRAMS
American Chemical Society
Competitions/Field Experience

The society offers several competitions and programs for high school students who are interested in chemistry—including ChemClub, the Chemistry Olympiad, and Project SEED.

The society offers more than 185 ChemClubs around the United States for students who are interested in chemistry. In these clubs, students "participate in after-school activities, get involved in community building, learn about chemistry careers, enjoy social events, and better understand how chemistry plays a role in our everyday lives." Members also receive bonus items such as T-shirts and copies of *ChemMatters* and the *Journal of Chemical Education.* Membership in ChemClub is free, and the society provides a lot of information at its Web site about starting a club if one is not available near you.

In the Chemistry Olympiad, high school students from around the world compete to prove who has the best knowledge and skills in chemistry. Students first compete in local Chemistry Olympiad competitions, with winners moving on to compete at the national and international level. The goal of the competitions is to help students develop their chemistry skills, allow students who share a love of chemistry to interact with other like-minded students and teachers, and foster cross-cultural experiences. Contact the society for complete details regarding eligibility and competitions.

Project SEED is a summer research program for economically disadvantaged students. Rising high school juniors and seniors get the chance to work with "scientist-mentors on research projects in industrial, academic, and federal laboratories, discovering new career paths as they approach critical turning points in their lives." The program lasts eight to 10 weeks. Students receive a fellowship of $2,500 to $3,000, and they are also eligible to apply for a one-year, nonrenewable college scholarship of up to $5,000. Applications are typically due in late January. Contact the society for more information on eligibility requirements and other details.

American Chemical Society
1155 16th Street, NW
Washington, DC 20036-4839

800-227-5558
help@acs.org
http://www.chemistry.org

American Collegiate Adventures at the University of Wisconsin

College Courses/Summer Study/ Employment and Internship Opportunities

American Collegiate Adventures (ACA) offers high school students the chance to experience and prepare for college during their summer vacation. Adventures are based at the University of Wisconsin in Madison; programs last for two, three, four, or six weeks. On weekdays, participants take college-level courses that are taught by university faculty. On weekends, they visit other regional colleges and recreation sites. All students live in comfortable en suite accommodations, just down the hall from an ACA resident staff member. Recent enrichment courses include Bone-Up on Biology, Chemistry and Chemical Attraction, Save the Planet, Get Moving With Physics, and SAT and ACT Prep.

Tuition (which includes room and board) for the two-week program is approximately $2,895; the three-week program, $4,395; the four-week program, $5,595; and the six-week program, $6,995. Contact American Collegiate Adventures for current course listings and application procedures.

American Collegiate Adventures
1811 West North Avenue, Suite 201
Chicago, IL 60622-1488
800-509-7867

info@acasummer.com
http://www.acasummer.com

American Geophysical Union Bright STaRS (Students Training as Research Scientists) Program

Conferences

If you participate in after-school and summer research experiences in the earth and space sciences, you are eligible to apply for the Bright StaRS program. Participants present their research findings at the American Geophysical Union (AGU) fall conference and get an opportunity to learn about education, research, and career opportunities in the geosciences. They also get their research published in a meeting program; are invited to attend technical sessions and exhibits; receive access to the Academic Showcase, which provides information on 30 institutions offering geoscience educational programs; and are invited to attend a luncheon with scientists and symposium speakers. Contact the AGU for more information.

American Geophysical Union
2000 Florida Avenue, NW
Washington, DC 20009-1277
202-777-7508
icifuentes@agu.org
http://www.agu.org/outreach/
    education/brightstars.shtml

American Society of Limnology and Oceanography Minority Student Directory

Employment and Internship Opportunities

Minority high school (junior and senior years) and undergraduate and graduate students can post information about their educational backgrounds and aquatic science interests in the Minority Student Directory, which is available at the society's Web site. Listings include your name, current student status, an overview of your interests in the field, and a statement detailing your background and goals. Participating in the directory will help you meet other people in the field, as well as possibly obtain internships and employment.

American Society of Limnology and Oceanography

5400 Bosque Boulevard, Suite 680
Waco, TX 76710-4446
800-929-2756
http://www.aslo.org/mas/directory. html

Aquatic Sciences Adventure Camp at Southwest Texas State University

Camps

The Aquatic Sciences Adventure Camp is run by the Edwards Aquifer Research and Data Center at Southwest Texas State University, San Marcos. It offers students ages nine to 15 the chance to explore and conduct research on various bodies of water, from artesian wells, to ponds, to rivers. You will get the chance to learn about aquatic biology and water chemistry via a variety of activities. During the weeklong residential camp, your days start early (around 6:45 A.M.) and include snorkeling and scuba lessons, lectures, videos, and evening recreational activities (including cave tours, swimming and tubing in the San Marcos River,

swimming in a spring-fed pool, a raft trip on the Guadalupe River, and a trip to Sea World). Each session costs about $450, which includes room, board, equipment, and field trips. Students are accepted into each session on a first come, first served basis. All participants should be accustomed to moderate physical activity and be comfortable around water, and preferably have the ability to swim.

Aquatic Sciences Adventure Camp

Texas State University, San Marcos
248 Freeman Building
San Marcos, TX 78666-4616
512-245-2329
Aqscicamp@txstate.edu
http://www.eardc.txstate.edu/ aboutcamp.html

Association of Zoos and Aquariums (AZA)

Conferences/Membership/Volunteer Programs

The association offers an associate membership category "for zoo and aquarium professionals, as well as other interested parties, who want to support and forward the mission, vision, and goals of AZA." Members receive a subscription to *CONNECT*, the association's monthly magazine; free and discounted admission to AZA-accredited zoos and aquariums; and discounts on conferences.

The AZA does not offer volunteer opportunities, but it does offer links to its member organizations that do. Visit http://www.aza.org/Education/KidsAnd Families/detail.aspx?id=278 to find volunteer opportunities at a zoo or aquarium near you. Volunteering at a zoo or aquarium is a good way to learn about careers in the field. Volunteers learn about zoos and aquariums via classroom activities and hands-on work in animal care, conservation education, conservation and research, and visitor services. In addition to learning firsthand how zoos and aquariums work, there are other benefits to volunteering. Volunteers often receive discounts on admission and membership, get to participate in field trips and other activities, make valuable contacts with zoo and aquarium professionals, and meet new friends.

Association of Zoos and Aquariums

8403 Colesville Road, Suite 710
Silver Spring, MD 20910-3314
301-562-0777
http://www.aza.org

Astronomical Society of the Pacific
Membership

This nonprofit educational and scientific organization offers membership for students and amateur astronomers. Members receive *Mercury* magazine and Astronomy Beat, "a twice-monthly, online column written by 'insiders' from the worlds of astronomy research and outreach."

Astronomical Society of the Pacific

390 Ashton Avenue
San Francisco, CA 94112-1722
415-337-1100
http://www.astrosociety.org

Bureau of Land Management Volunteer Opportunities/Student Educational Employment Program
Employment and Internship Opportunities/Volunteer Programs

The Bureau of Land Management (BLM) is the division of the U.S. Department of the Interior responsible for managing the land and resources of more than 258 million acres of public-owned property. It offers volunteer opportunities to people of all ages and skill levels. As a volunteer, you can take part in research projects, help monitor wilderness areas, perform office work, or participate in any number of activities designed to conserve and preserve the land's natural and historic resources. Depending on your interests and the BLM's needs, you can work alone or in a group, on a prearranged project or on one of your own devising, for a few hours or every day, just once, or on a continuing basis. (Note: Information on volunteer opportunities with other federal environmental agencies—including the Bureau of Reclamation, Fish & Wildlife Service, Forest Service, National Park Service, Natural Resources Conservation Service, U.S. Army Corps of Engineers, and U.S. Geological Survey—can be found at http://www.volunteer.gov/gov.)

Additionally, you can participate in the federal government's Student Educational Employment Program (SEEP). High school students in SEEP are employed in entry-level positions with the BLM and other federal agencies that match their interests and career goals. Applicants must be U.S. citizens or residents of American Samoa or Swains Islands. Successful completion of

SEEP may lead to permanent opportunities in federal service upon completion of other educational requirements (namely, a college degree). College students at the undergraduate and graduate levels are also eligible to participate in SEEP. For further information, visit http://www.opm.gov/employ/students.

Bureau of Land Management
U.S. Department of the Interior
1849 C Street, Room 406-LS
Washington, DC 20240-0001
http://www.blm.gov/wo/st/en.html

Canon Envirothon
Competitions
The Envirothon is a series of competitions, established in 1979, for ninth- through 12th-graders who want to increase their knowledge of the natural sciences and environmental issues. Progressing from local to state/provincial/territorial to national competitions, teams of five students perform experiments and activities and then work together to answer the questions they are given. Competition questions come from five subjects: soils and land use, aquatic ecology, forestry, wildlife, and a current wildlife issue that changes each year. State/provincial/territorial competitions feature questions about the local environment, regulations, and concerns in addition to general knowledge questions. While the goal of the Envirothon is to develop knowledgeable, environmentally active adults, the program is also designed to be fun for all participants. Teams are headed by high school teachers or other youth leaders and may draw members from schools or from other organizations and associations. At the national level, the Envirothon is sponsored by Canon USA; at the regional levels, usually by state EPAs, forest services, and game and parks commissions. More than $100,000 in scholarships and prizes is awarded at the national competition. For information about the Envirothon program in your area, contact the relevant state agencies, or speak to your science teacher or guidance counselor. You may also contact the national executive director at the address below.

Envirothon
Attn: National Director
PO Box 855
League City, TX 77574-0855
800-825-5547
http://www.envirothon.org

The Center for Excellence in Education USA Biology Olympiad/ Research Science Institute
Competitions/Field Experience
The goal of the Center for Excellence in Education (CEE) is to nurture future leaders in science, technology, and business. And it won't cost you a dime: All of the CEE's programs are free (except for transportation costs).

All high school students are eligible to participate in the USA Biology Olympiad (USABO). To participate, you must be nominated by your teacher. If you score well on a multiple-choice exam, and then subsequently excel on another exam, you will make the final group of 20 finalists who are eligible to compete at the USABO

National Finals at a leading university. The National Finals consist of two weeks of intensive practical and theoretical tutorials, where you will get the opportunity to work with leading biologists in the United States. At the end of the two weeks, you will take a theoretical and practical exam to compete for one of the four positions on the U.S. team that will compete in the International Biology Olympiad. Contact Marcy Reedy, the program manager, via email (mreedy@cee.org) for more information.

Since 1984, the CEE has sponsored the Research Science Institute, a six-week residential summer program held at the Massachusetts Institute of Technology. Seventy-five rising high school seniors with scientific and technological promise are chosen from a field of more than 700 applicants to participate in the program, conducting projects with scientists and researchers. You can read more about specific research projects online.

The Center for Excellence in Education
8201 Greensboro Drive, Suite 215
McLean, VA 22102-3813
703-448-9062
http://www.cee.org

College and Careers Program at the Rochester Institute of Technology

College Courses/Summer Study

The Rochester Institute of Technology (RIT) offers its College and Careers Program for rising high school seniors who want to experience college life and explore career options in computing and informa-

tion sciences; engineering and engineering technology; environmental studies; social sciences; science, mathematics, and medical sciences; and other areas. Recent classes include Bioinformatics: Enabling Discovery; Biotechnology/Genetic Engineering: How to Clone a Dinosaur; Chemistry: The Wonders of Chemistry; Computer Science: Overview of Computing; Criminal Justice; Imaging Science: Big Bang and Black Holes; Imaging Science: Create Your Own Holograms; Mathematical Sciences: Let's Make A Deal; Mischief Managed-Digital Mapping and Environmental Science; and Physics of Sound and Hearing. The program, in existence since 1990, allows you to spend a Friday and Saturday on campus, living in the dorms and attending up to four sessions in the career areas of your choice. In each session, participants work with RIT students and faculty to gain hands-on experience in the topic area. The program is held twice each summer, usually once in mid-July and again in early August. The registration deadline is one week before the start of the program, but space is limited and students are accepted on a first-come, first-served basis. For further information about the program and specific sessions on offer, contact the RIT admissions office.

College and Careers Program
Rochester Institute of Technology
Office of Undergraduate Admissions
60 Lomb Memorial Drive
Rochester, NY 14623-5604
585-475-6631
admissions@rit.edu
http://ambassador.rit.edu/careers/
    sessions.php

Collegiate Scholars Program at Arizona State University

College Courses/Summer Study/ Employment and Internship Opportunities

The Collegiate Scholars Program allows high school students to earn college credit during summer academic sessions. Recent classes include Principles of Bio-Chemistry, Linear Algebra, Aviation Meteorology, Advanced Chemistry, Calculus, Statistics, and Public Speaking. Students get the opportunity to explore careers and interact with college professors, as well as receive access to internships, mentoring programs, and research opportunities. Online classes are also available. Arizona high school seniors may apply, and they are evaluated for admission based on their "high school GPA and/or class rank, test scores, high school schedules, and involvement in other programs offering college credit." Contact the Collegiate Scholars executive coordinator for information on program costs and other details.

Collegiate Scholars Program

Arizona State University
Attn: Executive Coordinator
480-965-2621
mark.duplissis@asu.edu
http://promise.asu.edu/csp

Early Experience Program at the University of Denver

College Courses/Summer Study

The University of Denver invites academically gifted high school students in grades 10–12 to apply for its Early Experience Program, which involves participating in university-level classes (including science classes) during the school year and especially during the summer. This is a commuter-only program. Interested students must submit a completed application (with essay), official high school transcript, standardized test results (PACT/ ACT/PSAT/SAT), a letter of recommendation from a counselor or teacher, and have a minimum GPA of 3.0. Tuition is approximately $1,850 per four-credit class. Financial aid is available. Contact the Early Experience Program coordinator for more information.

University of Denver

Early Experience Program
Attn: Coordinator
2197 South University Boulevard
Denver, CO 80208-4711
800-525-9495
http://admission.du.edu/admissions/
apply/earlyexperience.asp

Earthwatch Institute

Conferences/Field Experience/ Employment and Internship Opportunities/Membership

Earthwatch Institute is the organization for people whose spirit of adventure is as great as their commitment to the earth's well-being. A nonprofit membership organization founded in 1971, Earthwatch's major activity is linking volunteers with scientific research expeditions that need them. There are about 130 different expeditions every year, covering all continents but Antarctica, each lasting anywhere from five days to almost three weeks. If you are 16 or 17, you can join a Teen Team and participate in an expedition researching Costa Rican caterpillars, for example, or Australia's fossil forests. Whichever expedition you choose, you work with five to 10 other people under the guidance of a research scientist (often a university professor working in his or her field of expertise).

Living and working conditions vary widely among the expeditions; you might stay in a hotel or a tent, remain at one site or hike to several locations while carrying a heavy backpack. Expenses also vary widely, from about $199 to $4,000, depending on travel, accommodation and eating arrangements, and other necessary provisions. Earthwatch reminds potential volunteers, however, that your payment of expenses (along with the donation of your time) is really an investment in environmental research. Of course, you're also investing in your own future. With so many expeditions to choose from, you'll be able to gain experience in career fields from ecology to national park service, from natural history to wildlife preservation. Contact Earthwatch for its annual catalog listing all the details.

Even if you're not up for one of their demanding expeditions, Earthwatch invites you to become a member at the standard rate of $35 per year. High school students can benefit from the organization's own scholarship, fellowship, and grant opportunities. You can also attend Earthwatch's annual conference or apply for an internship at its offices in Oxford, England; Melbourne, Australia; or Tokyo, Japan. Contact the organization for more information.

Earthwatch Institute
Three Clock Tower Place, Suite 100
PO Box 75
Maynard, MA 01754-2549
800-776-0188
info@earthwatch.org
http://www.earthwatch.org

Environmental Studies Summer Youth Institute at Hobart and William Smith Colleges
College Courses/Summer Study

Hobart and William Smith Colleges sponsor the Environmental Studies Summer Youth Institute (ESSYI) for rising high school juniors and seniors. Academically talented students are invited to participate in this examination of environmental issues from scientific, social, and humanistic perspectives. Running for two full weeks beginning in July, the ESSYI is comprised of classroom courses, laboratory procedures, outdoor explorations, and plenty of time to discuss and think about integrating these many approaches to understanding the environment. Lectures encompass ecology, philosophy, geology, literature, topography, and art, among other areas of study, and are conducted by professors from Hobart and William Smith Colleges. Your study of the environment and how humans relate to it also includes field trips to such places as quaking bogs, organic farms, the Adirondack Mountains, and Native American historical sites. Participants also make use of the *HMS William F. Scandling,* the colleges' 65-foot research vessel, as they explore the ecology of nearby Seneca Lake. ESSYI students live on campus and have access to all the colleges' recreational facilities. Those who complete this intellectually and physically challenging program are awarded college credit. The fee for the program is $2,200. For information on financial aid and application procedures, contact the institute director.

Environmental Studies Summer Youth Institute

Hobart and William Smith Colleges
Attn: Director
Geneva, NY 14456-3397
315-781-4401
essyi@hws.edu
http://academic.hws.edu/enviro

Exploration Summer Programs: Senior Program at Yale University
College Courses/Summer Study

Exploration Summer Programs (ESP) has been offering academic summer enrichment programs to students for more than three decades. Rising high school sophomores, juniors, and seniors can participate in ESP's Senior Program at Yale University. Two three-week residential and day sessions are available. Participants can choose from more than 80 courses. Recent courses include Crime Scene Investigation-Forensic Science; Mad Scientist Mother Nature-Environmental Chemistry; A Bone to Pick-Anatomy + Physiology; Cracking the Code-Genetic Engineering; Mechanized Miracles-Physics Of Motion; Beyond the Matrix-Philosophy of Physics; and B3h1nd th3 Numb3rs-Professional Mathematics. All courses and seminars are ungraded and not-for-credit. In addition to academics, students participate in extracurricular activities such as tours, sports, concerts, weekend recreational trips, college trips, and discussions of current events and other issues. Students who stay on cam-

pus reside in residence halls in suites that house from two to nine students. Basic tuition for the Residential Senior Program is approximately $4,555 for one session and $8,390 for two sessions. Day session tuition ranges from approximately $2,100 for one session to $3,820 for two sessions. A limited number of need-based partial and full scholarships are available. Programs are also available for students in grades four through nine. Contact ESP for more information.

Exploration Summer Programs

932 Washington Street
PO Box 368
Norwood, MA 02062-3412
781-762-7400
http://www.explo.org

High School Field Ecology Program at the Teton Science School
College Courses/Summer Study/Field Experience

The Teton Science School operates an intense High School Field Ecology summer program for rising high school juniors and seniors. The program lasts four weeks and, while based in Jackson Hole, Wyoming, includes time at Yellowstone and Grand Teton National Parks. In the program, you "learn field ecology by doing field ecology," and are expected to maintain a high level of physical activity while conducting research and exploring the ecosystem. Working with instructors, scientists, and representatives of federal agencies, you learn proper field investigation techniques as well as how to keep a field journal, read and make maps, and explore the wilderness without harming the environment. The program culminates with a major independent research project that addresses a current conservation issue. Each participant is formally assigned a grade and given a written evaluation for his or her work in the program, so this is a suitable source of high school credit. You live in log cabin-style dormitories with modern facilities, except during a backpacking trip through the mountains. Most outdoor gear and all meals are covered by the tuition fee of around $3,600; some financial assistance is available. You must have completed a biology class and received favorable teacher recommendations to be considered. The Teton Science School also runs a Middle School Field Ecology program; a Field Natural History program for rising high school freshmen, sophomores, and juniors; and various programs for adults and teachers. All correspondence should be directed to the registrar.

High School Field Ecology Program

Teton Science School
700 Coyote Canyon Road
Jackson, WY 83001-8501
303-733-1313
http://www.tetonscience.org

High School Honors Program/ Summer Challenge Program/ Research Internship in Science & Engineering/Summer Preview at Boston University

College Courses/Summer Study

Boston University offers four summer educational opportunities for high school students: the High School Honors Program, the Summer Challenge Program, the Research Internship in Science & Engineering Program, and the Summer Preview Program.

Rising high school seniors can participate in the High School Honors Program, which offers six-week, for-credit undergraduate study at the university. Students take two for-credit classes (up to eight credits) alongside regular Boston College students, live in dorms on campus, and participate in extracurricular activities and tours of local attractions. Classes are available in more than 50 subject areas, including astronomy, biology, chemistry, communications, foreign languages, geography and environment, mathematics, physics, and statistics. The program typically begins in early July. Tuition for the program is approximately $4,120, with registration/program/application fees ($550) and room and board options ($1,900 to $2,060) extra. Students who demonstrate financial need may be eligible for financial aid.

Rising high school sophomores, juniors, and seniors in the university's Summer Challenge Program learn about college life and take college classes in a noncredit setting. The program is offered in three sessions. Students choose two seminars (which feature lectures, group and individual work, project-based assignments, and field trips) from a total of about 15 program options. Past seminars include Engineering, Infectious Diseases, and Topics in Ethics. The cost of the program is approximately $3,070 (which includes tuition, a room charge, meals, and sponsored activities). No financial aid is available

High school students who are entering their senior year can participate in the Research Internship in Science & Engineering Program, a six-week honors program in which participants have the "opportunity to conduct university-level research in state-of-the-art laboratories, alongside some of the sharpest scientific minds in the country." Students can conduct research in the following areas: astronomy, biology, chemistry, engineering, medicine, physics, and psychology. Tuition for the program is $3,500, plus a nonrefundable $50 application fee and a $500 registration and program fee. Room and board for residential students is extra and ranges from $1,897 to $2,055 depending on the number of meals included in the plan. Financial aid is available.

Rising high school freshmen and sophomores can participate in the one-week Summer Preview Program. This noncredit, commuter program introduces students to college life and a particular area of study. Recent seminars include Medicine and Society, Graphic Design, Learning the Art of Writing, and Film Studies. The cost of the program is $1,100 (which includes tuition, textbooks, lunch, and activities). No financial aid is available.

Boston University High School Programs

755 Commonwealth Avenue,
  Room 105
Boston, MA 02215-1401
617-353-1378
buhssumr@bu.edu
http://www.bu.edu/summer/
  high-school-programs

High School Summer College at Stanford University
College Courses/Summer Study

Students who have completed their junior or senior year of high school can apply to Stanford University's High School Summer College. The program will also accept applications from "accomplished and mature" sophomores. This competitive program welcomes students from around the world who are ready to explore a challenging university environment and prepare for their college careers. Participants commute or live on campus and attend a selection of regular undergraduate classes from mid-June to mid-August. Course offerings vary from year to year, but recent courses include Introduction to Biology; Introduction to Biology Lab; Introduction to Human Physiology; Introduction to Biological Research Methods; Biochemistry, Genetics, and Molecular Biology; Chemical Principles; Structure and Reactivity; Organic Monofunctional Compounds; Organic Chemistry Laboratory; The Oceans: An Introduction to the Marine Environment; Calculus; The Nature of the Universe; Modern Physics with Laboratory; Astronomy Laboratory and Observational Astronomy; Statistical Methods in Engineering and the Physical Sciences; and Data Mining and Analysis. As you would expect from an institution like Stanford, the coursework is demanding and the grading stringent, but university credit is awarded upon successful completion of your courses. When not in class, you can enjoy the many activities on campus and you also participate in College Admission 101, which is designed to help you through the difficult process of choosing and successfully applying to colleges. The cost of the High School Summer College ranges from $6,697 to $9,733 depending on the number of course units taken, and includes room and board as well as tuition and program fees. Financial aid is available. For application information and current course offerings, contact the staff of the Stanford Summer Session; materials are usually available in late January, and rolling admissions are then open until mid-May.

Summer Session Office
Stanford University
482 Galvez Street
Stanford, CA 94305-6079
650-723-3109
summersession@stanford.edu
http://summersession.stanford.edu/
    highschool/overview.asp

High School Summer Scholars Program at Washington University in St. Louis

College Courses/Summer Study

Rising sophomores and juniors can earn up to seven units of college credit by participating in the High School Summer Scholars Program. Two five-week sessions are available. More than 60 college courses are offered. Recent courses include Introduction to Human Evolution; Introduction to Problem-Based Learning in Biology; Topics in General Chemistry; Geology of National Parks; The Solar System; Resources of the Earth; General Physics; Introduction to Statistics; and several foreign languages. Students spend 16–20 hours each week in class; during the rest of the time, they do

homework, participate in planned social activities, and explore the campus and the St. Louis area. Applicants must have a B+ average and have a combined SAT score of at least 1800, a combined PSAT score of 180, or an ACT or PLAN composite score of at least 25. Tuition for the program is about $5,935, which includes the classes, housing in a campus residence hall, three meals a day, and access to student health services. Financial aid is available. The average award is $2,300, and 80 percent of students receive financial aid. Contact the program director for more information, including details on application deadlines.

**Washington University in
    St. Louis**
High School Summer Scholars
    Program
Attn: Program Director
One Brookings Drive
Campus Box 1145, January Hall,
    Room 100
St. Louis, MO 63130-4862
866-209-0691
mhussung@artsci.wustl.edu
http://ucollege.wustl.edu/programs/
    highschool

High School Summer Workshop at the University of Wisconsin—Madison

College Courses/Summer Study

The University of Wisconsin—Madison's Cooperative Institute for Meteorological Satellite Studies offers a four-day workshop for high school students who are interested in atmospheric science, earth science, astronomy, and remote sensing. The workshop is typically held in late July. Students stay in dorms on campus. The cost of the workshop is $475 (which includes housing, meals, and activities). Contact the institute for more information.

University of Wisconsin— Madison

Cooperative Institute for
   Meteorological Satellite Studies
High School Summer Workshop
1225 West Dayton Street
Madison, WI 53706-1612
608-263-7435
http://cimss.ssec.wisc.edu/student
   workshop

Internship Connection
Employment and Internship Opportunities

Internship Connection provides summer or "gap year" internships to high school and college students in Boston and New York City. Internships are available in biotechnology, environment, and more than 30 other fields. As part of the program, participants learn how to create a resume, participate in a job interview, and develop communication and personal skills that are key to success in the work world. They also get the chance to make valuable contacts during their internships that may help them land a job once they complete college. The program fee for interns in New York is $2,500. Those who attend the program in Boston pay $2,000. Contact Internship Connection for more information.

Internship Connection
17 Countryside Road
Newton, MA 02459-2915
617-796-9283

carole@internshipconnection.com
http://www.internshipconnection.com

Junior Scholars Program at Miami University—Oxford
College Courses/Summer Study

Academically talented high school seniors can earn six to eight semester hours of college credit and learn about university life by participating in the Junior Scholars Program at Miami University—Oxford. Students may choose from more than 40 courses, including Plants Humanity & Environment; Microorganisms and Human Disease; Pre-Calculus; Calculus; Introduction to Computer Concepts and Programming; Statistics; and various foreign languages. In addition to academics, scholars participate in social events, recreational activities, and cocurricular seminars. Program participants live in an air-conditioned residence hall. Fees range from approximately $2,348 to $3,526 depending on the number of credit hours taken and the applicant's place of residence. (Ohio residents receive a program discount.) There is an additional fee of approximately $200 for books. The application deadline is typically in mid-May. Visit the program's Web site for additional eligibility requirements and further details.

Miami University—Oxford
Junior Scholars Program
202 Bachelor Hall
Oxford, OH 45056-3414
513-529-5825
juniorscholars@muohio.edu
http://www.units.muohio.edu/
   jrscholars

Junior Science and Humanities Symposium (JSHS)
Competitions/Conferences

The Junior Science and Humanities Symposium (JSHS) encourages high school students (grades nine through 12) who are gifted in engineering, mathematics, and the sciences to develop their analytical and creative skills. Competition categories include Environmental Science/Earth and Space Science; Engineering; Physical Sciences (including astronomy, chemistry, and physics); Life Sciences; Medicine and Health/Behavioral and Social Sciences; and Mathematics and Computer Science. There are approximately 48 regional symposia held throughout the United States so that each year some 12,000 students are able to participate. Funded by the U.S. Army Research Office since its inception in 1958 (and by the U.S. Army, Navy, and Air Force since 1995), the JSHS has little to do with the military and everything to do with research. At each individual symposium, researchers and educators from various universities and laboratories meet with the high school students (and some of their teachers) to study new scientific findings, pursue their own interests in the lab, and discuss and debate relevant issues. Participants learn how scientific and engineering research can be used to benefit humanity, and they are strongly encouraged to pursue such research in college and as a career. To provide further encouragement, one attendee at each symposium will win a scholarship and the chance to present his or her own research at the national Junior Science and Humanities Symposium. Finalists from each regional JSHS win all expense paid trips to the national symposium, where the top research students can win additional scholarships and trips to the prestigious London International Youth Science Forum. For information about the symposium in your region and eligibility requirements, contact the national Junior Science and Humanities Symposium.

Junior Science and Humanities Symposium
Academy of Applied Science
24 Warren Street
Concord, NH 03301-4048
603-228-4520
http://www.jshs.org

Learning for Life Exploring Program
Field Experience

Learning for Life's Exploring Program is a career exploration program that allows young people to work closely with community organizations to learn life skills and explore careers. Opportunities are available in Arts & Humanities, Aviation, Business, Communications, Engineering, Fire Service, Health, Law Enforcement, Law & Government, Science, Skilled Trades, and Social Services. Each program has five areas of emphasis: Career Opportunities, Service Learning, Leadership Experience, Life Skills, and Character Education.

To be eligible to participate in this program, you must have completed the eighth grade and be 14 years old *or* be 15 years of age but have not reached your 21st birthday. This program is open to both males and females.

To find a Learning for Life office in your area (there are more than 300 throughout the United States), contact the Learning for Life Exploring Program.

Learning for Life Exploring Program

1329 West Walnut Hill Lane
PO Box 152225
Irving, TX 75015-2225
972-580-2433
http://www.learningforlife.org/
exploring

Marine Science Institute

Camps

Students entering grades nine through 12 can participate in Project Discovery, a weeklong summer exploration program, where they receive the opportunity to study the San Francisco Bay. You will use scientific equipment to study fish, invertebrates, plankton, and water. You will also get a chance to kayak and spend a day aboard the institute's research vessel, the *R/V Robert G. Brownlee*. The cost for the commuter program is $599 (which includes lunch). Financial aid is available. (Note: The institute also offers programs for students in grades K–8.) Contact the institute for more information.

Marine Science Institute

500 Discovery Parkway
Redwood City, CA 94063-4715
650-364-2760
julie@sfbaymsi.org
http://sfbaymsi.org/marinecamp.html

Marine Technology Society (MTS) Summer Internship Program for High School Students

Employment and Internship Opportunities/Membership

High school students who are at least 16 years old and have a GPA of at least 3.5 can participate in a six-week summer internship (which is sponsored by the society's San Diego section). Participants receive "hands-on, science/technology experience, and build important scientific, technical, and employment skills under the direction of a workplace mentor." After they complete the program, they receive a stipend of $1,920.

Junior and high school students can become MTS Club Members for free; members at this level receive the *MTS Club Newsletter*. There are also membership categories for college students and anyone who is interested in marine technology.

Marine Technology Society

PO Box 371348
San Diego, CA 92137-1348
410-884-5330
http://www.mtsociety.org

Mars Student Imaging Project at Arizona State University

Field Experience

Students in grades five through college sophomore level can participate in the Mars Student Imaging Project. The program is operated by NASA and Arizona State University (ASU). Participants will have the "opportunity to work with scientists, mission planners, and educators on the THEMIS team at ASU's Mars Space Flight Facility, to image a site on Mars using the THEMIS visible wavelength camera onboard the *Mars Odyssey* spacecraft which is currently orbiting Mars every two hours." They learn on-site at the Mars Space Flight Facility in Tempe, Arizona, and via distance education. There is no charge to participate in the project, and students from across the United States can take part. Contact the project director for more information.

Mars Student Imaging Project
Mars Education Program
Mars Space Flight Facility
Arizona State University
Moeur Building, Room 131
PO Box 876305
Tempe, AZ 85287-6305
480-965-1788
msip@asu.edu
http://msip.asu.edu

National Ground Water Association
Membership
If you are interested in groundwater resources, you can become an associate member of the association; the cost is $105 a year. Members receive access to association publications and the opportunity to participate in interest groups and volunteer events.

National Ground Water Association
PO Box 73124
Cleveland, OH 44193-0002
800-551-7379
customerservice@ngwa.org
http://www.ngwa.org/membership/membership.aspx

National Oceanic and Atmospheric Administration
Employment and Internship Opportunities
The National Oceanic and Atmospheric Administration offers a variety of summer programs and paid internships for young people. Examples of opportunities for high school students include an employment and internship program for students with disabilities; an apprenticeship program in Florida that allows students to gain experience at the Atlantic Oceanographic and Meteorological Laboratory and Southeast Fisheries Science Center; and an engineering and science career orientation summer program for students in the Washington, D.C., area. Contact the administration for more information on these and other programs.

National Oceanic and Atmospheric Administration
1401 Constitution Avenue, NW, Room 5128
Washington, DC 20230-0001
http://www.oesd.noaa.gov/noaa_student_opps.html

National Park Service Student Educational Employment Program/Youth Programs/Volunteers-In-Parks
Employment and Internship Opportunities/Field Experience/Volunteer Programs
The federal government's Student Educational Employment Program is available to high school, college, and professional degree students. Participants are paid a salary and gain valuable work experience while attending school, which may lead to future employment with the National Park Service (NPS) or other federal agencies after graduation. Applicants must be U.S. citizens or residents of American Samoa or Swains Islands. For fur-

ther information, visit http://www.opm. gov/employ/students.

The NPS offers more than 25 programs for people between the ages of five and 24. The programs, such as the Youth Conservation Corps and Public Land Corps, will help educate you about the environment while you work with conservation workers to improve national parks. Visit the NPS Web site to learn about the wide range of programs that are available and to view photos of past projects.

You can also protect and preserve America's natural and cultural heritage by becoming a park volunteer. You might work as a volunteer at a visitor center in Acadia National Park or help out in the office at Big Cypress National Preserve, or perform a variety of other tasks. Visit the NPS Web site to search for volunteer opportunities by state and national park.

National Park Service
U.S. Department of the Interior
1849 C Street, NW
Washington, DC 20240-0001
202-208-3818
http://www.nps.gov/gettinginvolved

National Science Bowl for High School Students
Competitions
The National Science Bowl, which is sponsored by the U.S. Department of Energy, is an academic competition that tests your knowledge of all science and math fields. Teams of students are quizzed using a style that is similar to the television show *Jeopardy.* High school and middle school students may participate. Contact the U.S. Department of Energy

for more information about this annual competition.

U.S. Department of Energy
http://www.scied.science.doe.gov/ nsb

Natural Resources Conservation Service (NRCS) Earth Team Volunteers
Volunteer Programs
If you are at least 14 years of age, you can become an Earth Team Volunteer. Program participants help NRCS professionals conserve soil, water, and other natural resources. Contact the NRCS for more information.

Natural Resources Conservation Service
U.S. Department of Agriculture
5140 Park Avenue, Suite C
Des Moines, IA 50321-1280
888-526-3227
landcare@usda.gov
http://www.nrcs.usda.gov/feature/ volunteers

New Jersey Governor's School on the Environment
College Courses/Summer Study
The New Jersey Governor's School on the Environment is a summer program for gifted and talented rising high school seniors. To participate in this program, you should have an interest in environmental issues, but do not need to excel academically in the sciences. Guided by experienced faculty, you perform research activities on such topics as pollution and public health, pesticides, environmental law, and global

ecosystems. You will attend daily intensive courses on such topics as "pinelands ecology and policy, environmental protection and economic development, geographic information systems, community design, pollution and public health, the quality of urban life, air and water pollution, marine science, biodiversity, alternate energy sources, environmental ethics, and global environmental issues." You will also participate in integrative seminars and field experiences. There are also opportunities to watch and participate in performing arts events, and you experience campus life by living at Stockton State College. Admission to the Governor's School on the Environment is highly selective. You must first be recommended by your principal and/or guidance counselor, who consider GPA, test scores, curriculum, and extracurricular activities to determine whether you possess the established characteristics of the talented and gifted. Their recommendations along with essays you have written are then considered by county and state selection committees, which ultimately decide who will attend. This residential program is fully funded by the New Jersey Department of Education. In New Jersey, contact the Governor's School on the Environment or your principal or guidance counselor for further details. Outside New Jersey, contact your governor's office or state department of education to see if a similar program is available.

New Jersey Governor's School on the Environment
Richard Stockton College of
  New Jersey
PO Box 195

Pomona, NJ 08240-0195
609-652-4924
gschool@stockton.edu
http://intraweb.stockton.edu/eyos/
  page.cfm?siteID=102&pageID=2

Pre-College Programs at the University of California—Santa Barbara
College Courses/Summer Study

The University of California—Santa Barbara offers four programs for high school students who are interested in science and other fields: Early Start, Academic & Enrichment, Enrichment, and Research Mentorship.

In the Early Start Program, which lasts six weeks, students take two college-level courses to help them explore career options and prepare for college study. Students interested in science can take General Chemistry, General Chemistry Labs, Concepts of Biology, Human Development, Introduction to Environmental Studies, Oceanic and Atmospheric Processes, Geology & Environment, Principles of Physical Geology, Dinosaurs, Concepts of Biology, Biology of Cancer, Human Disease, and Statistics. Applicants must have completed the 10th, 11th, or 12th grades and have a GPA of at least 3.3 to be eligible for the program.

Students in the six-week Academic & Enrichment Program take one for-credit course and one noncredit, skills-based enrichment course. Applicants must have completed the 10th, 11th, or 12th grades and have a GPA of at least 3.15 to be eligible for the program. A typical 1+1 pairing for students interested in science might consist of Crime Scene Investigation (noncredit) and Introduction to Law and Society or Introduction to Archaeology (credit). Another option might consist of Aqualogy (noncredit) and Aquatic Science (credit).

Students in the Enrichment Program take one or more noncredit courses that meet two to four times a week for approximately 1.5 to two hours. Recent courses include Aqualogy, Forensics-CSI: Santa Barbara; and SAT or ACT Prep. Applicants must have completed the 10th, 11th, or 12th grades and have a GPA of at least 2.75 to be eligible for the program.

Students in the Research Mentorship Program take one laboratory course and one lecture course. They conduct research in a variety of topics including astronomy, biology, chemistry, ecology, environmental studies, geology, marine biology, marine ecology, mathematics, neuroscience, and physics and materials. Applicants must have completed the 10th, 11th, or 12th grades and have a GPA of at least 3.5 to be eligible for the program. Residential and commuter options are available.

Students in these programs live in Santa Cruz Residence Hall, which is located near the Pacific Ocean. The rooms feature high-speed Internet access. Other amenities in the residence halls and on-campus include a recreation center, a pool table, video games, a multi-station computer center, and laundry room. The cost for the Early Start, Academic & Enrichment, and Enrichment programs is approximately $6,770 (which includes tuition, housing, three daily meals, and extracurricular activities). Tuition for the Research Mentorship Program is $7,100 for residential students and $3,100 for commuter students. A nonrefundable application fee of $95 is also required for all programs.

University of California—Santa Barbara

c/o Summer Discovery
1326 Old Northern Boulevard
Roslyn, NY 11576-2244
805-893-2377
http://www.summer.ucsb.edu/
precollegeprograms.html

Science Olympiad
Competitions

The Science Olympiad is a national competition based in schools. School teams feed into regional and state tournaments, and the winners at the state level go on to the national competition. Some schools have many teams, all of which compete in their state Science Olympiad. Only one team per school, however, is allowed to represent its state at the national contest, and each state gets a slot. There are five divisions of Science Olympiad: Divisions A1, A2, and A3 for younger students, Division B for grades six through nine, and Division C for grades nine through 12. There is no national competition for Division A. Recent competition areas for Division C include Life, Personal, and Social Science; Earth and Space Science; Physical Science and Chemistry; Technology and Engineering; and Inquiry and Nature of Science.

A school team membership fee must be submitted with a completed membership form 30 days before your regional or state tournament. The fee entitles your school to a copy of the *Science Olympiad Coaches and Rules Manual* plus the eligibility to have up to 15 students at the first level of your state or regional contest. Fees vary from state to state. The National Science Olympiad is held in a different site every year, and your school team is fully responsible for transportation, lodging, and food.

Specific rules have been developed for each event and must be read carefully. There are numerous different events in each division. You and your teammates can choose the events you want to enter and prepare yourselves accordingly. Winners receive medals, trophies, and some scholarships.

For a list of all Science Olympiad state directors and a membership form, go to the Science Olympiad Web site. You can also write or call the national office for information.

Science Olympiad
National Office
Two Trans Am Plaza Drive, Suite 415
Oakbrook Terrace, IL 60181-4290
630-792-1251
http://www.soinc.org

Secondary School Program at Harvard University
College Courses/Summer Study

High school students who have completed their sophomore, junior, or senior years may apply to Harvard's Secondary School Program. The program is held for six weeks each summer, and participants earn college credit. Students who live on campus take either two four-credit courses or one eight-credit course for college credit. Commuting students may take two concurrent four-credit courses or one eight-credit course. Recent courses include Space Exploration and Astrobiology: Planets, Moons, Stars, and the Search for Life in the Cosmos; Fundamentals of Contemporary Astronomy: Stars, Galaxies, and the Universe; Introductory Biology; Principles of Biochemistry; Principles and Techniques of Molecular Biology; Principles of Genetics; Marine Life and Ecosystems of the Sea; General Chemistry; Organic Chemistry; Global Climate Change: The Science, Social Impact, and Diplomacy of a World Environmental Crisis; Precalculus Mathematics; Calculus; Principles of Physics; and several foreign languages. In addition to academics, students can participate in extracurricular activities such as intramural sports, a trivia bowl, a talent show, and dances. Tuition for the program ranges from $2,475 (per four-unit course) to $4,950 (per eight-unit course). A nonrefundable registration fee ($50), health insurance ($165), and room and board ($4,250) are extra. Contact the program for more information.

In addition to the aforementioned on-site offerings, Harvard also offers selected online classes to students who can't attend classes on campus.

Secondary School Program
Harvard University
51 Brattle Street
Cambridge, MA 02138-3722
617-495-4024
summer@dcemail.harvard.edu
http://www.summer.harvard.edu/

Secondary School Training Program/Life Science Summer Program at the University of Iowa
College Courses/Summer Study

The University of Iowa offers two interesting youth programs for those who are interested in science: the Secondary School Training Program and the Life Science Summer Program.

Those who have completed grade 10 or 11 can apply to the Secondary School Training Program (SSTP). The program allows students to explore a particular area of science, such as biochemistry, biology, chemistry, computer science, hydro science, microbiology, and physics and astronomy, while conducting scientific research. Participants work with university faculty in one of the many laboratories on campus, studying and conducting research projects for approximately 40 hours per week. At the end of the program, which usually runs from late June to early August, you present your project to a formal gathering of faculty, staff, and fellow SSTP participants. Throughout the program you also take part in various seminars on career choices and the scientific profession, and a variety of recreational activities designed especially for SSTP participants. Students live in University of Iowa dormitories and use many of the facilities on campus. The admissions process is highly competitive and is based on an essay, transcript, and recommendations. Those who complete the program have the option of receiving college credit from the University of Iowa. Applications are due in March, and applicants will be notified of the decisions by mid-May. Tuition fees, room, and board generally total around $2,360; spending money and transportation to and from the university are not included. Financial aid is available. For an application form, financial aid information, and to discuss possible research projects, contact the Secondary Student Training Program.

Rising high school freshmen and sophomores who are interested in biology can participate in the Life Science Summer Program. The program, which is sponsored by The Center for Diversity & Enrichment (CDE), is held for two weeks each July. Applicants must demonstrate aptitude and interest for biology. In the program, you will "participate in hands-on laboratory training and classroom instruction covering a wide range of topics in the area of developmental biology." Participants live on campus in air-conditioned residence halls. The cost for the program is $25 plus transportation costs to and from the university. Contact the CDE for more information about the program.

Secondary School Training Program
Attn: Will Swain
University of Iowa
E203 Seashore Hall
Iowa City, IA 52242-0001
319-335-3876
william-swain@uiowa.edu
http://www.continuetolearn.uiowa.
  edu/SSTP

Life Science Summer Program
University of Iowa
The Center for Diversity &
  Enrichment
24 Phillips Hall
Iowa City, IA 52242-1323
319-335-3555
cde@uiowa.edu
http://cde.uiowa.edu/index.php/
  life-science-summer-program.html

SkillsUSA

Competitions

SkillsUSA offers "local, state and national competitions in which students demonstrate occupational and leadership skills." Students who participate in its SkillsUSA Championships can compete in categories such as Community Service, Crime Scene Investigation, Extemporaneous Speaking, and Job Interview. SkillsUSA works directly with high schools and colleges, so ask your counselor or teacher if it is an option for you. Visit the SkillsUSA Web site for more information.

SkillsUSA
14001 SkillsUSA Way
Leesburg, VA 20176-5494
703-777-8810
http://www.skillsusa.org

Summer @ Brown at Brown University

College Courses/Summer Study

High school students in the Pre-College Courses Program at Brown can take one or more interesting college-level courses. Classes, which last anywhere from one to four weeks, are held Monday through Friday. More than 200 classes are available—some are available for credit. Students spend three hours a day in class, and the remaining time studying, interacting with professors and fellow students, and participating in cultural and social activities. A wealth of fascinating courses have been offered in recent years, including Introduction to Stem Cells and Tissue Engineering; Techniques in DNA-Based Biotechnology; Introduction to Bio-Medical Science: Cells, Tissues and Organs; Fundamentals for Calculus: Functions and Equations; Research Techniques in Biomedical Fields; Stem Cells, Cloning, Regenerative Medicine: Changing the Face of Biology; True-Life Forensic Investigation: How to Solve a Crime; Introduction to Biochemistry; Genetics and Human Behavior; Techniques in DNA-Based Biotechnology; Exploring the Interface of Nanotechnology and Biology; Nature vs. Nurture: Genes and Environment in Human Biology; and Exploring the Planets. There are also classes that will help students develop their communication or study skills or better prepare for the college admissions process including Cracking the AP Code (one week); Putting Ideas Into Words (one week); Persuasive Communication (one week); Writing the Academic Essay (three weeks); and Writing the College Admissions Essay (one week). Program participants live in residence halls that are within walking distance of classes and other activities. Students who are interested in taking Pre-College Courses must have intellectual curiosity, be emotionally mature, and have strong academic records. The following tuition rates are charged for Pre-College Courses: one week residential ($2,153), one week commuter ($1,652); two week residential ($3,265), two week commuter ($2,255); three week residential ($4,702), three week commuter ($3,200); four week residential ($5,454), four week commuter ($3,449). Housing and meals are included in the residential tuition. A limited amount of financial aid is available.

Rising high school seniors can take a variety of for-credit classes in the Summer Session Credit Program, including Basic Physics; Introductory Calculus; and The

Brain: An Introduction to Neuroscience. Each class last seven weeks. Commuter and residential options are available; students who choose the residential option must take two courses. The cost for one course for commuter students is about $3,200 and $5,990 for two classes. Tuition for residential students is about $9,200.

Contact the Office of Summer & Continuing Studies for more information on these programs.

Office of Summer & Continuing Studies

Brown University
42 Charlesfield Street, Box T
Providence, RI 02912-9063
401-863-7900
http://brown.edu/scs/pre-college/
pre-college-courses.php

Summer @ Georgetown University for High School Students

College Courses/Summer Study

Academically gifted high school students can earn up to 12 college credits by participating in Georgetown University's Summer College. Rising sophomores, juniors, and seniors may apply. More than 100 courses are available, including Introductory Biology, General Chemistry Lecture, General Chemistry Lab, Introduction to Computer Science, Basic Physics, Pre-Calculus, Principles of Physics Lab, Principles of Physics Lecture, Public Speaking, Statistics With Exploratory Data Analysis, and foreign languages (Arabic, Chinese, French, German, Italian, Japanese, Persian, Spanish).

Tuition for the program is $1,018 per credit hour. Other costs include a pre-college fee ($398 per session), room ($782),

and a meal plan ($864). Financial aid is available for "exceptional" students who can demonstrate financial need.

A one-week Environmental Science Workshop is also available. The cost is $1,800 for students who live on campus and $1,575 for commuter students.

Students who live on campus stay in air-conditioned residence halls. Access to laundry facilities is provided. In their off hours, students can attend dances, movie nights, ice cream socials, and other activities, as well as explore the campus and the Washington, D.C., area. Contact the university for more information.

Summer Programs for High School Students

Georgetown University
Box 571006
Washington, DC 20057-1006
202-687-8700
scsspecialprograms@georgetown.edu
http://www12.georgetown.edu/scs/
degrees-and-programs/summer-and-special-programs.cfm

Summer College for High School Students at Syracuse University

College Courses/Summer Study

Students who have completed their sophomore, junior, or senior year of high school are eligible to apply to the Summer College for High School Students at Syracuse University, which runs for six weeks from early July to mid-August. Commuter and residential options are available. The program has several aims: to introduce students to the many possible majors and study areas within their interest area; to help them match their aptitudes with possible careers; and to prepare them for college, both academically and socially. Students attend classes, listen to lectures, and take field trips to destinations that are related to their specific area of interest. All students are required to take two for-credit courses during the program, and they receive college credit if they successfully complete the courses.

There are eight programs available, including one in Forensic Science. Students learn about the field via classes, guest speakers, and participation as a member of a forensic science team that gathers evidence at a simulated crime scene. Topics covered include "blood analysis, organic and inorganic evidence analysis, microscopic investigations, hair analysis, DNA, forensic psychology, drug chemistry and toxicology, fiber comparisons, paints, glass compositions and fragmentation, fingerprints, soil comparisons, and arson investigations, among others."

Admission is competitive and is based on recommendations, test scores, and transcripts. The total cost of the residential program is about $6,995; the commuter option costs about $4,995. Some scholarships are available. The application deadline is in mid-May, or mid-April for those seeking financial aid. For further information, contact the Summer College.

Syracuse University
Summer College for High School
  Students
700 University Avenue
Syracuse, NY 13244-2530
315-443-5000
sumcoll@syr.edu
http://summercollege.syr.edu

Summer Program for High School Students at Columbia University
College Courses/Summer Study

Rising ninth through 12th graders can participate in Columbia University's weeklong Summer Program for High School Students. More than 65 classes are available. Recent Junior-Senior Division Courses include Biomedical Engineering: Physical Effects on Cells, Explorations in Genetics and Molecular Biology, Intensive Seminars in Modern Chemistry, Investigations in Theoretical and Experimental Physics, Issues in Biological Conservation, Survey of Modern Mathematics, and Issues in Biological Conservation. A course on college preparation is also available. All courses are rigorous, but are unavailable for college credit. During the week, students take classes from 10:00 A.M. to 12:00 P.M.; break for lunch and activities from 12:00 to 2:30 P.M.; and return to class from 2:30 to 4:30 P.M. In the evenings and on weekends, residential students participate in a wide variety of extracurricular activities, including on-campus events (such as parties, a talent show, a scavenger hunt, an open mic night, and organized sports) and off-campus excursions in and around New York City (such as guided walking tours, films, and trips to museums, concerts, restaurants, beaches, and amusement parks). Participants also have access to university libraries, computer labs, a fitness center, a student activity center, and other facilities. Commuter students pay approximately $3,400 per session. Residential students pay $6,225, which includes housing and dining. All students pay an additional fee of $135 for activities and health coverage. The university also suggests that residential students bring an additional $700 in spending money.

Additionally, study abroad programs are available in Barcelona, Spain, and the Middle East. Contact the School of Continuing Education for more information.

Columbia University
Summer Program for High School Students
School of Continuing Education
203 Lewisohn Hall
2970 Broadway, Mail Code 4119
New York, NY 10027-6902
212-854-9666
http://www.ce.columbia.edu/hs

Summer Program for High School Students at New York University
College Courses/Summer Study
Rising high school juniors and seniors in the New York City-area can participate in the university's Summer Program for High School Students. During this commuter program, students take one or two courses for college credit (for up to eight credits) and get a feel for college life. (A noncredit writing workshop is also available.) Some of the classes that were recently offered include Human Evolution, Human Physiology, Living Environment, Introduction to Computers and Programming, Calculus I, Linear Algebra, Food Microbiology, and various foreign languages. Students are not allowed to live on campus, and must find living arrangements within commuting distance of the campus. Tuition varies by class credit amount and subject area. The application deadline is typically in mid-April. Financial aid is available. Contact the Office of Undergraduate Admissions for more information.

Summer Program for High School Students
New York University
Office of Undergraduate Admissions
22 Washington Square North
New York, NY 10011-9191
212-998-4500
http://www.nyu.edu/summer/2009/highschool/program.html

Summer Programs for Youth at Southern Methodist University
College Courses/Summer Study
Southern Methodist University (SMU) offers several opportunities for high school students.

Gifted and highly motivated high school students who have completed the 10th or 11th grades can participate in the College Experience Program. This five-week residential program allows students to experience college-level instruction and earn up to six college credits. Students take two courses (such as Pre-Calculus Mathematics or Calculus With Analytical Geometry) from the SMU summer school schedule. Applicants must submit an academic transcript, recommendations, an essay, and PSAT, SAT, or ACT scores. Tuition for the program is approximately $2,470. An additional $1,600 for room and board and a nonrefundable registration fee of $35 are also required.

There are also several other programs for high school students, including the Summer Youth Program (for students ages five through 18); Girls Talk Back:

Making Yourself Heard; Summer Sports Camps; Engineering Camp for Girls; Academic-Skills Enhancement Workshops; and Visioneering (an engineering exploration program that is held each spring). Contact the university for more information.

Southern Methodist University
College Experience Program
PO Box 750383
Dallas, TX 75275-0383
214-768-0123
gifted@smu.edu
http://www.smu.edu/continuing_
education/youth

Summer Scholars Institute at Pace University
College Courses/Summer Study
Rising high school juniors and seniors can participate in Pace University's Summer Scholars Institute, a two-week program that allows them to take college-level courses and get a taste of college life. Each major features two classes—one in the morning, and one in the afternoon. In the evenings, students participate in activities that help them learn how to write better college essays and applications, as well as explore the culture of New York City. Two recent majors of interest to readers of this book were forensic science, and biology and biological sciences. Forensic science featured the following classes: Skeleton Keys: Unlocking the Secrets of the Dead, and Crime Solvers: A Look Inside a Real Forensic Laboratory. Students who majored in biology and biological sciences took International Public Health,

and Demystifying the Science of Toxicology. The cost of the program is $1,000 for commuters (which includes one meal a day and social events) and $2,000 for residents (which includes room, two meals a day, and social events). Financial aid is available. Applications are typically due in mid-June.

Pace University
Summer Scholars Institute
Attn: Program Coordinator
Pforzheimer Honors College
W207E Pace Plaza
New York, NY 10038-1598
212-346-1192
summerscholar@pace.edu
http://www.pace.edu/page.cfm?doc_
id=17156

Summer Scholars Program at the University of Notre Dame
College Courses/Summer Study
The Summer Scholars Program consists of nearly 15 two-week classes for rising high school juniors and seniors. One interesting class is Life Sciences, in which participants study two major subareas in this discipline: Ecology and Environmental Science and the Molecular Genetics of Disease. Students participate in interactive lectures, collaborative learning, laboratory work, group discussions, and field trips to nature areas and science-related museums in Chicago. The application deadline for the program is typically in early March. Tuition for this mandatory residential program is $2,500 (which includes room/board and meals), plus a $45 application fee

and a $150 lab fee. A limited amount of financial aid is available. Contact the Office of Pre-College Programs for more information.

University of Notre Dame
Office of Pre-College Programs
202 Brownson Hall
Notre Dame, IN 46556-5601
574-631-0990
precoll@nd.edu
http://precollege.nd.edu/
   summer-scholars

Summer Science Program
College Courses/Summer Study
High school juniors who excel in math and science can participate in the Summer Science Program, a six-week residential program in which they complete a "challenging, hands-on research project in celestial mechanics." (Note: A very small number of high-achieving sophomores are also accepted to the program.) Participants study college-level astronomy, calculus, physics, and programming during the day. At night, they work in teams to "take a series of telescopic observations of a near-earth asteroid, and write software to convert those observations into a prediction of the asteroid's orbit around the sun." Guest speakers and field trips (Very Large Array, Sunspot/Apache Point Observatory, NASA Jet Propulsion Laboratory, and Mt. Wilson Observatory) also provide participants with knowledge about these fields. In addition to study six days a week, students also participate in recreational excursions, talent shows, sports, and games. The program is held on two campuses: New Mexico Institute of Mining and Technology in Socorro, and Besant Hill School in Ojai, California. Participants stay in campus residence halls. Applications are typically due in March. Tuition for the program is $3,750, which covers room and board, local transportation, and supplies. One-third of participants receive financial aid, which averages $3,000 per individual. Contact the program for more information.

Summer Science Program
108 Whiteberry Drive
Cary, NC 27519-5135
866-728-0999
info@summerscience.org
http://www.summerscience.org

Summer Seminars/Summer Science Camp for High School Women at the University of Southern California
College Courses/Summer Study
Rising high school sophomores, juniors, and seniors who are interested in science and other subjects can get a taste of college life by participating in four-week Summer Seminars at the University of Southern California. Commuter and residential options are available. Recent seminars include BodyWorks: Human Physiology in Health & Disease; The Brain: Cognition, Creativity and Cerebral Function; and Discovering Engineering. A typical schedule involves lectures from 9:00 A.M. to 12:00 P.M., a break for lunch, a workshop from

1:30 to 4:30 P.M., a study session from 4:00 to 6:00 P.M., dinner, and free time in the evening. In addition to classes, workshops, and studying, students participate in a variety of recreational activities (dancing, karaoke, a movie night) and field trips (the Hollywood Walk of Fame, a youth symphony concert, Disneyland, Knott's Berry Farm, the J. Paul Getty Museum, the Santa Monica Pier, a Dodgers baseball game, or a visit to the beach). Participants who choose the residential option stay in dormitories on campus that have a common hallway with bathroom and showers. Each room has analog phone ports, Ethernet ports, a Microfridge (a half-sized refrigerator with attached microwave), and cable TV hookup. Students must bring their own telephones, televisions, cables for Internet hookup, linens, and toiletry items. The cost of attendance for residential students is about $6,105 (and includes room and board and lab, program, and health center fees). The cost of attendance for commuter students is about $4,300 (and includes a meal plan and lab, program, and health center fees). Financial aid is available. The application deadline is typically in late March.

Female high school students who are entering grades nine through 11 who are interested in marine biology and oceanography can participate in the one-week Summer Science Camp for High School Women. This residential camp is held on Catalina Island. Participants explore ecological and biological principles through field and laboratory research, educational simulations, and self-guided experiments. Educational activities/topics include algae pressing, astronomy, biodiversity, botany, data collection, environmental physiology, fish printing, fish surveys, geology of Catalina group science projects, journaling, kelp forest ecology, natural communities, nature printing, and plankton tows. In addition to educational activities, campers also have the opportunity to participate in recreational activities such as arts and crafts, relaxation on the beach, games, hiking, kayaking, snorkeling, swimming, and volleyball. Tuition is $1,800 and includes room, board, and transportation to and from the University of Southern California and Catalina Island.

University of Southern California
Continuing Education and
   Summer Programs
3415 South Figueroa Street,
   Suite 107
Los Angeles, CA 90089-0874
213-740-5679
summer@usc.edu
http://cesp.usc.edu

Summer Studies at the University of Richmond
College Courses/Summer Study
The University of Richmond offers several exploration programs for high school students, including the Summer Scholars Program. The Summer Scholars Program seeks to provide high school students with a "realistic, first-hand experience of college including the challenges and rewards that come with it, all

while experiencing 'life on campus.'" Rising juniors and seniors are eligible to participate in this three-week, for-credit residential program. Approximately five courses are offered each summer. One recent course of interest was Biogenetics and Contemporary Issues in Biology, in which students learned about "microbiology, genetics, gene transfer, gene therapy, cloning, stem cell research, pathogenesis, genetically modified organisms, and the transfer of antibiotic resistance" via hands-on research, lectures, and other activities. Applicants must have a competitive grade point average and enjoy intellectual stimulation and academic challenges. Program participants stay in air-conditioned residence halls and have access to study lounges, vending machines, and laundry facilities. The cost of the program is $4,200 (which includes tuition, textbooks and classroom supplies, residence hall lodging, a meal plan, and extracurricular activities). Financial assistance is available. Students also can use on-campus facilities such as the library, computer labs, and a sports center. The application deadline is typically in early May. Contact the director of summer programs for more information.

University of Richmond
School of Continuing Studies
Director of Summer Programs
28 Westhampton Way
Richmond, VA 23173-0001
804-289-8133
http://summer.richmond.edu/
scholars

Summer Study at Pennsylvania State University
College Courses/Summer Study
Students who have completed the ninth, 10th, and 11th grades can apply to participate in the university's Summer Enrichment Program. The program offers three-and-a-half week and two-week options and recently featured classes in a variety of subject areas including algebra, calculus, community service workshop, forensic science, Kaplan SAT or ACT prep course, pre-calculus, study skills, and TOEFL Prep by Kaplan.

There is also a six-and-a-half-week for-credit program that features more than 75 college credit courses and more than 25 noncredit enrichment classes. Rising high school juniors and seniors and recent graduates may apply. Recent for-credit courses include Astronomical Universe; Basic Writing Skills; College: Algebra I; General View of Mathematics; Finite Mathematics; Genetics, Ecology, and Evolution; Human Body: Form and Function; Introductory Biological Anthropology; Introductory Meteorology; and Statistical Concepts & Reasoning. Noncredit courses include CSI: Penn State-Forensic Science; Don't Be Irrational: Pre-Calculus; The Hills Are Alive: Environmental Studies; Test Tube Tactics: Chemistry; What's Your Function?: Calculus; and You Can Count On Me: Algebra.

Tuition for the Summer Enrichment Program is approximately $6,995 for the six-and-a-half-week program; $4,495 for the three-and-a-half-week program; and $2,495 for the two-week program. Limited financial aid is available. Contact the Summer Study Program for more information.

Summer Study Program
The Pennsylvania State University
900 Walt Whitman Road
Melville, NY 11747-2293
800-666-2556
info@summerstudy.com
http://www.summerstudy.com/
 pennstate

Summer Term/Young Scholars Program at the University of Maryland

College Courses/Summer Study

Rising high school juniors and seniors with a GPA of at least 3.0 may take one or more classes for credit in the University of Maryland's Summer Term program. Two six-week sessions and four three-week sessions are available. College credit is awarded to students who satisfactorily complete coursework. Recent classes include Introduction to Astronomy, Biochemistry, The World of Biology, Principles of Biology, Chemistry I: Fundamentals of General Chemistry, Elementary Mathematical Models, and various foreign languages. Participants live in residence halls at the University of Maryland and take their meals on campus or in selected College Park restaurants. A commuter option is also available. Contact the Office of Extended Studies for information on current tuition costs and application deadlines.

Students in the Young Scholars Program spend three weeks in July exploring various fields and taking a college-level course. College credit is awarded to those who satisfactorily complete the class. Past courses include Environmental Biology, Environmental Geology, and Biopharmaceutical Production. Program participants commute or live in the residence halls at the University of Maryland and take their meals on campus or in selected College Park restaurants. To apply, you must be a rising high school junior or senior and submit an application form, an essay, two letters of recommendation, a current transcript, and an application and enrollment fee of $205 by mid-May. Admissions decisions are based primarily on the recommendations, the applicant's academic record (they must have a GPA of 3.0 or higher), and overall academic ability. Residential tuition for the program is about $2,935; tuition for commuters is approximately $1,815. For further details and an application form, contact the Office of Extended Studies.

Office of Extended Studies
University of Maryland
0132 Main Administration Building
College Park, MD 20742-5000
301-405-7762
http://www.summer.umd.edu

Summer University at Johns Hopkins University

College Courses/Summer Study

Rising high school juniors and seniors and recent graduates can participate in the Summer University program. Participants live on Hopkins' Homewood campus for five weeks beginning in early

July. Classes leading to college credit are available in more than 30 areas. Past courses include Introduction to Biological Molecules, Introductory Chemistry, Introductory Chemistry Laboratory, Introduction to Public Health and Biomedical Informatics, Our Changing Planet, An Introduction to Neuroscience, Subatomic World, Stars & the Universe, Statistical Analysis, Discrete Mathematics, Introduction to Biostatistics, Introduction to Calculus, Oral Presentations, Technical Communication, and foreign language (Arabic, French, German, and Spanish) courses. Students who live in the greater Baltimore area have the option of commuting. Applicants must submit an application form, essay, transcript, two recommendations, and a nonrefundable application fee (rates vary by date of submission). Tuition for residential students is $6,300 (for two courses, room and board, and up to six credits). Commuter students pay $630 per credit hour (books, supplies, meals, and special activities are not included in this price). Applicants must have at least a 3.0 GPA (on a 4.0 scale). Contact the Office of Summer Programs for more information.

Johns Hopkins University
Pre-College Program
Office of Summer Programs
3400 North Charles Street
Shaffer Hall, Suite 203
Baltimore, MD 21218-2685
800-548-0548
summer@jhu.edu
http://www.jhu.edu/~sumprog

Summer Youth Explorations at Michigan Technological University
College Courses/Summer Study

Michigan Technological University (MTU) offers the Summer Youth Explorations program for students in grades six through 12. Participants attend one of five weeklong sessions, choosing either to commute or to live on campus. Students undertake an Exploration in one of many career fields through laboratory work, field trips, and discussions with MTU faculty and other professionals. Some recent Explorations include Aquatic Ecology, Aquatic Ecology: Field Study at Gratiot Lake, Wolf Ecology, Astronomy, Forensic Science and CSI, Clinical Laboratory Science, Space Science: Rocketry, Genetic Engineering and Biotechnology, Wide World of Chemistry, and Learning to Lead: A Leadership Introduction for Everyone. The cost of the Summer Youth Program is $650 for the residential option, $395 for commuters. Applications are accepted up to one week before the Exploration begins.

Summer Youth Explorations
Michigan Technological University
Youth Programs Office,
   Alumni House
1400 Townsend Drive
Houghton, MI 49931-1295
906-487-2219
http://youthprograms.mtu.edu/syp

U.S. Fish and Wildlife Service
Volunteer Programs

Volunteers of all ages are welcomed by the U.S. Fish & Wildlife Service. Volunteers may be tasked with conducting wildlife population surveys, leading tours, helping with laboratory work, banding ducks at a National Wildlife Refuge, restoring wildlife habitat, performing clerical tasks, and photographing natural and cultural resources. Contact the U.S. Fish & Wildlife Service for more information.

U.S. Fish and Wildlife Service

U.S. Department of the Interior
Division of Human Resources
4401 North Fairfax Drive, Room 634
Arlington, VA 22203-1610
800-344-9453
http://www.fws.gov/volunteers
http://volunteer.gov/gov

Yosemite Institute
Camps/Field Experience

The Yosemite Institute, established in 1971, works in cooperation with the National Park Service to offer several programs for youth. Overnight Wilderness Backpacking Trips consist of one- to three-night camping adventures that encourage young people to "appropriately challenge themselves while exploring the wilderness and practicing Leave No Trace ethics." Led by professional naturalist guides, you explore Yosemite's high peaks, deep canyons, alpine lakes, and other features rarely seen by other visitors. You learn about the area's abundant wildlife and unique cultural and natural history while hiking four to six miles per day at elevations of 6,000–10,000 feet. Only 12 participants are accepted for each Overnight Wilderness Backpacking Trip. The program fee

includes meals and group overnight gear (tents, cooking pots, etc.). You must provide your own personal gear, however, including sleeping bag, water bottle, and utensils.

Teens who participate in the institute's two-week Field Research Course can earn college credit by creating their own ecology research project. You will learn "wilderness survival and backpacking skills; Sierra Nevada natural history and ecology; how to record field observations and identify patterns; how to generate answerable questions and hypotheses; how to collect data that will answer your question; and how to analyze and present your data to other scientists." To participate, you must be at least 16 years old and have completed at least one year of high school biology. The cost of the program is $1,900 for California residents and $2,400 for out-of-state participants. Participants will receive three college credits when they complete the program.

Additionally, young women between the ages of 15 and 18 can participate in the Armstrong Scholars Program, which "seeks to inspire young women to reach their highest potential and develop a stronger sense of self and community and a stronger connection to nature." The nine-day program costs $150 (the remaining costs are covered by a scholarship).

The Yosemite Institute also offers environmental workshops for teachers, and various programs throughout the year. Contact the institute for further information and for details on available scholarship funds.

Yosemite Institute

Yosemite Backcountry Adventure
PO Box 487
Yosemite, CA 95389-0487
209-379-9511
http://www.yni.org/yi

Zoological Association of America

Membership

The association "promotes conservation, preservation, and propagation of animals in both private and public domains." It offers a membership category for those who support its goals. The membership fee is $40. Members receive access to the members-only section of the association's Web site.

Zoological Association of America

PO Box 511275
Punta Gorda, FL 33951-1275
813-449-4356
info@zaa.org
http://www.zaa.org

Read a Book

When it comes to finding out about science, don't overlook a book. (You're reading one now, after all.) What follows is a short, annotated list of books and periodicals related to science. The books range from fiction and personal accounts to biographies of the greats and career-oriented publications. Don't be afraid to check out the professional journals, either. The technical stuff may be way above your head right now, but if you take the time to become familiar with one or two, you're bound to pick up some of what is important to science professionals, not to mention begin to feel like a part of their world, which is what you're interested in, right?

We've tried to include recent materials as well as old favorites. Always check for the most recent editions, and, if you find an author you like, ask your librarian to help you find more. Keep reading good books!

❏ BOOKS

Ahrens, C. Donald. *Meteorology Today: An Introduction to Weather, Climate, and the Environment.* 8th ed. Florence, K.Y.: Brooks Cole, 2006. Ahrens provides an interesting and introspective look into the study of meteorology, incorporating stories, interviews, and other learning tools to keep readers engaged and up to speed. Each chapter includes discussion ideas, review points, and exercises to encourage student understanding.

Barnes-Svarney, Patricia L., and Michael R. Porcellino. *Through the Telescope: A Guide for the Amateur Astronomer.* 2d ed. New York: McGraw-Hill, 1999. This award-winning book originally written by Porcellino and most recently updated by Barnes-Svarney provides and up-to-date guide on exploring the solar system from your backyard. Authors give tips on spotting all types of sky wonders, such as comets, star clusters, supernovas, and asteroids. The book also includes lists of Web sites for exploration and more.

Barr, Nevada. *Endangered Species.* Reprint ed. New York: Berkley Books, 2008. This is one in a series of ecological mysteries featuring Anna Pigeon, park ranger. In the Cumberland Island National Seashore in Georgia, in a world of loggerhead turtles and wild ponies, Anna finds herself embroiled in a plot involving espionage, airplane crashes, eccentric islanders, and many twists and turns of plot before she can unravel the mystery.

Bertino, Anthony J. *Forensic Science: Fundamentals and Investigations.* Florence, Ky.: South-Western Educational Publishing, 2008. Written by a 40-year science expert and educator, Bertino shares his knowledge of forensic science in this guide for early explorers. Includes hands-on activities to apply lessons in a fun and interactive manner.

Bortz, Fred. *Beyond Jupiter: The Story of Planetary Astronomer Heidi Hammel.* Washington, D.C.: J. Henry Press, 2006. This series of books is perfect for the young space explorer, delving into the lives of inspiring scientists. This book details Heidi Hammel's life, from her down-to-earth upbringing to her famous studies of Neptune and Uranus. *Beyond Jupiter* also includes full color photos of Hammel from her own personal photo collection.

Brown, Theodore E., H. Eugene LeMay, Bruce E. Bursten, and Catherine Murphy. *Chemistry: The Central Science.* 11th ed. Upper Saddle River, N.J.: Prentice Hall, 2008. Heralded as the expert resource on chemistry, this text makes a complicated subject into a more manageable read.

Camenson, Blythe. *Opportunities in Forensic Science Careers.* 2d ed. New York: McGraw-Hill, 2008. Guide includes tips on breaking into forensic science, detailing different careers in the field, salary statistics, and online resources for more information.

Chartrand, Mark. *The Night Sky: A Guide To Field Identification.* New York: St. Martin's Press, 2001. This book, perfect for the casual stargazer or aspiring astronomer, covers the range of constellations visible far and wide, from those large enough to be spotted with the naked eye, to those requiring binoculars or a home telescope. Special section includes eclipse schedules and tips for safe viewing.

Cobb, Cathy, and Monty L. Fetterolf. *The Joy of Chemistry: The Amazing Science of Familiar Things.* Amherst, N.Y.: Prometheus Books, 2005. This guide is a good crash course on all areas of chemistry, including general, organic, inorganic, analytical, forensic, and biochemistry. Wide scope also includes hands-on experiments at the start of each chapter using ingredients found in the home. Also includes a separate lab section.

Crane, Kathleen. *Sea Legs: Tales of a Woman Oceanographer.* New York: Basic Books, 2004. An informative and inspiring autobiography from a pioneer in the study of underwater volcanic activity. Crane details the wonders of the sea and the challenges of being a women in a male-dominated field.

DeGalan, Julie. *Great Jobs for Environmental Studies Majors.* 2d ed. New York: McGraw-Hill, 2008. This book will help environmental science majors develop winning job-search strategies and explore career options in the field.

Easton, Thomas. *Careers in Science.* 4th ed. New York: McGraw-Hill, 2004. This book covers a wide range of jobs in the sciences and includes details on educational and certification requirements needed for the most common jobs. From education to government to the life and social sciences, the author covers the hot jobs in each wide-ranging field. The book also includes a chapter on job search tips and tricks for launching your science career.

Funkhouser, John. *Forensic Science for High School Students.* Dubuque, Iowa: Kendall Hunt Publishing Company, 2005. This introduction to the forensic sciences includes details on career options, lab exercises for hands-on learning, and lists of resources for more exploration.

Goldstein, Mel. *The Complete Idiot's Guide to Weather.* New York: Alpha Books, 2002. Another easy-to-read introduction from the Idiot's line of books, this guide is a great read for anyone interested in meteorology. It covers basics on the origins of wind, rain, storms and hot topics such as global warming, air pollution, and more.

Guch, Ian. *The Complete Idiot's Guide to Chemistry.* 2d ed. New York: Alpha Books, 2006. Written for high school and college students looking to brush up on their chemistry basics, this guide is a good primer and complement to any chemistry text. It includes practice problems and even some humor to make chemistry less threatening and more enjoyable.

Harrington, Philip S. *Star Ware: The Amateur Astronomer's Ultimate Guide to Choosing, Buying, & Using Telescopes and Accessories.* 4th ed. Hoboken, N.J.: Wiley, 2007. This book includes reviews and ratings on all makes and models of stargazing equipment, from telescopes to cameras, from lenses to star charts. Harrington also breaks down what is essential and what are "add-ons" for the amateur astronomer and details how to best maintain this specialized equipment so that it lasts for years of enjoyment.

Heitzman, Ray. *Opportunities in Marine Science and Maritime Careers.* Rev. ed. New York: McGraw-Hill, 2006. This book provides an overview of educational requirements, earnings, and career options for a variety of marine science and maritime careers.

Hunter, Malcolm L., David Lindenmayer, and Aram Calhoun. *Saving the Earth as a Career: Advice on Becoming a Conservation Professional.* Hoboken, N.J.: Wiley-Blackwell, 2007. Professionals provide advice on choosing and landing a career in conservation biology.

James, Stuart H., and Jon J. Nordby. *Forensic Science: An Introduction to Scientific and Investigative Techniques.* 3d ed. Boca Raton, Fla.: CRC Press, 2009. This book covers a wide range of topics in forensic science and gives insight into new developments in the field, such as the increased use of technology in forensics, including specialized photography, DNA analysis, and forensic pathology.

Kaplan, Eugene H. *Sensuous Seas: Tales of a Marine Biologist.* Princeton, N.J.: Princeton University Press, 2006. These wonderful essays by a Hofstra University educator serve as an excellent introduction to the beauty, mysteries, and science of the sea. Highly recommended for aspiring marine biologists.

Klass, David. *California Blue.* New York: Scholastic Paperbacks, 1996. When 17-year-old John Rodgers discovers a new subspecies of butterfly that may necessitate closing the lumber mill where his dying father works, he and his father find themselves on opposite sides of the environmental conflict. A gripping novel that brings to life the heated emotions on both sides of an environmental issue.

Lowman, Margaret D., Edward Burgess, and James Burgess. *It's A Jungle Up There: More Tales from the Treetops.* New Haven, Conn.: Yale University Press, 2008. A rainforest biologist, nicknamed "Canopy Meg" because she often climbs to the top of the rainforest to conduct research, details the rewards of working in rainforests in Peru, India, and Samoa alongside her sons. (Note: For more information on Canopy Meg, visit http://www.canopymeg.com.)

Lutgens, Frederick K. *The Atmosphere: An Introduction to Meteorology.* 10th ed. Upper Saddle River, N.J.: Prentice Hall, 2006. Lutgens includes introductory and specialized material in this comprehensive look at the study of the world's atmosphere. Hot topics include an in-depth look into Florida's hurricane season, the causes and concerns of the ozone depletion, the science behind thunderstorms and lightning, and more.

Mackay, Richard. *The Atlas of Endangered Species.* Berkeley, Calif.: University of California Press, 2008. This illustrated guide to the world's endangered species provides an overview of the major threats to biodiversity (loss of habitat, war, hunting, global warming) and the steps conservation scientists are taking to slow the destruction of wildlife.

McIvor, Don. *Curiosity's Destinations: Tales & Insights from the Life of a Geologist.* Greenwich, Conn.: Grindstone Press, 2005. Written by a scientist exploring the world in search of oil, this guide details his travels on almost every continent, covering his discoveries about the land, culture, and life.

Platt, Richard. *Crime Scene: The Ultimate Guide to Forensic Science.* New York: DK Adult, 2006. Platt provides an insider's guide to the job of the forensic scientist. With color photographs throughout displaying the tools and tricks of the trade for both the "good guys" and the criminals, this text makes for an interesting read. Also includes detail on major headline-making events, such as the Oklahoma City bombing.

Robbins-Roth, Cynthia. *Alternative Careers in Science: Leaving the Ivory Tower.* 2d ed. St. Louis, Mo.: Academic Press, 2005. A good percentage of graduates in the sciences remain in academia, in research positions or the lab. This guide explores other alternatives in industries such as pharmaceuticals, biotechnology, business, and government. Each chapter highlights a different "alternative" position, including day-in-the-life stories from insiders in the career, as well as educational and certification prerequisites to getting the job.

Robinson, Tara Rodden. *Genetics For Dummies.* Hoboken, N.J.: For Dummies, 2005. This book explores the basics of genetics, its role in causing and preventing disease, and even the ethics surrounding genetic research. Covers hot topics such as the science behind cloning and the Human Genome Project.

Schwarcz, Joe. *Radar, Hula Hoops, and Playful Pigs: 67 Digestible Commentaries on the Fascinating Chemistry of Everyday Life.* New York: Holt Paperbacks, 2001. Schwarcz takes an often dull and complicated subject such as chemistry and infuses it with fun lessons to teach readers that this science is approachable and even enjoyable. The book begins with a good overview of chemicals and gaseous substances and follows with playful experiments and eye-opening discoveries.

Stephens, Lester D., and Dale R. Calder. *Seafaring Scientist: Alfred Goldsborough Mayor, Pioneer in Marine Biology.* Columbia, S.C.: University of South Carolina Press, 2006. This biography details the fascinating life of the Harvard-trained scientist who founded the first tropical marine biology laboratory in the Western hemisphere.

Tarbuck, Edward J., and Frederick K. Lutgens. *Earth Science.* 12th ed. Upper Saddle River, N.J.: Pearson Prentice Hall, 2008. Spanning the sciences of geology, meteorology, astronomy, and oceanography, this book is a good overview for the beginning student or a refresher tool for those returning to the sciences. Full color photographs and detailed illustrations augment lessons and enhance learning.

VanCleave, Janice. *Janice VanCleave's Solar System: Mind-Boggling Experiments You Can Turn Into Science Fair Projects.* San Francisco: Jossey-Bass, 2000. For the younger scientists-in-training, this fun read poses different scientific questions and answers them through experimentation. Each chapter highlights a project and lists tools and ingredients needed (all readily available), steps for the experiment with special attention to safety, and how to draw the conclusion from each lesson.

Wilbraham, Anthony C., Dennis D. Staley, Michael S. Matta, and Edward L. Waterman. *Prentice Hall Chemistry.* Upper Saddle River, N.J.: Pearson Prentice Hall, 2007. Often used in chemistry classrooms, this text provides a good overview of this science with sample problems in each chapter. Includes color photos and illustrations.

Williams, Judith. *Forensic Scientist: Careers Solving Crimes and Scientific Mysteries.* Berkeley Heights, N.J.: Enslow Publishers Inc., 2009. With each chapter, Williams explores a different aspect of the forensic science field and provides a look inside the careers in this exciting field. The book also includes an extensive glossary and lists of online and other resources for further exploration.

Williams, Linda. *Earth Science Demystified.* New York: McGraw-Hill Professional, 2008. Earth science is broken down into easy to digest and fun to read lessons in this good introduction or refresher book. Includes sections on rocks and minerals, fossils, volcanoes, glaciers, oceans, and more. Each major section includes a test to quiz students on their readings and also includes a final exam at the close of the book.

Winter, Charles. *Opportunities in Biological Science Careers.* New York: McGraw-Hill, 2004. This book explores the many branches of biology, how to enter these fields, and areas with the most job opportunities. Includes an interesting discussion on bioethics and how it affects the study of science.

❏ PERIODICALS

American Journal of Human Genetics. Published monthly by Elsevier (Customer Service Department, 3251 Riverport Lane, Maryland Heights, MO 63043-4816, 800-545-2522, usbkinfo@elsevier.com, http://www.cell.com/AJHG) for The American Society of Human Genetics (ASHG), this is the official publication of the ASHG. It features peer-reviewed articles about human genetics.

The Astronomical Journal. Published monthly by IOP Publishing (c/o AIP, PO Box 503284, St. Louis, MO 63150-3284, 800-344-6902, subs@aip.org,

http://www.iop.org/EJ/journal/aj) for the American Astronomical Society, this publication features "original astronomical research, with an emphasis on significant scientific results derived from observations, including descriptions of data capture, surveys, analysis techniques, and astrophysical interpretation." Recent articles include "Chaotic Diffusion of Resonant Kuiper Belt Objects," "Why Are There Normal Slow Rotators Among A-Type Stars?," and "Ring Edge Waves and the Masses of Nearby Satellites."

The Astrophysical Journal. Published 36 times annually by IOP Publishing (c/o AIP, PO Box 503284, St. Louis, MO 63150-3284, 800-344-6902, subs@aip.org, http://www.iop.org/EJ/home/AP) for the American Astronomical Society, this magazine features scholarly articles that will be of interest to astrophysicists.

Audubon. Published bimonthly by the National Audubon Society (225 Varick Street, 7th Floor, New York, NY 10014-4396, 212-979-3000). This attractive magazine is available to members of the society, which seeks to "conserve and restore natural ecosystems." Visit http://audubonmagazine.org to read sample articles.

ChemMatters. Published quarterly by the American Chemical Society (Office of Society Services, 1155 16th Street, NW, Room 520, Washington, DC 20036-4839, 800-227-5558, help@acs.org), this publication is geared toward high school chemistry students. Recent articles include "Rainforests: A Disappearing Act," "Those Blooming Algae!," "Air Pollution: What Weather Satellites Tell Us," and "Using Chemistry to Protect the Environment." Each issue also includes a teacher's guide that provides classroom demonstrations, hands-on activities, and other resources. Visit http://portal.acs.org to read sample articles.

Clinical Chemistry. Published monthly by the American Association for Clinical Chemistry (AACC Customer Service, 1850 K Street, NW, Suite 625, Washington, DC 20006-2213, 800-892-1400, custserv@aacc.org), this publication features articles about clinical chemistry, editorials, reviews, and letters to the editor. It is the most cited journal in its field. Visit http://www.clinchem.org/subscriptions/sample.shtml to read a sample issue.

CONNECT. Published monthly by the Association of Zoos and Aquariums (8403 Colesville Road, Suite 710, Silver Spring, MD 20910-3314, 301-562-0777), this publication for association members features articles about new exhibits, conservation developments, and other topics. Recent articles include "Latino Outreach at The Phoenix Zoo," "Saving the Critically Endangered Mississippi Gopher Frog," "Not a Laughing Matter: Conservation Effects of Media Portrayals," and "Significant Efforts in Conservation Exhibits." Visit http://www.aza.org/AZAPublications to read sample articles.

Earth. Published monthly by the American Geological Institute (4220 King Street, Alexandria, VA 22302-1507, 703-379-2480, subscriptions@agiweb.org), this magazine features articles about earth science and geology, editorial commentary, and career listings. Recent articles include "Giant Dunes, Not Mega Tsunami Deposits," "Sand Dunes Threaten Southwest Plants," and "Getting a Master's in Social Geology." Visit http://www.earthmagazine.org to read sample articles.

Earthwatch Journal. This is a member publication of the Earthwatch Institute (Three Clock Tower Place, Suite 100, Box 75, Maynard, MA 01754-2549, 800-776-0188, info@earthwatch.org, http://www.earthwatch.org/newsandevents/publications). Topics discussed range from acid rain to endangered species.

Electronic Journal of Operational Meteorology. Published five times annually by the National Weather Association (228 West Millbrook Road, Raleigh, NC 27609-4304), this online publication offers articles that summarize operational meteorological studies and contains content that is especially suited for electronic publication. Recent articles include "Significant Nighttime Tornadoes in the Plains Associated with Relatively Stable Low-Level Conditions," "Emerging Technologies in the Field to Improve Information in Support of Operations and Research," and "Anticipating the Initiation, Cessation, and Frequency of Cloud-to-Ground Lightning." Visit http://nwas.org/ej to read sample issues.

Endangered Species Bulletin. Published online three times annually by the U.S. Fish and Wildlife Service (4401 North Fairfax Drive, Room 634, Arlington, VA 22203-1610, 703-358-1735, esb@fws.gov), the bulletin provides fascinating stories about endangered species and efforts to save them. Recent stories include "Chiricahua Leopard Frog Inches Toward Recovery," "Jump Starting a Rabbit's Recovery," and "Fisheries and Habitat Conservation." Issues are available for free at http://www.fws.gov/endangered/bulletin.html. A highlights edition is also published.

Environmental & Engineering Geoscience. Published quarterly by the Association of Environmental & Engineering Geologists and the Geological Society of America, this scholarly journal publishes "peer reviewed manuscripts that address issues relating to the interaction of people with hydrologic and geologic systems." Visit http://eeg.geoscienceworld.org to read abstracts and to obtain subscription information.

Environmental Career Opportunities. Published bimonthly by Environmental Career Opportunities Inc. (700 Graves Street, Charlottesville, VA 22902-5722, 866-750-9777, ecosubscriptions@mindspring.com, http://ecojobs.com), this newsletter provides job listings in a variety of environmental fields, including environmental science and engineering, renewable energy, law, and natural resources and conservation.

Frontiers in Ecology and the Environment. Published 10 times annually by the Ecological Society of America (1990 M Street, NW, Suite 700, Washington, DC 20036-3415, 202-833-8773, esahq@esa.org, http://www.esajournals.org/loi/fron), this professional publication focuses on ecology and related disciplines.

Genetics. Published monthly by the Genetics Society of America (9650 Rockville Pike, Bethesda, MD 20814-3998, 412-268-1812, genetics-gsa@andrew.cmu.edu, http://www.genetics.org), this publications covers a wide range of topics relating to inheritance, such as population and evolutionary genetics, developmental and behavioral genetics, cellular genetics, genome integrity and transmission, and genome and systems biology.

Geology. Published monthly by GSA Sales & Service (3300 Penrose Place, PO Box 9140, Boulder, CO 80301-9140, 888-443-4472, gsaservice@geosociety.org) for the Geological Society of America, this publication offers more than 20 refereed short scientific papers on earth science in each issue. Visit http://geology.gsapubs.org to read sample articles.

Journal of Applied Meteorology and Climatology. Published monthly by the American Meteorological Society (45 Beacon Street Boston, MA 02108-3693, http://www.ametsoc.org/pubs/journals/jam), this publication covers topics of interest to meteorologists, including physical meteorology, satellite meteorology, radar meteorology, weather modification, boundary layer processes, air pollution meteorology, agricultural and forest meteorology, and applied climatology.

Journal of Clinical Microbiology. Published monthly by the American Society for Microbiology (1752 N Street, NW, Washington, DC 20036-2904, 202-942-9244, journals@asmusa.org, http://jcm.asm.org), this resource "publishes the most current research on the microbiological aspects of human and animal infections and infestations, with emphasis on their etiologic agents, diagnosis, and epidemiology." It features articles, mini-reviews, commentaries, and case reports.

Journal of Environmental Quality. Published bimonthly by the American Society of Agronomy, Crop Science Society of America, and Soil Science Society of America (677 South Segoe Road, Madison, WI 53711-1086, 608-273-8080, journals@agronomy.org, http://agron.scijournals.org), this professional journal covers a wide variety of environmental topics, including plant and environment interactions, surface and groundwater water quality, ecosystem restoration, waste management, and biodegradation and bioremediation.

Journal of Forensic Sciences. Published bimonthly by Wiley-Blackwell (Journal Customer Services, John Wiley & Sons Inc., 350 Main Street, Malden, MA 02148-5089, http://www.aafs.org) for the American Academy of Forensic Sciences, this scholarly publication covers a wide range of topics of interest to forensic science professionals.

Journal of Forestry. Published eight times annually by the Society of American Foresters (400 Grosvenor Lane, Bethesda, MD 20814-2198, 866-897-8720, safweb@safnet.org), this publication covers a plethora of forestry-related topics, including economics, education and communication, entomology and pathology, fire, forest ecology, geospatial technologies, history, international forestry, measurements, policy, recreation, silviculture, social sciences, soils and hydrology, urban and community forestry, utilization and engineering, and wildlife management. Recent articles include "Is Sustainable Development Sustainable?," "Wood Science and Forestry-Partners in Progress to a New World," and "Guide for Classifying Lands for Greenhouse Gas Inventories." Visit http://www.safnet.org/publications/jof to read sample articles.

Journal of the American Chemical Society. Published weekly by the American Chemical Society (1155 16th Street, NW, Washington, DC 20036-4839, 800-333-9511, service@acs.org), this professional resource provides comprehensive coverage of developments in chemistry as well as ancillary fields such as neurochemistry, biology, materials, and single molecule chemistry. It is considered the leading journal in its field. Visit http://pubs.acs.org to read a sample issue.

Journal of the Atmospheric Sciences. Published monthly by the American Meteorological Society (45 Beacon Street, Boston, MA 02108-3693), this scholarly publication "covers basic research related to the physics, dynamics, and chemistry of the atmosphere of the earth and other planets, with emphasis on the quantitative and deductive aspects of the subject." Visit http://www.ametsoc.org/pubs/journals/jas to read article abstracts.

Limnology and Oceanography. Published bimonthly by the American Society of Limnology and Oceanography (5400 Bosque Boulevard, Suite 680, Waco, TX 76710-4446, 800-929-2756, business@aslo.org, http://www.aslo.org/publications.html), this professional journal features original articles about limnology and oceanography and seeks to promote an understanding of aquatic ecosystems.

Mercury. Published quarterly by the Astronomical Society of the Pacific (390 Ashton Avenue, San Francisco, CA 94112-1722, 415-337-1100), this digital-only resource features articles about the latest scientific discoveries, observation techniques, and archaeoastronomy, among other topics. Recent articles include "The Universe: Yours to Discover," "What Galileo Saw-and More!," "Dark Skies are a Universal Resource," and "Armchair Astrophysics." Visit http://www.astrosociety.org/pubs/mercury/mercury.html to read article excerpts.

National Parks. Published quarterly by the National Parks Conservation Association (1300 19th Street, NW, Suite 300, Washington, DC 20036-1628), this attractive publication for the general public includes information about national parks and reserves in the United States and the conservation of natural resources. Visit http://www.npca.org/magazine to read select articles.

National Wildlife. Published six times annually by the National Wildlife Federation (11100 Wildlife Center Drive, Reston, VA 2019-5361, 800-822-9919), this is a popular magazine devoted to wildlife conservation issues. Visit http://www.nwf.org/nationalwildlife to read sample articles.

Nature Conservancy. Quarterly publication of The Nature Conservancy (4245 North Fairfax Drive, Suite 100, Arlington, VA 22203-1606, 800-628-6860), a "conservation organization working around the world to protect ecologically important lands and waters for nature and people." Visit http://www.nature.org/magazine to read sample articles.

Oceanography. Published four times annually by The Oceanography Society (PO Box 1931, Rockville, MD 20849-1931, 301-251-7708, magazine@tos.org, http://www.tos.org/oceanography), this magazine discusses current issues involving ocean science worldwide.

Perspectives in Genetic Counseling. Published quarterly by the National Society of Genetic Counselors (4061 Paysphere Circle, Chicago, IL 60674-0040, http://www.nsgc.org/resources/pgc_newsletter.cfm), this newsletter provides updates on development in genetics and other issues of interest to genetic counselors. Sample column titles include: "The Creative Job Search," "The Larger Genetics Community," "Media Watch," and "Global Perspective."

Physics Today. Published monthly by the American Institute of Physics (One Physics Ellipse, College Park, MD 20740-3842, 301-209-3040), this publication is considered one of the most influential physics magazines in the world. Recent articles include "The Amiable Einstein and Nordström," "Analysis Quantifies Effects of Tides in Jupiter and Io," "Encouraging Good Science on the Web," and "U.S. Public Likes Scientists, Poll Finds." Visit http://www.physicstoday.org to read sample articles.

The Professional Geologist. Published bimonthly by the American Institute of Professional Geologists (1400 West 122nd Avenue, Suite 250, Westminster, CO 80234-3499, 303-412-6205), this publication for new and experienced geologists, as well as geology students, covers a wide range of topics in geology. Recent articles include "A Mudlogging Geologist," "Earth Science Education," and "Students and Recent Graduates-How to Become a Valuable Employee." Visit http://www.aipg.org/StaticContent/anonymous/pubs/tpgs_public.htm to read sample issues.

Wildlife Conservation Magazine. Published bimonthly by the Wildlife Conservation Society (2300 Southern Boulevard, Bronx, NY 10460-1068, 718-220-5100), this publication is available to members of the society, which seeks to protect wildlife and wild lands. Visit http://www.wcs.org/magazine to read sample articles.

The Wildlife Professional. Published quarterly by The Wildlife Society (5410 Grosvenor Lane, Suite 200, Bethesda, MD 20814-2144, 301-897-9770, http://joomla.wildlife.org), this publication provides information for professionals in wildlife management and conservation.

Surf the Web

You must use the Internet to do research, to find out, to explore. The Internet is the closest you'll get to what's happening now all over the place. This chapter gets you started with an annotated list of Web sites related to science. Try a few. Follow the links. Maybe even venture as far as asking questions in a chat room. The more you read about and interact with science professionals, the better prepared you'll be when you're old enough to participate as a professional.

One caveat: You probably already know that URLs change all the time. If a Web address listed below is out of date, try searching on the site's name or other key words. Chances are if it's still out there, you'll find it. If it's not, maybe you'll find something better!

❏ THE SITES

About.com: Environmental Issues
http://environment.about.com

Everything you ever wanted to know about environmental issues—from global warming and green living to renewable energy and environmental law/policy—is available on this appropriately named Web site. The site has four main sections: Environmental Issues, What's at Risk, What to Do (which provides advice on living green and reducing global warming), and Global Warming. You might also want to sign up to receive a free environmental issues newsletter to keep abreast of the latest developments in the field. In the Community Forum section, you can register to participate in conversations with others interested in learning about topics in the field.

American Academy of Forensic Sciences: So You Want to Be a Forensic Scientist!
http://www.aafs.org/default.asp?section_id=resources&page_id=choosing_a_career

This section of the American Academy of Forensic Sciences Web site outlines several worthwhile topics that will be of interest to students contemplating a career in forensic science. So You Want to Be a Forensic Scientist! briefly explains what forensic science is and provides detailed information on the different disciplines within the field recognized by the academy, including criminalistics, odontology, pathology, physical anthropology, psychiatry, and toxicology. The Web site also describes the type of work a forensic scientist does and where they typically work. In addition, the Web site provides a comprehensive list of other forensic-related resources, including numerous links to other useful Web sites.

American Chemical Society: High School Student Programs and Resources
http://portal.acs.org

High school students interested in chemistry will enjoy perusing the High School Student Programs and Resources section of the American Chemical Society's Web site. Useful material includes information on the American Chemical Society's ChemClub, the Chemistry Olympiad competition, and Project SEED, a summer program for high school juniors and seniors who come from an economically disadvantaged background. In addition, select content from *ChemMatters,* an award-winning magazine geared toward high school chemistry students, is available for free on the Web site. Students leaning toward pursuing a chemistry degree will find the Web site's College Planning section especially useful—it details the types of chemistry degrees available, typical course work, financial aid opportunities, and how to get started on a chemistry degree at a community college.

American Meteorological Society: A Career Guide for the Atmospheric Sciences
http://www.ametsoc.org/ atmoscareers

The American Meteorological Society (AMS) offers a comprehensive career guide on its Web site. Content includes suggestions on the types of course work and training to consider during the college years, various career opportunities (not all meteorologists work on television or radio news shows!), typical employers and workplaces, job and salary outlook statistics, and certification information. Anyone interested in working in the field of meteorology will find the information presented in the AMS's Career Guide for the Atmospheric Sciences to be both interesting and useful.

Ask the Space Scientist
http://image.gsfc.nasa.gov/poetry/ ask/askmag.html

A plethora of fascinating space-related information can be found on the Ask the Space Scientist page of the National Aeronautics and Space Administration's Web site. Ask the Space Scientist delivers information in a straightforward manner, presenting several lists of Frequently Asked Questions in such topic areas as The Sun, Earth-Rotation, Solar Storms, Earth-Atmosphere, and Aurora Science. The Web site is limited in its visual appeal (it is primarily all text), but it is a solid go-to source for when you want to quickly find answers (provided by a NASA scientist!) to your space-related questions. There are also several links to other NASA educational resources, as well as to other space-related Web sites.

Astronomy Today
http://www.astronomytoday.com

Anyone interested in astronomy will enjoy the material available at Astronomy Today's Web site, which is filled with astronomy-related information written in clear, easy to understand language. A collection of astronomy-related articles is browsable by such topics as Astronomy, Interviews with Amateur Astronomers, Solar System, Space Exploration, Cosmology, and Constellations and Stars of the Sky. In addition, the Web site provides reviews of astronomy-related products as well as a guide to selecting and purchasing a telescope. The Web site's popular Sky Guide provides observation information for many types of astronomical events, such as lunar and solar eclipses and meteor showers, and on what days you'll find the best opportunities for viewing of the planets.

CanopyMeg.com
http://www.canopymeg.com

Who is Canopy Meg, you ask? She's Dr. Meg Lowman, a pioneer of *canopy ecology,* the study of wildlife and plant life found within the layers of a group of mature tree crowns. Browse her Web site to get a glimpse of her many travels and studies—from the Amazon rain forest to the tropical ecosystems of Panama. One of the most interesting sections is Photos & Multimedia. Here you can really get a feel for Meg's work and how it has affected people around the world. You'll see pictures ranging from a treetop camp held in New York, to a photo and blog from a middle school student's history project on Canopy Meg.

Careers in Forestry & Natural Resources
http://www.forestrycareers.org

This site, which is sponsored by the National Science Foundation, provides a wealth of information about careers in the following subdisciplines in the field: Fish & Wildlife Management; Parks, Recreation, and Tourism; Management and Conservation; Policy and Planning; Forestry & Natural Resources Sciences; Environmental Science and Technology; Wood and Paper Science; and Genetics and Biotechnology. Each section offers a list of possible careers, brief interviews with forestry and natural resources workers in the field, photographs of workers in the field, and links to other Web sites. There is also a useful Education section (which features information on schools that offer degrees in forestry or natural resources) and a Diversity section that encourages people of color to enter the field.

Careers in Human Genetics
http://www.ashg.org/education/careers_overview.shtml

The American Society of Human Genetics maintains a comprehensive Web site, including the Careers in Human Genetics section. Career information is presented clearly and concisely, covering the most common career choices in this field in greater detail while mentioning other options as well. A Frequently Asked Questions sections deals with such topics as salary, job availability, and a typical week in the life of a human geneticist. Of particular interest to students aspiring to a career in human genetics are the profiles of human geneticists, detailing their current job, education, career path, and advice for those pursuing a career in this field.

Career Voyages
http://www.careervoyages.gov

Anyone considering a career in science should check out the Career Voyages site, a joint effort between the U.S. Departments of Labor and Education. The Web site features several sections that will be of interest to readers of this book, including Biotechnology and Emerging Industries (Geospatial Technology and Nanotechnology). Each section contains an overview of the particular subindustry; a thorough list of education and training options; links to schools offering relevant training; a list of in-demand occupations for each subindustry; and other career information, including videos.

College Navigator
http://nces.ed.gov/collegenavigator

College Navigator is sponsored by the National Center for Education Statistics, an agency of the U.S. Department of Education. At the site, users can search for information on nearly 7,000 postsecondary institutions in the United States. Searches can be conducted by school name, state, programs/majors offered (including Biological and Biomedical Sciences, Natural Resources and Conservation, Physical Sciences, and Science Technologies/Technicians), level of award, institution type, tuition, housing availability, campus settings, percentage of applicants who are admitted, test scores, availability of varsity athletic teams, availability of extended learning opportunities, religious affiliation, and specialized mission. Additionally, users can export the results of their search into a spreadsheet, save the results of their session, and compare up to four colleges in one view. This is an excellent starting place to conduct research about colleges and universities.

CoolWorks.com
http://www.coolworks.com

Can you picture yourself saddling up burros at the Grand Canyon or working as a tour guide at Mount Rushmore this summer? Cool Works quickly links you to a wealth of information about seasonal employment at dozens of national and state parks, preserves, monuments, and wilderness areas. There are also listings of jobs and volunteer opportunities at ski areas, private resorts, cruise ships, and summer camps. Most of the national and state jobs require that applicants be 18 years or older. Most national and state parks listed here have seasonal positions available in similar departments. Specific job descriptions can also be accessed by searching a pull-down menu of U.S. states and regions or international locations. While only some jobs allow you to apply directly online, many have downloadable application forms.

Cyber-Sierra's Natural Resources Job Search
http://www.cyber-sierra.com/nrjobs

This site is overflowing with up-to-date information to assist job seekers in the fields of forestry, water resources, and other environmental careers. In spite of its abundance of data, the site has a friendly tone and seems to have the interests of a job seeker in mind. Take the time to read the Overview page for insights into how to best use this site and general advice about looking for work. Even if you're only at the preliminary stage of exploring options for your future, there's plenty to glean from this site. Besides seeing the scope of career possibilities, you can link to many environmental organizations, online courses, and reference tools.

Ecological Society of America: Ecology as a Career
http://esa.org/education_diversity/explore.php

The Ecological Society of America's Web site is full of information and resources that eco-leaning students will find interesting and useful. Particularly of note for students is the Ecology as a Career section, which breaks down information into subsections explaining what ecologists do and the different types of ecological careers that are available. Career information covers additional topics such as the type of educational background that is necessary, job outlook, and activities that an interested high school student or college undergraduate can do now to further explore a career in ecology.

The Encyclopedia of Earth
http://www.eoearth.org

The Encyclopedia of Earth is written by environmental scholars, profession-als, educators, and experts. The articles, which are peer-reviewed, are written in nontechnical language for easy understanding by students and the general public. There are thousands of detailed entries on a variety of topics and well-known individuals in the field, including acid rain, the Exxon Valdez oil spill, the Ocean Dumping Act, Rachel Carson, species diversity, wind farms, and the Yapen rain forests. There are also news articles on the latest environmental developments and a forum where you can comment on issues ranging from man-made chemicals in drinking water to the ecological impacts of climate change.

GradSchools.com
http://www.gradschools.com

This site offers listings of graduate schools searchable by field of study (such as Biological Science, Earth Science, Environment, and Physical Science), format (campus, online, or both), and location (U.S. and international locations). From the home page, use the drop-down menu to choose the subject of your interest. For example, under Biological Science you can choose from Biochemistry, Ecology, Microbiology, and other majors. Listings include program info, degrees offered, school Web site, and email contact.

Her Lab In Your Life: Women in Chemistry
http://www.chemheritage.org/women_chemistry

This attractive and intriguing Web site, maintained by the Chemical Heritage

Foundation, is full of examples of how women in chemistry have left their impact on everyday life. Profiles of female chemists are organized by the subject areas in which they have worked, such as Health and Safety, where you can read about Alice Hamilton, who identified many hazardous substances in the workplace and was an early champion of industrial medicine; Stuff, where you can find the profile of Stephanie Kwolek, the inventor of Kevlar, a lightweight polymer used in many applications, including bulletproof and flame-resistant clothing; and Universe, which houses the profile of Marie Curie, who won two Nobel Prizes for her scientific advancements. There is also a fun Careers section, which uses the profiles of women in chemistry to showcase the wide range of workplace settings in which a chemist might work. Although the site focuses on the accomplishments of women, anyone interested in the applications of chemistry will find this site interesting and informative.

How Stuff Works
http://www.howstuffworks.com

If you spend a lot of time wondering how stuff you use or see every day actually works, then this site should be on your short list of Web sites to explore, as it covers how "stuff," as varied and timely as tsunamis to identity theft to satellite radio, works. Complex concepts are carefully broken down and examined, including photos and links to current and past news items about the subject. Topics of interest to those interested in science include How Hydrology Works, How

Lunar Eclipses Work, How Animal Camouflage Works, How the Earth Works, How Experiments Work, and more.

National Park Service: Nature and Science: Views of the National Parks
http://www.nature.nps.gov

Views of the National Parks is a multimedia program that "presents the natural, historical, and cultural wonders associated with national parks." Users can learn about parks in the system (such as the Badlands, Devil's Tower, and the Grand Canyon), listen to interviews about the parks and their features, and view photos of the parks.

National Weather Service
http://www.nws.noaa.gov

This Web site, sponsored by the National Oceanic and Atmospheric Administration, is a good, solid source for all things weather-related. The National Weather Service provides a variety of forecast information—such as forecasts for local, aviation, and marine weather; flooding; and air quality—much of which is presented with simple graphics on easy-to-read maps, including some that utilize radar or satellite imagery. The Web site also keeps up-to-date information and warnings on hurricanes, tornados, conditions conducive to fires, and other types of severe weather.

Occupational Outlook Handbook
http://stats.bls.gov/search/ooh.htm

Every two years, the U.S. Department of Labor publishes a guide to career options in various U.S. industries. Hundreds of jobs are covered, including these and other science-related careers: Atmospheric Scientists, Biological Scientists, Chemists and Material Scientists, Environmental Scientists and Hydrologists; Geoscientists, Medical Scientists, Physicists and Astronomers, and Science Technicians. Each article contains the following sections: Significant Points; Nature of the Work; Training, Other Qualifications and Advancement; Employment; Job Outlook; Earnings; Related Occupations; and Sources of Additional Information. This is a good site to visit to locate trustworthy information about science careers.

Peterson's Summer Camps and Programs
http://www.petersons.com/
summerop/code/ssector.asp

This Web site offers great information about academic and career-focused summer programs. Finding a camp that suits your interests is easy enough at this site; just search Peterson's database by activity (Academics, Arts, Sports, Wilderness/ Outdoors, Special Interests), geographic region, category (Day Programs in the U.S., Residential Programs in the U.S., Travel in the U.S. and to Other Countries, Special Needs Accommodations), keyword, or alphabetically. By conducting a keyword search using words such as "science," "biology," or "astronomy," you'll find a list of links to hundreds of programs. Click on a specific program or camp for a quick overview description. In some instances you'll get a more in-depth description, along with photographs, applications, and online brochures.

Physics To Go
http://www.physicstogo.org

If you are looking for a variety of physics-related content that is routinely updated, check out Physics To Go. The Web site is home to an online physics magazine that is published every two weeks and includes sections on Physics in Your World, From Physics Research, Physics at Home, and Worth a Look. You can also view previous issues through the Web site's archive feature. In addition to the magazine, Physics To Go maintains a database of more 600 physics-related Web sites, which can be browsed by focusing on subject headings such as Astronomy, Education Practices, Fluids, Light, Quantum Physics, and other topics.

Public Broadcasting Service: American Field Guide
http://www.pbs.org/americanfield
guide

This fascinating Web site features more than 14,000 videos in the following environmental categories: Animals, Ecosystems, Human History, Livelihoods, Earth & Space, Plants, Public Policy, and Recreation. For example, under Ecosystems you can view videos of tidal pools in South Carolina; the Blanton Forest, the largest old-growth forest in Kentucky; and Saguaro cacti and other desert life in Saguaro National Park in Arizona. This is an excellent place to learn more about the environment.

Sea Grant Marine Careers
http://www.marinecareers.net

Interested in a career as a marine biologist, oceanographer, or ocean engineer? If so, you've come to the right place. Sea Grant Marine Careers provides detailed information on careers, educational requirements, typical work settings, earnings, and much more. There are also profiles of workers in the field (such as marine biotechnologists, aquatic chemists, geological oceanographers, and environmental engineers), answers to frequently asked questions, and photographs of marine science professionals at work.

Society of Physics Students: Careers Using Physics
http://www.spsnational.org/cup

Students interested in physics will find lots of interesting and relevant information on the Society of Physics Students' Web site, especially the Careers Using Physics section. A variety of career-related information is organized into subsections such as Profiles, which offers glimpses of people with physics careers; Advice, which provides assistance in choosing academic and career goals, tips on networking, and more; Resources, which includes a variety of materials, ranging from general physics information to information geared toward students at various stages

of education; and Summer Research Jobs, a browsable database of summer research opportunities.

Space Weather.com
http://www.spaceweather.com

This fascinating Web site provides information on the current conditions for solar wind, solar flares, sunspots, and more, as well as providing space weather forecasts, information on meteor showers, aurora (such as the Northern Lights), space traffic, and other planets. You can sign up for a free email alert that will let you know when something exciting is happening, such as when an eclipse will occur or when a comet might streak across the night sky. There are also several photo galleries of space weather-related phenomenon, submitted by people in countries around the world.

U.S. Fish & Wildlife Service Students' Page
http://www.fws.gov/educators/students.html

This site provides links to information on a variety of environmental resources—from birds and fish, to habitat and endangered species, to plants and wildlife. There is also a FAQ section and links to the service's photo and video libraries.

Ask for Money

By the time most students get around to thinking about applying for scholarships, grants, and other financial aid, they have already extolled their personal, academic, and creative virtues to such lengths in essays and interviews for college applications that even their own grandmothers wouldn't recognize them. The thought of filling out yet another application fills students with dread. And why bother? Won't the same five or six kids who have been competing for academic honors for years walk away with all the really good scholarships?

The truth is, most of the scholarships available to high school and college students are being offered because an organization wants to promote interest in a particular field, encourage more students to become qualified to enter it, and finally, to help those students afford an education. Certainly, having a great grade point average is a valuable asset. More often than not, however, grade point averages aren't even mentioned; the focus is on the area of interest and what a student has done to distinguish himself or herself in that area. In fact, sometimes the only requirement is that the scholarship applicant must be studying in a particular area.

❏ GUIDELINES

When applying for scholarships there are a few simple guidelines that can help ease the process considerably.

Plan Ahead

The absolute worst thing you can do is wait until the last minute. For one thing, obtaining recommendations or other supporting data in time to meet an application deadline is incredibly difficult. For another, no one does his or her best thinking or writing under the gun. So get off to a good start by reviewing scholarship applications as early as possible—months, even a year, in advance. If the current scholarship information isn't available, ask for a copy of last year's version. Once you have the scholarship information or application in hand, give it a thorough read. Try to determine how your experience or situation best fits into the scholarship, or if it even fits at all. Don't waste your time applying for a scholarship in geology, for example, if you hate working outside—where geologists often work to collect rock samples and conduct research.

If possible, research the award or scholarship, including past recipients and, where applicable, the person in whose name the scholarship is offered. Often, scholarships are established to memorialize an individual who majored in science, but in other cases, the scholarship is to memorialize the *work* of an individual. In those cases, try to get a feel for the spirit of the person's work. If you have any similar interests, experiences, or abilities, don't hesitate to mention these.

Talk to others who received the scholarship, or to students currently studying in the same area or field of interest in which the scholarship is offered, and try to gain insight into possible applications or work related to that field. When you're working on the essay asking why you want this scholarship, you'll have real answers—"I would benefit from receiving this scholarship because studying biology will help me become a better biologist."

Take your time writing the essays. Make sure that you answer the question or questions on the application and not merely restating facts about yourself. Don't be afraid to get creative; try to imagine what you would think of if you had to sift through hundreds of applications: What would you want to know about the candidate? What would convince you that someone was deserving of the scholarship? Work through several drafts and have someone whose advice you respect—a parent, teacher, or counselor—review the essay for grammar and content.

Finally, if you know in advance which scholarships you want to apply for, there might still be time to stack the deck in your favor by getting an internship, volunteering, or working part time. Bottom line: The more you know about a scholarship and the sooner you learn it, the better.

Follow Directions

Think of it this way: Many of the organizations that offer scholarships devote 99.9 percent of their time to something other than the scholarship for which you are applying. Don't make a nuisance of yourself by pestering them for information. Simply follow the directions as they are presented to you. If the scholarship application specifies that you should write for further information, then write for it—don't call.

Pay close attention to whether you're applying for a grant, a loan, an award, a prize, or a scholarship. Often these words are used interchangeably, but just as often they have different meanings. A loan is financial aid that must be paid back. A grant is a type of financial aid that does not require repayment. An award or prize is usually given for something you have done: built a park or helped distribute meals to the elderly; or something you have created: a science project, a musical composition, a design, a scientific paper, a film, or an invention. On the other hand, a scholarship is frequently a renewable sum of money that is given to a person to help defray the costs of college. Scholarships are given to candidates who meet the necessary criteria based on essays, eligibility, grades, or creative work, or sometimes all four. They do not have to be paid back.

Supply all the necessary documents, information, and fees, and make the deadlines. You won't win any scholarships by forgetting to include a recommendation from a teacher or failing to postmark the application by the deadline. Bottom line: Get it right the first time, on time.

Apply Early

Once you have the application in hand, don't dawdle. If you've requested it far enough in advance, there shouldn't be any reason for you not to turn it in well in advance of the deadline. You never know, if it comes down to two candidates, your timeliness just might be the deciding factor. Bottom line: Don't wait.

Be Yourself

Don't make promises you can't keep. There are plenty of hefty scholarships available, but if they all require you to study something that you don't enjoy, you'll be miserable in college. And the side effects from switching majors after you've accepted a scholarship could be even worse. Bottom line: Be yourself.

Don't Limit Yourself

There are many sources for scholarships, beginning with your school counselor and ending with the Internet. All of the search engines have education categories. Start there and search by keywords, such as "financial aid," "scholarship," and "award." But don't be limited to the scholarships listed in these pages.

If you know of an organization related to or involved with the field of your choice, write a letter asking if they offer scholarships. If they don't offer scholarships, don't stop there. Write them another letter, or better yet, schedule a meeting with the executive director, education director, or someone in the public relations department and ask them if they would be willing to sponsor a scholarship for you. Of course, you'll need to prepare yourself well for such a meeting because you're selling a priceless commodity— yourself. Don't be shy, be confident. Tell them all about yourself, what you want to study and why, and let them know what you would be willing to do in exchange— volunteer at their favorite charity, write up reports on your progress in school, or work part time on school breaks, full time during the summer. Explain why you're a wise investment. Bottom line: The sky's the limit.

❏ ONE MORE THING

We have not listed financial aid that is provided by colleges and universities. Why? There are two reasons. First, because there are thousands of schools that offer financial aid for students who are interested in studying science-related majors, and we couldn't possibly fit them all in this book. Second, listing just a few schools wouldn't be helpful to the vast majority of students who do not plan to attend these institutions. This means that it is up to you to check with the college that you want to attend for details on available financial aid. College financial aid officers will be happy to tell you what types of resources are available.

❏ THE LIST

Advancing Hispanic Excellence in Technology, Engineering, Math and Science Foundation

c/o Scholarship Program
University of Texas at Arlington
College of Engineering, Box 19019
Nedderman Hall, Room 634
Arlington, TX 76019-0019
817-272-1116
ahetems@shpe.org
http://www.ahetems.org

The foundation offers scholarships to Hispanic high school seniors and under-graduate and graduate students who plan to or who are currently pursuing degrees in engineering, mathematics, science, and computer science. Visit its Web site for more information.

American Chemical Society (ACS)

ACS Scholars Program
1155 16th Street, NW
Washington, DC 20036-4839
800-227-5558, ext. 6250
scholars@acs.org
http://www.chemistry.org

African American, Hispanic/Latino, and American Indian students interested in pursuing undergraduate college degrees in chemical sciences and chemical tech-nology are eligible to participate in the ACS Scholar Program. Graduating high school seniors and college freshmen, sophomores, and juniors are eligible to apply. Applicants must have a GPA of at least 3.0 and demonstrate financial need. Scholarship recipients receive up to $5,000. Visit the ACS Web site for an application and additional details.

American Ground Water Trust

Scholarship Application
50 Pleasant Street
Concord, NH 03301-4073
603-228-5444
http://www.agwt.org/scholarships. htm

The trust offers three scholarships for high school seniors who are interested in pursuing careers in groundwater. Schol-arships range from $1,000 to $2,000. Applicants must be U.S. citizens or legal residents, have a GPA of at least 3.0, and "either have completed a science/envi-ronmental project in high school which directly involved ground water resources or, have had vacation/out of school work experience that is related to the environ-ment and natural resources." Visit the trust's Web site for more information and to download an application.

American Indian Science and Engineering Society (AISES)

PO Box 9828
Albuquerque, NM 87119-9828
505-765-1052, ext. 105
tina@aises.org
http://www.aises.org/Programs/ ScholarshipsandInternships/ Scholarships

The AISES offers several scholarships for Native American students at the under-graduate and graduate level who are studying engineering, the natural/physical sciences, natural resources, computer science, and other fields. Applicants must be student members and demonstrate proof of tribal membership. Contact the society for more information and to download applications.

American Institute of Professional Geologists (AIPG)

1400 West 122nd Avenue, Suite 250
Westminster, CO 80234-3499
303-412-6205
aipg@aipg.org
http://www.aipg.org

College sophomores, juniors, or seniors who are majoring in geology or earth science can apply for scholarships from the AIPG. Applicants must be attending a four-year accredited institution in the United States and be participating student members of the AIPG (they may also apply for membership by application). Scholarship winners must also agree to submit a 600- to 800-word article for publication in *The Professional Geologist*. Contact the AIPG for more information.

American Legion Auxiliary

8945 North Meridian Street
Indianapolis, IN 46260-5387
317-569-4500
alahq@legion-aux.org
http://www.legion-aux.org/scholar
ships/index.aspx

Various state auxiliaries of the American Legion, as well as its national organization, offer scholarships to help students prepare for a variety of careers. Most require that candidates be associated with the organization in some way, whether as a child, spouse, etc., of a military veteran. Interested students should contact the auxiliary for further information.

American Meteorological Society (AMS)

45 Beacon Street
Boston, MA 02108-3693
617-227-2425
http://www.ametsoc.org/
amsstudentinfo/scholfeldocs

The society offers several scholarships to high school seniors and college students. The AMS/Industry Minority Scholarship is open to minority students who have been traditionally underrepresented in the sciences, especially Native American, Hispanic, and Black/African-American students. Applicants must be high school seniors who plan to pursue a career in the atmospheric or related oceanic and hydrologic sciences. The AMS/Freshman Undergraduate Scholarship is available to high school seniors who plan to study atmospheric or related oceanic or hydrologic sciences in college. Visit the society's Web site for more information and to download applications.

American Physical Society

One Physics Ellipse
College Park, MD 20740-3841
http://www.aps.org/programs/
minorities/honors/scholarship

High school seniors or college freshman or sophomores who are planning to or currently studying physics can apply for scholarships from the society. Applicants must be U.S. citizens or permanent residents and African American, Hispanic American, or Native American. Contact the society for more information.

Association on American Indian Affairs

Attn: Director of Scholarship
  Programs
966 Hungerford Drive, Suite 12-B
Rockville, MD 20850-1743
240-314-7155
lw.aaia@verizon.net
http://www.indian-affairs.org

Undergraduate and graduate Native American students who are pursuing a wide variety of college majors (including science) can apply for several different scholarships of $1,500. All applicants must provide proof of Native American heritage. Visit the association's Web site for more information.

CollegeBoard: Scholarship Search

http://apps.collegeboard.com/
  cbsearch_ss/welcome.jsp

This testing service (PSAT, SAT, etc.) also offers a scholarship search engine at its Web site. It features scholarships worth nearly $3 billion. You can search by specific major (such as biology, physics, and science) and a variety of other criteria.

CollegeNET: MACH 25-Breaking the Tuition Barrier

http://www.collegenet.com/mach25/
  app

CollegeNET features 600,000 scholarships worth more than $1.6 billion. You can search by keyword (such as science) or by creating a personality profile of your interests.

FastWeb

http://www1.fastweb.com

FastWeb is one of the best-known scholarship search engines around. It features 1.3 million scholarships worth more than $3 billion. To use this resource, you will need to register (free).

Foundation for the Carolinas

Office of Scholarships
217 South Tryon Street
Charlotte, NC 28202-3201
704-973-4537
tcapers@fftc.org
http://www.fftc.org

The foundation administers more than 105 scholarship programs that offer awards to high school seniors and undergraduate and graduate students who plan to or who are currently pursuing study in a variety of disciplines. (Note: Some scholarships require residency in North or South Carolina.) Visit the foundation's Web site for a list of awards.

The Garden Club of America

14 East 60th Street, 3rd Floor
New York, NY 10022-7147
212-753-8287
scholarships@gcamerica.org
http://www.gcamerica.org/
  scholarships.php3

The club offers several scholarships and fellowships to college students who are interested in studying field botany, ornamental horticulture, ecological restoration, urban forestry, tropical botany, horticulture, and other environmental fields. Funds are available for study during the summer and the regular school year. Visit the club's Web site for detailed information about available awards.

GuaranteedScholarships.com

http://www.guaranteed-scholarships.com

This Web site offers lists (by college) of scholarships, grants, and financial aid that "require no interview, essay, portfolio, audition, competition, or other secondary requirement."

Hawaii Community Foundation

1164 Bishop Street, Suite 800
Honolulu, HI 96813-2817
888-731-3863
khasegawa@hcf-hawaii.org
http://www.hawaiicommunity
foundation.org/scholar/scholar.php

The foundation offers scholarships for high school seniors and college students planning to or currently studying a variety of majors in college. There are several scholarships for college students interested in math, physics, science, technology, and the biological sciences. Applicants must be residents of Hawaii, demonstrate financial need, and attend a two- or four-year college. Visit the foundation's Web site for more information and to apply online.

Hispanic College Fund (HCF)

1301 K Street, NW,
  Suite 450-A West
Washington, DC 20005-3317
800-644-4223
hcf-info@hispanicfund.org
http://www.hispanicfund.org

The Hispanic College Fund, in collaboration with several major corporations, offers many scholarships for high school seniors and college students planning to or currently attending college. Applicants must live in the United States (including Puerto Rico) and have a GPA of at least 3.0 on a 4.0 scale. Contact the HCF for more information.

Illinois Career Resource Network

http://www.ilworkinfo.com/icrn.htm

Created by the Illinois Department of Employment Security, this useful site offers a scholarship search engine, as well as detailed information on careers (including science-related options such as astronomer, biologist, chemist, forensic science technician, forestry technician, geologist, geophysist, meteorologist, physicist, and science technician). You can search for scholarships based on major (such as astronomy, biological sciences, physics, etc.), and other criterion. This site is available to everyone, not just Illinois residents; you can get a password by simply visiting the site. The Illinois Career Resource Network is just one example of the type of sites created by state departments of employment security (or departments of labor) to assist students with financial- and career-related issues. After checking out this site, visit your state's department of labor Web site to see what it offers.

Imagine America Foundation

1101 Connecticut Avenue, NW,
  Suite 901
Washington, DC 20036-4303
202-336-6800
http://www.imagine-america.org/
  scholarship/a-about-scholarship.asp

The Imagine America Foundation (formerly the Career College Foundation) is a nonprofit organization that helps students pay for college. It offers three $1,000 scholarships each year to high school students or recent graduates. Applicants must have a GPA of at least 2.5 on a 4.0 scale, have financial need, and demonstrate voluntary community service during their senior year. Scholarships can be used at more than 500 career colleges in the United States. These colleges offer a variety of fields of study, including biology technician/biotechnology laboratory technician, computer engineering, computer programming, computer science, criminal justice/police science, engineering technology, fire science/firefighting, forensic science and technology, gene/genetic therapy, genetic counseling/counselor, genetics, nursing, and petroleum technology/technician. Visit the foundation's Web site for more information.

Marine Technology Society

Student Scholarship
5565 Sterrett Place, Suite 108
Columbia, MD 21044-2606

410-884-5330
http://www.mtsociety.org/education/
  scholarships.aspx

The society offers approximately $59,000 in scholarship funds annually to high school, undergraduate, graduate, and two-year college students who are interested in pursuing careers in a marine-related field. Visit its Web site for detailed information on available scholarships.

Morris K. Udall Foundation

Morris K. Udall Scholarship
  Program
130 South Scott Avenue
Tucson, AZ 85701-1922
520-901-8500
info@udall.gov
http://www.udall.gov

The foundation awards approximately 80 scholarships to college students in their sophomore or junior year who have outstanding potential and intend to pursue environmental careers. The foundation "seeks future leaders across a wide spectrum of environmental fields, including policy, engineering, science, education, urban planning and renewal, business, health, justice, and economics." Visit its Web site for more information.

National Association of Secondary School Principals (NASSP)

c/o National Honor Society
1904 Association Drive
Reston, VA 20191-1537
703-860-0200
http://www.nhs.us

The NASSP has awarded the National Honor Society (NHS) Scholarships since 1946. It has provided more than $10 million in scholarships to NHS members. Students cannot apply directly, but are nominated through their school's NHS chapter. High school seniors who are members in good standing of their school chapter can be considered for nomination. State finalists receive $1,000 scholarships; state winners, $1,500 scholarships; regional winners, $2,500 scholarships; and the national winner, a $13,000 scholarship. Contact the NHS or your local high school NHS chapter for more information.

National Ground Water Association

National Ground Water Research
    and Educational Foundation
Attn: Scholarship Coordinator
601 Dempsey Road
Westerville, OH 43081-8978
bhowell@ngwa.org
http://www.ngwa.org/ngwref/assante

High school seniors and college undergraduates are eligible to apply for scholarships from the Len Assante Scholarship Fund. Applicants must be "entering a field of study that serves, supports, or promotes the ground water industry" and have a GPA of at least 2.5 on a 4.0 scale. Visit the association's Web site for details and to download an application.

Sallie Mae

http://www.collegeanswer.com/
    paying/scholarship_search/pay_
    scholarship_search.jsp

Sallie Mae offers a scholarship database of more than 3 million awards worth more than $16 billion. You must register (free) to use the database.

Scholarship America

One Scholarship Way
Saint Peter, MN 56082-0297
800-537-4180
http://www.scholarshipamerica.org

This organization works through its local Dollars for Scholars chapters throughout the United States. In 2008, it awarded more than $219 million in scholarships to students. Visit Scholarship America's Web site for more information.

ScholarshipExperts.com

http://scholarshipexperts.com

ScholarshipExperts.com offers a free scholarship search engine, although you must register to access it. The database features 2.4 million scholarships worth more than $14 billion. The Web site also offers several of its own scholarships each year to students who are seeking funds for college. Scholarship themes and award amounts change annually. Visit ScholarshipExperts.com for details.

Scholarships.com

http://www.scholarships.com

Scholarships.com offers a free college scholarship and grant search engine (although you must register to use it) and financial aid information. Its database of awards features 2.7 million listings worth more than $19 billion in aid.

Society of Exploration Geophysicists Foundation

PO Box 702740
Tulsa, OK 74170-2740
918-497-5500
scholarships@seg.org
http://www.seg.org

High school seniors and college students who are planning to or currently studying the geosciences, physics, geology, or earth and environmental sciences may apply for scholarships from the foundation. Contact the foundation for more information regarding specific scholarships.

Society of Satellite Professionals International

55 Broad Street, 14th Floor
New York, NY 10004-2501
212-809-5199
http://www.sspi.org/
?page=Scholarships

The Society of Satellite Professionals International offers a scholarship program for high school seniors and college students who are committed to pursuing education and career opportunities in the satellite industry or a field making direct use of satellite technology. Past scholarship winners have pursued studies in broadcasting, business, distance learning, energy, government, imaging, meteorology, navigation, remote sensing, space law, and telecommunications. Scholarships range from $2,500 to $3,500. Applicants must demonstrate academic and leadership achievement, show potential for a major contribution to the satellite communications industry, and be mem-

bers of the society. Contact the society for more information.

Sodexho Foundation

9801 Washingtonian Boulevard
Gaithersburg, MD 20878-5355
http://www.sodexofoundation.org/
hunger_us/scholarships/scholar
ships.asp

The Sodexho Foundation offers $5,000 STOP Hunger Scholarships to "recognize and reward students who have made a significant impact in the fight against hunger and its root causes in the United States." Applicants must be enrolled in an accredited education institution (kindergarten through graduate school) in the United States, have demonstrated volunteer service to non-family members that impacts hunger, and be citizens or permanent residents of the United States. Contact the foundation for more information.

United Negro College Fund (UNCF)

8260 Willow Oaks Corporate Drive
PO Box 10444
Fairfax, VA 22031-8044
800-331-2244
http://www.uncf.org/forstudents/
scholarship.asp

Visitors to the UNCF Web site can search for information on thousands of scholarships and grants, many of which are administered by the UNCF. Its search engine allows you to search by major (such as anthropology, applied mathematics, biochemistry, biological science, biology, biotechnology, chemistry, computer science, criminal justice, criminology, ecology, forensic science, forest and natural resources, general science, geoenvironmental, geology, geophysics, hydrology/hydrogeology, mathematics, microbiology, natural science, nursing, physical sciences, physics, plant and soil sciences, science, science technology, and wood science), state, scholarship title, grade level, and achievement score. High school seniors and undergraduate and graduate students are eligible.

U.S. Department of Education
Federal Student Aid
800-433-3243
http://www.federalstudentaid.ed.gov
http://studentaid.ed.gov/students/pub
    lications/student_guide/index.html

The U.S. government provides a wealth of financial aid in the form of grants, loans, and work-study programs. Each year, it publishes *Funding Education Beyond High School,* a guide to these funds. Visit the Web sites listed above for detailed information on federal financial aid.

Look to the Pros

The following professional organizations offer a variety of materials—from career brochures, to lists of accredited schools, to salary surveys. Many publish journals and newsletters that you should become familiar with. Some also have annual conferences that you might be able to attend. (While you may not be able to attend a conference as a participant, it may be possible to "cover" one for your school or even your local paper, especially if your school has a related club.)

When contacting professional organizations, keep in mind that they all exist primarily to serve their members, be it through continuing education, certification, political lobbying, or just "keeping up with the profession." While many are strongly interested in promoting their profession and sharing information with the general public, these busy professional organizations do not exist solely to provide you with information. Whether you call your write, be courteous, brief, and to the point. Know what you need and ask for it. If the organization has a Web site, check it out first: what you're looking for may be available there for downloading, or you may find a list of prices or instructions, such as sending a self-addressed stamped envelope with your request. Finally, be aware that organizations, like people, move. To save time when writing, first confirm the address, preferably with a quick phone call to the organization itself: "Hello, I'm calling to confirm your address. . . ."

❏ THE SOURCES

Academy of Board Certified Environmental Professionals
PO Box 42564
Towson, MD 21284-2564
866-767-8073
office@abcep.org
http://www.abcep.org

This organization offers certification to environmental professionals.

American Academy of Forensic Sciences
410 North 21st Street
Colorado Springs, CO 80904-2712
719-636-1100
http://www.aafs.org

The academy was founded in 1948 and has members in 53 countries. Its members include toxicologists, physical anthropologists, document examiners, psychiatrists, physicists, physicians, attorneys, dentists, engineers, criminalists, educators, digital evidence experts, and other forensic science professionals. Visit its Web site for comprehensive information on careers and colleges and universities that offer courses and degrees in forensic science-related fields, membership for college students, and the *Journal of Forensic Sciences.*

American Association for Clinical Chemistry
1850 K Street, NW, Suite 625
Washington, DC 20006-2215
800-892-1400
http://www.aacc.org

Visit the association's Web site for information on publications and to read industry news.

American Association of Petroleum Geologists
1444 South Boulder
Tulsa, OK 74119-3604
800-364-2274
http://www.aapg.org

Visit the association's Web site for information on membership for college students and answers to frequently asked questions about the field.

American Astronomical Society
2000 Florida Avenue, NW, Suite 400
Washington, DC 20009-1231
202-328-2010
aas@aas.org
http://www.aas.org

This is the primary membership organization for astronomers, but also has physicists, mathematicians, geologists, and engineers among its membership. Visit its Web site for job listings and information on careers and publications.

American Board of Genetic Counseling
PO Box 14216
Lenexa, KS 66285-4216
913-895-4617
info@abgc.net
http://www.abgc.net

Visit the board's Web site for information on certification, an overview of the career of genetic counselor, and a list of accredited graduate schools.

American Board of Medical Genetics
9650 Rockville Pike
Bethesda, MD 20814-3998
301-634-7315
abmg@abmg.org
http://www.abmg.org

Contact the board for information on training and certification for medical geneticists.

American Chemical Society
1155 16th Street, NW
Washington, DC 20036-4839
800-227-5558
help@acs.org
http://www.chemistry.org

Visit the society's Web site for a career blog and information on approved education programs, careers, earnings, professional journals, competitions and programs for high school students (including the Chemistry Olympiad and a summer research program for economically disadvantaged students), and membership and scholarships for college students.

American Chemistry Council

1300 Wilson Boulevard
Arlington VA 22209-2323
703-741-5000
http://www.americanchemistry.com

The American Chemistry Council offers a great deal of information about the chemical industry, and maintains an informative Web site.

American Geological Institute (AGI)

4220 King Street
Alexandria, VA 22302-1502
703-379-2480
http://www.agiweb.org

The AGI is a "nonprofit federation of 45 geoscientific and professional associations that represents more than 120,000 geologists, geophysicists, and other earth scientists." Visit its Web site for information on educational programs, scholarships, careers, and member organizations, and to read the latest edition of the *Status of the Geoscience Workforce*.

American Geophysical Union

2000 Florida Avenue, NW
Washington, DC 20009-1277
800-966-2481
http://www.agu.org

The union offers education programs to encourage young people (especially students of color) to enter the field. Visit its Web site for more information.

American Institute of Biological Sciences

1444 I Street, NW, Suite 200
Washington, DC 20005-6535

202-628-1500
http://www.aibs.org

The institute is a membership organization for biologists and professional biology societies and organizations. Visit its Web site for information on careers and publications.

American Institute of Hydrology

Southern Illinois University—Carbondale
Engineering D, Mail Code 6603
1230 Lincoln Drive
Carbondale, IL 62901-4335
618-453-7809
aih@engr.siu.edu
http://www.aihydrology.org

The institute offers information on certification for hydrology professionals and technicians, college student chapters, and job listings at its Web site.

American Institute of Physics

One Physics Ellipse
College Park, MD 20740-3843
301-209-3100
http://www.aip.org

This organization is a resource for professionals who work in many physics disciplines, including astronomy. Visit its Web site for job listings, information on careers and education, publications, and an online archive of historical interviews with renowned physicists.

American Institute of Professional Geologists

1400 West 122nd Avenue, Suite 250
Westminster, CO 80234-3499

303-412-6205
http://www.aipg.org

Visit the institute's Web site for information on careers, certification, scholarships for college students, and membership for college students and those who "have an avocational or general interest in the geological sciences."

American Meteorological Society

45 Beacon Street
Boston, MA 02108-3693
617-227-2425
http://www.ametsoc.org

Visit the society's Web site for information on careers, certification, and membership and scholarships for college students; a searchable database of postsecondary training programs in meteorology; and answers to frequently asked questions about meteorology.

American Petroleum Institute

1220 L Street, NW
Washington, DC 20005-4070
202-682-8000
http://www.api.org

The institute represents the professional interests of oil and natural gas companies. Visit its Web site for career information and facts and statistics about the petroleum industry.

American Physical Society

One Physics Ellipse
College Park, MD 20740-3841
301-209-3100
http://www.aps.org

The society's mission is to "to advance and diffuse the knowledge of physics." Visit its Web site for information on careers, publications, educational programs, membership for college students, and summer programs for high school students.

American Physiological Society

9650 Rockville Pike
Bethesda, MD 20814-3991
301-634-7164
http://www.the-aps.org

Visit the society's Web site for career-related articles, a list of institutions that award academic degrees with a major in physiology, and information on publications and membership for college students.

American Society for Microbiology

1752 N Street, NW
Washington, DC 20036-2904
202-737-3600
http://www.asm.org

Visit the society's Web site for information on education and careers.

American Society of Human Genetics

9650 Rockville Pike
Bethesda, MD 20814-3998
301-634-7300
society@ashg.org
http://www.ashg.org

Visit the society's Web site for information on educational programs, membership for college students, and for the guide *Careers in Human Genetics*.

American Society of Limnology and Oceanography
5400 Bosque Boulevard, Suite 680
Waco, TX 76710-4446
800-929-2756
business@aslo.org
http://www.aslo.org

The society offers information on careers, volunteer positions, publications, and internships and jobs for college students. It also offers diversity programs to encourage students of color to enter the field.

Association for Women Geoscientists
1400 West 122nd Avenue, Suite 250
Westminster, CO 80234-3499
303-412-6219
office@awg.org
http://www.awg.org

Visit the association's Web site for an overview of careers in the geosciences, information on internships and scholarships for college students, answers to frequently asked questions about women in the geosciences, and profiles of women in the geosciences.

Association of Environmental and Engineering Geologists
PO Box 460518
Denver, CO 80246-0518
303-757-2926
aeg@aegweb.org
http://aegweb.org

Visit the association's Web site for resources for high school and college students (including summer geology camps), a list of colleges and universities that offer geology programs, and information on its Visiting Professionals Program, publications, and membership and scholarships for college students.

Association of Environmental Engineering and Science Professors
2303 Naples Court
Champaign, IL 61822-3510
217-398-6969
http://www.aeesp.org

Visit the association's Web site for information on colleges and universities that offer degrees in environmental engineering or science.

Association of Zoos and Aquariums (AZA)
8403 Colesville Road, Suite 710
Silver Spring, MD 20910-3314
301-562-0777
http://www.aza.org

Visit the association's Web site for information on conservation programs and careers in aquatic and marine science, job listings, a list of accredited zoos throughout the world, and to read *CONNECT* magazine. The AZA also offers an associate membership category "for zoo and aquarium professionals, as well as other interested parties, who want to support and forward the mission, vision, and goals of AZA."

Astronomical Society of the Pacific
390 Ashton Avenue

San Francisco, CA 94112-1722
415-337-1100
http://www.astrosociety.org

This nonprofit educational and scientific organization was founded in 1889. Visit its Web site for information on publications, education and careers, and membership for students and amateur astronomers.

Behavior Genetics Association
http://www.bga.org

The goal of the association is to "promote the scientific study of the interrelationship of genetic mechanisms and behavior, both human and animal." Visit its Web site for information on membership for college students.

Biotechnology Industry Organization
1201 Maryland Avenue, SW,
  Suite 900
Washington, DC 20024-2149
202-962-9200
info@bio.org
http://www.bio.org

Visit the Biotechnology Industry Organization Web site for information on biotechnology.

Bureau of Land Management (BLM)
U.S. Department of the Interior
1849 C Street, Room 5665
Washington, DC 20240-0001
202-208-3801
http://www.blm.gov

This U.S. government agency employs environmental professionals. Visit its Web site for information on its land holdings and career and volunteer opportunities.

Earthwatch Institute
Three Clock Tower Place,
  Suite 100
PO Box 75
Maynard, MA 01754-2549
800-776-0188
info@earthwatch.org
http://www.earthwatch.org

This organization offers international environmental expeditions that educate people about biodiversity, sustainability, habitat loss, coral reef health, indigenous cultures, climate change, and other environmental issues. Students can become members of the institute and participate in summer activities.

Ecological Society of America (ESA)
1990 M Street, NW, Suite 700
Washington, DC 20036-3415
202-833-8773
esahq@esa.org
http://esa.org

In addition to certification and membership for college students, the ESA offers a wide variety of publications, including *Issues in Ecology, Careers in Ecology*, and fact sheets about specific ecological concerns.

Friends of the Earth
1717 Massachusetts Avenue,
  Suite 600

Washington, DC 20036-2002
877-843-8687
http://www.foe.org

This group offers internships and fellowships for college and graduate students with an interest in environmental issues. Membership in the organization is also available.

Genetics Society of America

9650 Rockville Pike
Bethesda, MD 20814-3998
301-634-7300
http://www.genetics-gsa.org

Visit the society's Web site for information on publications and membership for graduate students, as well as to read *Careers in Genetics.*

Geological Society of America

PO Box 9140
Boulder, CO 80301-9140
888-443-4472
gsaservice@geosociety.org
http://www.geosociety.org

Visit the society's Web site for information on careers, programs for high school and college students, publications, and membership for college students.

Institute of Professional Environmental Practice

600 Forbes Avenue
339 Fisher Hall
Pittsburgh, PA 15282-0001
ipep@duq.edu
http://www.ipep.org

This organization offers certification to environmental professionals. Informa-

tion on certification and job listings are available at its Web site.

Marine Technology Society

5565 Sterrett Place, Suite 108
Columbia, MD 21044-2606
410-884-5330
http://www.mtsociety.org

Visit the society's Web site for information on programs for students in grades six–12, the publication *Education and Training Programs in Oceanography and Related Fields* (which is available for a small fee), and information on membership for college students and those with a general interest in the marine field.

National Association of Clean Air Agencies

444 North Capitol Street, NW,
  Suite 307
Washington, DC 20001-1512
202-624-7864
http://www.4cleanair.org

This association represents air pollution control agencies in 53 U.S. states and territories. Visit its Web site for information about air pollution and government pollution control boards.

National Association of Conservation Districts

509 Capitol Court, NE
Washington, DC 20002-4937
202-547-6223
http://www.nacdnet.org

This organization represents the 3,000 conservation districts in the United States.

National Association of Environmental Professionals
PO Box 460
Collingswood, NJ 08108-0460
856-283-7816
http://www.naep.org

The cross-disciplinary association offers job listings and information on internships at its Web site.

National Association of State Boards of Geology
PO Box 11591
Columbia, SC 29211-1591
803-739-5676
http://www.asbog.org

For information on the National Geology Examination, visit the association's Web site.

National Audubon Society
225 Varick Street, 7th Floor
New York, NY 10014-4396
212-979-3000
http://www.audubon.org

This is a membership organization for people and organizations that are committed to "conserving and restoring natural ecosystems, focusing on birds, other wildlife, and their habitats for the benefit of humanity and the earth's biological diversity." Visit its Web site for detailed information and illustrations of birds in the United States and an overview of its programs.

National Ground Water Association
601 Dempsey Road

Westerville, OH 43081-8978
800-551-7379
ngwa@ngwa.org
http://www.ngwa.org

Visit the association's Web site for job listings, a career-mentoring database, and information on certification, scholarships, and membership (for college students and anyone who is interested in groundwater resources).

National Oceanic and Atmospheric Administration
1401 Constitution Avenue, NW, Room 5128
Washington, DC 20230-0001
http://www.noaa.gov

The National Oceanic and Atmospheric Administration says that its reach "goes from the surface of the sun to the depths of the ocean floor." Visit its Web site for information on environmental topics such as climate monitoring, fisheries management, and coastal restoration, as well as details on careers, summer programs and paid internships for young people, and financial aid for college-level students.

National Park Service (NPS)
U.S. Department of the Interior
1849 C Street, NW
Washington, DC 20240-0001
202-208-3818
http://www.nps.gov

Visit the NPS Web site for information on national parks and other protected areas in the United States, careers, volunteer opportunities, internships, and youth programs.

National Parks Conservation Association

1300 19th Street, NW, Suite 300
Washington, DC 20036-1628
800-628-7275
npca@npca.org
http://www.npca.org

The association has a goal of protecting our national parks and historical sites. Visit its Web site for general information on national parks and to subscribe to *National Parks* magazine.

National Society of Genetic Counselors

401 North Michigan Avenue
Chicago, IL 60611-4255
312-321-6834
nsgc@nsgc.org
http://www.nsgc.org

Visit the society's Web site for comprehensive information on genetic counseling, including career information, a list of postsecondary training programs, and details on membership for college students.

National Weather Association

228 West Millbrook Road
Raleigh, NC 27609-4304
http://www.nwas.org

Visit the association's Web site for a list of schools with degree programs in meteorology or atmospheric science and information on scholarships and membership for college students.

National Weather Service (NWS)

1325 East West Highway

Silver Spring, MD 20910-3280
http://www.nws.noaa.gov

The NWS is an agency of the National Oceanographic and Atmospheric Administration. Visit its Web site for comprehensive information on weather forecasting and weather phenomena.

National Wildlife Federation

11100 Wildlife Center Drive
Reston, VA 20190-5362
800-822-9919
http://www.nwf.org

Visit the federation's Web site for information on internships, volunteerships, job opportunities, and *National Wildlife* magazine.

Natural Resources Conservation Service (NRCS)

U.S. Department of Agriculture
1400 Independence Avenue, SW
Washington, DC 20250-0002
http://www.nrcs.usda.gov

The NRCS "helps America's private land owners and managers conserve their soil, water, and other natural resources." Visit its Web site for information on volunteer opportunities and youth programs.

The Nature Conservancy

4245 North Fairfax Drive, Suite 100
Arlington, VA 22203-1606
800-628-6860
comment@tnc.org
http://nature.org

The Nature Conservancy's "mission is to preserve the plants, animals and natural communities that represent the diversity of life on earth by protecting the lands and waters they need to survive." It has protected more than 119 million acres of land and 5,000 miles of rivers throughout the world. Visit its Web site for information on conservation, careers, internships, membership, volunteerships, and more.

North American Association for Environmental Education (NAAEE)
2000 P Street, NW, Suite 540
Washington, DC 20036-6921
202-419-0412
http://www.naaee.org

The NAAEE is a "network of professionals, students, and volunteers working in the field of environmental education throughout North America and in over 55 countries around the world." Visit its Web site for information on membership for college students.

The Oceanography Society
PO Box 1931
Rockville, MD 20849-1931
301-251-7708
info@tos.org
http://www.tos.org

The society offers *Oceanography* magazine and membership for college students. Visit its Web site for more information.

Society for Integrative and Comparative Biology
1313 Dolley Madison Boulevard, Suite 402

McLean, VA 22101-3926
800-955-1236
SICB@BurkInc.com
http://www.sicb.org

Visit the society's Web site for information on careers, job listings, publications, and membership for college students.

Society of American Foresters (SAF)
5400 Grosvenor Lane
Bethesda, MD 20814-2198
301-897-8720
safweb@safnet.org
http://www.safnet.org

The SAF is a membership organization for foresters and forestry technicians. Visit its Web site for a wealth of information about careers and educational paths in forestry, including *Getting Started in Forestry, SAF-Accredited Professional Forestry Degree Programs, SAF-Recognized Forest Technology Degree Programs, The State of America's Forests,* and *Choose Forestry: Career Brochure.* Information on membership and scholarships for college students, a dictionary of forestry, and job listings are also available.

Society of Cosmetic Chemists
120 Wall Street, Suite 2400
New York, NY 10005-4088
212-668-1500
SCC@SCConline.org
http://www.scconline.org

Visit the society's Web site for information on careers in the cosmetics industry and membership for college students.

Soil and Water Conservation Society

945 SW Ankeny Road
Ankeny, IA 50023-9723
515-289-2331
http://www.swcs.org

The society provides information on soil conservation, job listings, college student membership, and publications (such as the *Journal of Soil and Water Conservation*) at its Web site.

Student Conservation Association (SCA)

689 River Road
PO Box 550
Charlestown, NH 03603-0550
603-543-1700
http://www.thesca.org

The SCA is a nonprofit environmental organization that offers summer trail crew opportunities to high school students and conservation internships to those age 18 and over. Visit its Web site for detailed information about these programs.

U.S. Environmental Protection Agency (EPA)

Ariel Rios Building
1200 Pennsylvania Avenue, NW
Washington, DC 20460-0001
202-272-0167
http://www.epa.gov

The EPA is a government agency that protects the environment and the health of people who live in the United States. Visit its Web site for general information about air quality and other environmental issues and employment opportunities.

U.S. Fish and Wildlife Service

U.S. Department of the Interior
4401 North Fairfax Drive, Room 634
Arlington, VA 22203-1610
800-344-9453
http://www.fws.gov/jobs

The U.S. Fish and Wildlife Service manages the 96 million-acre National Wildlife Refuge System. This system includes 550 National Wildlife Refuges, thousands of smaller wetlands, and other special management areas. Visit its Web site for information on careers, conservation, the *Endangered Species Bulletin*, and volunteer opportunities.

U.S. Geological Survey

12201 Sunrise Valley Drive
Reston, VA 20192-0002
703-648-4000
http://www.usgs.gov/education

This is a "multi-disciplinary science organization that focuses on biology, geography, geology, geospatial information, and water." It is an agency of the U.S. government. Visit its Web site for career and educational information about the geosciences.

Water Environment Federation

601 Wythe Street
Alexandria, VA 22314-1994
800-666-0206
http://www.wef.org

Contact the federation for information on water and sanitation, job listings, the Stockholm Junior Water Prize, details on membership for college students, and to read descriptions of 50 careers in the water environment field.

Wildlife Conservation Society
2300 Southern Boulevard
Bronx, NY 10460-1068
718-220-5100
http://www.wcs.org

The society seeks to save wildlife and wild lands. Visit its Web site to learn more about programs for teens and to read sample articles from *Wildlife Conservation Magazine.*

The Wildlife Society
5410 Grosvenor Lane, Suite 200
Bethesda, MD 20814-2144
301-897-9770
http://www.wildlife.org

The Wildlife Society offers *Careers in Wildlife Conservation,* which details more than 10 careers in the field. The publication is available at its Web site, along with information on other publications, student chapters, certification, and membership for college students or anyone who is interested in wildlife conservation and management.

Zoological Association of America
PO Box 511275
Punta Gorda, FL 33951-1275
813-449-4356
info@zaa.org
http://www.zaa.org

The association "promotes conservation, preservation, and propagation of animals in both private and public domains." It offers a membership category for those who support its goals.

Index

Entries and page numbers in **bold** indicate major treatment of a topic.

A